Q&A with

FB ATTORNEYS

Vol. 1

FAyaz A. Bhojani, Esq
BCom (McGill), LLB (London), LLM (Berkeley)

Gaudiosus Ishengoma, Esq
LLB (UDSM)

Dar es Salaam • Tanzania

This publication may be reproduced or transmitted, in any form, electronic, mechanical, photocopying, recording, scanning or otherwise, with appropriate acknowledgement given to FB Attorneys. Any enquiries about the book should be sent to FB Attorneys at this e-mail address: info@fbattorneys.com

Disclaimer: Information found in this book is intended to give you a general overview of the law. It is not a substitute for the role of your legal advisor. If you have legal issues, you are strongly urged to contact your Attorney. Also, kindly note that the laws which form the basis of our responses contained herein may have been amended over time.

Vol. 1
Printed and Published in the United Republic of Tanzania
ISBN 978-9976-89-924-5

FB

To my wife Shemina, and my daughters Alisa and Riana.
FAyaz A. Bhojani

To my family.
Gaudiosus Ishengoma

FB

Preface

Welcome to the first volume of 'Q&A with FB Attorneys'.

Q&A with FB Attorneys column was first published in the Daily News in 2009, making it one of the first interactive legal question and answer columns in East Africa. After having written the columns for more than eight years, and realising the thirst for legal knowledge out there, the authors embarked on this journey of compiling all columns since inception into a book.

This book, which covers questions and answers from 2009 to 2011 on Tanzanian and International Law, is a useful guide to readers, students, teachers, legal practitioners and the public. There are six chapters in the book and topics include relationships, Wills, employment disputes, consumer rights, commercial disputes, Court matters and crime.

The book aims to reach out to readers from all walks of life in an attempt to make the public aware of the law and the repercussions of not following the law. The law can confuse, frustrate and might sometimes not even work for you, but the general norm is that it must be followed. What the book does is to educate you on the law, your rights and the do's and don'ts.

As well as answering some serious questions on the law, this book has a sense of humour and the weekly columns published make for a good Monday morning read with a cup of coffee.

We thank the Daily News, the leading English newspaper in Tanzania that publishes the Q&A columns every Monday (www.dailynews.co.tz). It has been an excellent partnership between the Daily News and FB Attorneys.

We hope you enjoy reading the book.

FB Attorneys

FB Attorneys is a full service law firm based out of Dar es Salaam and brings with it a cumulative experience of over seventy years and a thorough knowledge of colloquial practices within the East African region. We cover all aspects of the law and specialise in Corporate and Commercial matters including Mining, Oil and Gas, Tax, Litigation, Banking, Competition, Real Estate, Intellectual Property Law and Land Law, amongst others.

We are held in high esteem throughout the region and internationally. Our stellar reputation has been built on successfully handling complex business transactions that consistently require a high level of sophistication. Frequently relied upon by clients as the preferred law firm for demanding legal cases, FB Attorneys offers unprecedented legal advice on a variety of corporate and commercial matters.

FB Attorneys has established long-standing relationships with some of the leading financial institutions, government entities, not-for-profit organisations, and other prominent public and private sectors in East Africa.

About the Authors

FAyaz A. Bhojani, Esq
BCom (McGill), LLB (London), LLM (Berkeley)

FAyaz Bhojani has seventeen years of experience in corporate affairs and heads the firm's Corporate Law department. He is a graduate of the world-renowned Berkeley Law School at the University of California. Having consulted for some of the leading banks, mining, oil and gas, and insurance companies, FAyaz brings a strong commercial sense to any legal transaction. Key specialisations include Corporate and Commercial Law with a focus on Mining Law, Oil and Gas, Tax Law, Banking and Mergers and Acquisitions. As an undergraduate, FAyaz studied actuarial science under the Society of Actuaries (SOA), bringing with him some sharp mathematical skills.

Gaudiosus Ishengoma, Esq
LLB (UDSM)

Having worked as a state attorney for eight years, Ishengoma has broad experience in high value litigation cases. In his legal career spanning twenty two years, he focuses on Land Law, Mining Law, and Contract Law. He has been involved in major cases before the High Court of Tanzania (Land Division), Commercial Court and the Court of Appeal. Ishengoma brings with him an excellent track record in bank recovery cases; he was trained by the British Council under a team from the House of Lords on prosecution skills.

Contents

Family, Relationships, Wills & Probate 1

Employment Disputes..31

Consumer and Claimant Rights...43

Commercial Disputes & Queries..81

Matters of Court Procedure & Ethics, Dealing with Lawyers 129

Crime 185

FB

Family, Relationships, Wills & Probate

The more time you spend away from your home and enjoy it, the higher the chances you will need a lawyer one day.

...for richer, for poorer in sickness and in health, till death do us part is the promise we make to our loved one when we marry. We promise to love and be faithful, we are not forced into this – we choose to do so. Making the promise is easy! Keeping it is another story. This chapter tackles some interesting questions on family relationships and examples of various case law used in answering these questions. The chapter also covers questions on Wills, probate and inheritance. To many of us, writing a Will is a reminder of the one guarantee life has to offer – death, which is inevitable so why not prepare for it!

Arrested for enticing a woman

For quite some time my neighbour has been accusing me of having an affair with his wife. In January 2010 there was a baptismal ceremony at another neighbour's house in which my family and that of my suspicious neighbour were invited. My neighbour found me standing outside the house with his wife, got very upset, and took her home after yelling at me in front of others. Shortly after they had left, some policemen arrived and arrested me. At the police station I was interrogated about the incident and released a day later. It is untrue that I am having an affair with the wife of my neighbour. Can I be arrested?

18th April 2011

The legendary James Bond would be in big trouble if enticing someone's wife was a criminal offence. But it is not, and hence you cannot be arrested for this. By answering in this manner, we are not giving relationship advice – there are other newspaper columns for that – we are merely advising you from a legal point of view. It is morally wrong to entice another man's wife – it is a tort, which is a civil wrong, not a criminal offence. The police have no right to arrest a man who is accused of such actions. In your case, you can sue both the policemen who arrested you and the neighbour for damages for false imprisonment. On the other hand, since such enticement is a tort, the husband can sue you for damages if he can prove a good cause of action against you.

Sexual relations with a pupil

I am a businessman and I have been sexually involved with a student of a certain secondary school. Last December, the father found out about our relationship and the girl confessed that we have been going out for two years and that she loves me. Surpris-

ingly, I was arrested by the police and have been charged with rape. I have never raped the girl – in fact the girl confesses that she consented to the sexual relations. I have a feeling that the police and magistrate have been compromised. What should I do?

28th March 2011

Due to the increased number of female students who drop out of school due to pregnancy and older men taking advantage of young girls, the law is plain and clear in that it is illegal to have sexual relations with a girl who is in primary or secondary school, or any girl who is below the age of 18. Any man having sexual relations with a pupil below 18 years of age will be guilty of rape regardless of whether she consented to it or not. The presumption of the law is that such a girl is incapable of understanding the situation and is thus incapable of consenting to sexual relations. We hence agree with the police and the Magistrate. Should you be convicted, be prepared to spend about thirty years in jail.

Prime property, no insurance

My father has had bad experiences with insurance companies. He believes they are the biggest crooks on earth. Because of his belief, we have major risk exposure on all assets our father owns. We are a family of eight with five brothers and three sisters. My father has a Will and has left a prime property for me to inherit. That property is currently leased to a company that is involved in mixing and supply of chemicals. This tenant poses a huge risk to the property – nonetheless my father is unwilling to insure the property. Since I am ultimately going to be the owner, can I insure the property to safeguard my interest?

21st March 2011

You must remember that this is not your property just yet. You merely have an expectation to inherit the property. You might have a moral certainty but you do not have full assurance, as the Will is changeable and you might die before your father. Unfortunately, since you do not own the property you cannot claim to have an insurable interest in the property, and hence cannot insure it in your name. If such an illusory insurance was available, it would be difficult to ascertain the limits on who could insure – for instance, your wife and children could also start insuring it, assuming the property will pass to them upon your demise.

Halving of rights, doubling of responsibilities

I was a very happy single man until I was forced into getting married five years ago. With my wife in the picture, my rights have been halved and responsibilities doubled. There is no peace of mind at home. My wife complains about me whenever she sees me. I just cannot seem to find the right formula to keep my family happy. What should I do?

14th March 2011

There are many aspects to your question that are beyond our scope of advice. There is no magic formula that we can think of that will please your wife. Problems between man and wife have existed since the time of Adam and Eve, and will likely continue to exist. If the marriage is so hopeless, you do have the option of separating and allowing time to reconcile, or proceed to file a petition for divorce. Life does go on even after a divorce, so you should keep that option on the drawing table. However, you might want to meet with a marriage counsellor before taking further action.

Fallen out of love

I got engaged to a man I loved. A few months after the engagement I changed my mind and now wish to call off the wedding. Can I do that? My friends tell me that I cannot, as legally I am bound to marry this man. What should I do?

21st February 2011

To begin with, you or your friends seem to think you are married. You are not. Engagement under the law is defined as a promise to marry, which is usually by way of an engagement ring. The law does not force you to get married and the engagement can be cancelled, contrary to what your friends tell you. It would be interesting to note what your so-called friends would say about divorce. The strict view they have on engagement means they may counsel others that divorce is illegal!

After all is said and done, if you intend to cancel the engagement and subsequently the marriage, you may be sued for damages for whatever loss that the other party has incurred in connection with the preparation of the marriage. Furthermore, the victim of such an act may sue for the return of the gifts given in expectation that marriage will take place. Be prepared for this.

Compulsion by husband

My husband is a controlling and strict man. He rules us with a heavy hand and a small mistake can lead to a severe beating to anyone, including me. I have no formal education and am entirely dependent on my husband for my livelihood, and hence cannot contemplate divorce. In a recent incident, our house girl left meat on the stove and forgot about it. The meat burnt, ruining the stove and causing a mess in the kitchen. When my husband got home and found out, he was furious. He ordered me to hit the house girl. I would not and he started hitting me and told me he would only stop if I hit the house girl. I hit her with a broom on the head a couple times and have now been charged with assault

with intention to cause Grievous Bodily Harm (GBH). After the arrest my husband decided to dump me and I was bailed out by my neighbour. What should I do?

7th February 2011

Such cruelty is not uncommon, and the law does come to your rescue. In the Penal Code, there is a provision which states that if a woman commits an offence (other than murder or treason), under the direct presence and compulsion of her husband, a sufficient defence is to prove beyond reasonable doubt that she only committed the offence because her husband forced her to do so. You should direct your defence in that direction. Assuming all that you have told us is the truth and can prove so in Court, it is likely that you will be acquitted.

We must, however, caution you that assault with intention to cause GBH, as opposed to common assault, is a very serious offence. GBH means serious bodily harm. In your case, it would depend on the size and weight of the broom, on what part of the body you struck the person, how sharp the assault weapon was, and why you decided to hit the maid on the head as opposed to any other part of the body. GBH also includes psychiatric injury but excludes mere emotions such as distress or fear.

Prenuptial agreement in Tanzania

I am a South African national and have lived in Tanzania for the last ten years. Over the years I have been dating a beautiful Tanzanian girl, whom I trust very much. Recently some lawyers from overseas were visiting our offices in Tanzania, and after I told them about my planned marriage, they suggested I enter into a prenuptial agreement with my girlfriend in case of divorce. Is this possible under Tanzanian law and are such contracts enforceable? What should I focus on in such an agreement? What are post nuptial agreements?

31st January 2011

A prenuptial agreement, also called antenuptial agreement or premarital agreement, is a contract entered into by the two parties prior to marriage. The contents of prenuptial agreements vary widely, but commonly include provisions for division of property and spousal support in the event of divorce or breakup of marriage. The agreement may also include terms for the forfeiture of assets as a result of divorce on the grounds of adultery.

Further conditions of guardianship may be included as well. When high net worth individuals enter into this agreement, frequently one of the more important provisions is that of assets owned before marriage would remain, in the event of divorce, with the party who owned them before the marriage. This provides an 'asset safety zone' for the party that could otherwise potentially end up paying billions in divorce settlement claims over property.

In some countries, particularly in Europe, people prefer these contracts, as they are regarded as (ahem) the ultimate test of love – the only way of knowing that one is truly loved, and not merely wanted because of his or her wealth. However, the contracts are not without opposition; many religious leaders consider them to be damaging to marriages because they are inconsistent with the principle of 'till death do us part'. In Tanzania, the Law of Marriage Act is silent on the issue. The Courts have also not been tested on this. Hence, our answer is based on our reading of the subject, in addition to the general legal framework in Tanzania.

The legality of these types of agreements in Tanzania will very likely depend on the way the prenuptial agreement is drafted. If it undermines morality or if it is against public policy, the agreement will likely be held to be void. The next question is what types of provisions would undermine morality or render the agreement antithetical to public policy. This will likely be a subjective test, and the background of the parties, their religion, and their culture will likely play a key role in determining this.

The law looks at marriage as a lifetime bond. This might have been a strong notion when the law came into effect in the early 1970s, but with the combination of decreasing tolerance levels amongst couples, increased level of openness, and increased awareness of the law has resulted in record high divorce rates. This is not only true in Tanzania, but all over the world. If the Courts were to look at a public policy from a broader angle, and consider the changing times (we are not sure if they would), we do not see why these agreements should be held illegal. However, as previously stated, this has not been tested in the Courts, and much as you would like us to, we cannot give you a firm answer.

There is, however, no harm in drafting this kind of agreement, and we highly recommend that you do so. It would not only save a lot of time, money and energy to litigants but also lessen the burden on Courts.

If the agreement is held not to be tenable or executable in a Court of Law, it can at best be an indication of the intent of the parties. A clause to exclude any provisions of the agreement that are held to be illegal should be included so that the other provisions of the agreement may be held to be enforceable.

To answer the last part of the question, post-nuptial agreements are similar to prenuptial agreements, except that they are entered into after a couple is married. Bargaining power after marriage is obviously much more limited, and we do not recommend you wait until after marriage to sign any such agreement.

Maintenance order against father

I have been in a relationship with a man for the past two years and have just delivered a baby boy. As is typical of males he has deserted me and I am left to look after the child alone. I am finding it hard to make ends meet. Should the father not also contribute to the well-being of the child? What options do I have?

17th January 2011

Under the Law of Child Act 2009, an application for maintenance order may be made against the alleged biological father to the Court in respect of the child by the expectant mother, at any time before the birth of the child; at any time within twenty four months from the birth of the child; at any time after the birth of the child upon proof that the man alleged to be the biological father of the child has within twenty four months after the birth of the child paid money for its maintenance; at any time within the twenty four months after the return to Mainland Tanzania of the man alleged to be a biological father of the child, upon proof that he ceased to reside in Tanzania before or after the birth of the child.

The Act further states that the Court shall refuse to grant a maintenance order unless it is satisfied that there is a reasonable cause to believe that the man alleged to be the father of the child is in truth the real father and that the application for a maintenance order is made in good faith and not for any purpose of intimidation and extortion; and the man alleged to be the father of the child has been requested by or on behalf of the applicant, to make provisions for maintenance of the child and has refused or neglected to provide maintenance, or has made inadequate provisions.

Based on the above, you have a good case and should proceed to make this application.

Same sex marriage

Does the law in Tanzania allow same sex marriage, and if so, can the partners adopt a child? I am informed that the marriage laws have been amended and such relationships are now recognised. If so, what is the procedure? What about temporary marriages? Can a man in Tanzania have more than one wife?

3rd January 2011

The Law of Marriage Act has not been amended, and same sex marriages, as is the case in most jurisdictions, is illegal. The law in Tanzania has defined marriage as a voluntary union of a man and a woman intended to last for the rest of their joint lives. With this definition, temporary marriages, whatever you mean by that, are not allowed.

A monogamous marriage is a union between one man and one woman to the exclusion of all others.

A polygamous marriage is a union in which the husband may be married to or marry another woman or women.

According to the law, there are two kinds of marriages: those that are monogamous or are intended to be monogamous, and those that are polygamous or potentially polygamous. As per the law, marriages contracted in Islamic form or according to rites recognised by customary law in Tanganyika, are presumed, unless the contrary is proved, to be polygamous or potentially polygamous. In any other case, the marriage is presumed to be monogamous, unless the contrary is proved. We thus answer the last part of your question in the affirmative, a man in Tanzania can have more than one wife.

My Will is in a safe overseas

I made a Will in Tanzania three years ago and deposited it in a bank vault in London for safekeeping. I am nearly 80 and do not expect to live very long. I wish to change my Will and sent a letter to the bank in London. But the bank wants me to be physically present to receive the envelope with the copy of the Will. I am very weak and cannot travel such distances any longer. The bank does not seem to be able to understand this. What should I do, as I desperately need to change my Will? What happens if there are two Wills?

13th December 2010

Before we answer your question we wonder why the bank in the UK is not releasing the Will. Perhaps they are unaware that the envelope contains a Will. We wonder what would have happened to the envelope in case you had passed away. Should the bank have acted like that when you were gone, it would have been pointless for you to have made a Will, as no one would have been able to access it. We suggest that you deposit the Will in a Will bank and inform the executor of the deposit being made there.

Your question is very simple – in order to make a new Will, you do not need to have the current Will. The new Will will automatically revoke any older Will. Hence, unless there are other reasons that you have not disclosed to us, there is no point in requesting the bank to send you the current Will. Proceed and draft a new Will, and make sure that it is kept in a place where the executor has access to it.

In the event there are two Wills, and both are genuine, the Will that was the latest prevails, as it revokes the older Will.

Compulsion to cohabitation

I was married in 1990 and our marriage is blessed with three children. In the last few months my wife and I have had frequent issues in our marriage, as my wife does not approve some of my habits. She has now gone back to her parents, and refuses to come back to our matrimonial home. Can the Court support me by issuing an order for her to return?

6th December 2010

Marriage is a voluntary union between a man and woman and contracted with the consent of both parties. The Law of Marriage Act 1971 is also clear that no proceedings may be brought to compel a wife to live with her husband or a husband with his wife. Therefore, the Court cannot compel the two of you to live together. The only remedy for you is to refer the matter to Marriage Conciliation Board. Alternatively, to save your marriage, you may want to change your habits, whatever they are.

Mother dead, father rich

My mother was a rich and famous business-woman in Mwanza who recently died. My father, with whom she did not get along very well, has produced a Will whereby to our utmost surprise she has given him more than we would have expected – he is now a rich man. How do we go about challenging the Will? At the bottom of the Will, my mother has signed as a testator of the Will. Is that not a fatal mistake?

15th November 2010

You have not mentioned whether you have any other Will that your mother made; your question is based on mere speculation. To verify that a Will is genuine, you can check with the witnesses who signed the Will. You can also get a forensic expert to look at the signature on the Will and confirm that it matches the signature of your mother. Your observation that your mother signed as a testator as opposed to a testatrix is interesting. However, in modern English, testator has become gender-neutral, like actor, juror, prosecutor and executor. We are not convin-ced that a Court will be perverse enough to

rule a Will invalid on the grounds that a female deceased had executed her Will as testator, especially in the face of the common statutory provision that in all documents the masculine includes the feminine and vice versa. You may need legal advice and we recommend you see your attorney.

Who can witness my Will?

I have prepared a Will and need a witness to sign it. Who can be a witness? Does it have to be a judge or lawyer or can it be anyone? I do not want my Will to be challenged.

1st November 2010

First and foremost, you require two witnesses and not one. It is not necessary that a judge or lawyer witness your Will. It is generally advised that a Will be witnessed by persons you know and are trustworthy, and if called upon, will be able to testify that the Will was signed by you in their presence.

A spouse, beneficiary, spouse of a beneficiary, blind person, minor and a person of unsound mind may not witness a Will. The witnesses should understand the nature and effect of what they are doing.

You must take note that both witnesses must be in the same room at the same time as you when they sign. Should one of your witnesses predeceases you, we would recommend that you immediately draw a new Will and get another witness. The law requires witnesses' verification at the time of applying for a probate and a dead witness may complicate and delay the process.

Claiming inheritance from my father

My father is a very rich man – one of the richest in the country. I am well taken care of and have access to pocket money, a car and all the works. My father, however, does not want to give me funds to start a business that I could manage on my own. He claims that upon his demise I shall get 50% of his wealth. I am turning 30 and would like to pre-claim this inheritance from my father and live my own life. I am also scared that he might change his mind in the Will as it is rumoured he has a mistress and children with her. I would like to confront him about this extramarital relationship. Please advise.

4th October 2010

We assume that you want us to advise you on whether you can claim under the Will and not whether you should confront your father about having a mistress. Unfortunately, if it is the latter, we are not qualified to answer.

To begin with, you are of a mature age and not a child by any definition. We know of no law in any jurisdiction that allows the beneficiary of a Will to pre-claim their portion of the testator's estate. A Will is an instrument that gets invoked upon the death of the testator. Fortunately (or unfortunately), your father is still alive and you cannot claim under the Will. It makes absolutely no difference if your father is the richest man in Tanzania or the richest man in Africa – amount of wealth does not change the law.

Also be informed that a Will is a changeable instrument and is not cast in stone. It can be changed at any time by the testator. Upsetting your father in any way can make him change his mind about you – do keep that in mind when you confront him about the mistress.

Divorcing a mentally challenged wife

I celebrated a Christian marriage with a girl five years ago. Our marriage is blessed with one boy who is nearly three. In January 2008 my wife fell sick with malaria and was mis-diagnosed and treated with the wrong medication. She then fell into a coma and was hospitalised for three months before being discharged. Ever since her discharge she is mentally challenged and cannot eat, take a bath or walk on her own. I have tried very hard to adjust, but have failed to keep up with this. I wish to support her for life, but wish to divorce her. Is this a sufficient grounds for divorce? What grounds for divorce can I come up with to be successful? Please note that two of my wife's brothers are lawyers.

27th September 2010

We are sorry to hear about your wife. We will take you down memory lane and remind you of the vows you made during your wedding ceremony when you undertook to live with your wife in any situation be it during happiness or sadness, sickness or good health. The same applies in law in that sickness is not ground for divorce, separation or annulment of a marriage. The case would have been different if your wife had this problem before you contracted your marriage and this was concealed from you. Had this been the case, your marriage would have been voidable and we could have advised you to go to Court for an annulment.

Since you have revealed the truth, we as officers of the Court are duty bound not to mislead any Court and do not see the need of discussing other grounds that you want to cook up. We have also taken note that two of your wife's brothers are lawyers – this fact is relevant to the extent that she will have good guidance on this matter and you should be aware of that.

Grant of letters of administration on urgent basis

My father passed away a few weeks ago without leaving behind a Will. Since I am the first born and our mother predeceased my father, I agreed with my younger brothers and sisters that I should apply for letters of administration for his estate. Before the letters of administration was granted, a woman appeared from out of the blue, and challenged my application, claiming she was also a wife of my father. I have never seen this woman in my life and the matter is before the Court. We have learned that a number of our father's properties are being misused in his absence. Other assets, including his car, are in the possession of his driver who does not seem to show good intentions. My father's business partners are also behaving weirdly and not disclosing details of certain transactions. The Court case will take a long time. What can we do at this juncture to stop this pilferage?

27th September 2010

The letters of administrations you have applied for will not be granted until the application made by this alleged wife of the deceased is disposed of. You have correctly pointed out that this will take time and time being of essence, you need to stop this pilferage and misuse of assets.

Our law allows the grant of letters of administration with limited powers. Such temporary letters of administration will give the administrator all the rights and powers of the general administrator, except the powers of distributing the estate. In law, this is referred to as grant of letters of administration *pendente lite*. We recommend that you immediately apply for letters of administration to preserve your late father's estates while you are settling matters in Court.

This application should be filed under 'certificate of urgency' for it to get a quick hearing date.

Husband has 'nyumba ndogo'

We have been married under a Christian marriage for the past fifteen years and blessed with five children. I can prove that my husband has another girl and house, *nyumba ndogo*, in his life. Is this not a criminal offence? What action can I take?

20th September 2010

The *nyumba ndogo* is an adulterous relation that your husband is engaged in. Adultery is defined as sexual intercourse between a married person with a person who is not that person's lawful spouse.

Unfortunately, this is not a criminal offence in Tanzania, meaning one cannot be arrested for being in this kind of a relationship.

If the behaviour does not change or your relation is beyond repair, this is grounds for divorce. You also have a right to sue the *nyumba ndogo* lady for damages, but such claim for damages can be thrown out by the Court if it can be convinced that you have done anything by your conduct or act or omission to induce or force your husband to behave in this manner.

Necessity of bride price

I entered into a Christian marriage with a woman. Strangely, her father came and took her away against her will, claiming that I had not paid bride price for her. I do not disagree with this, but the amount demanded is excessive. Is the father entitled to keep her away from me because of the unpaid bride price? Is bride price a mandatory requirement under the law? Please advise.

16th August 2010

Under the Law of Marriage Act bride price is not a mandatory requirement. In other words, there can be a valid marriage between a man and a woman, whether bride price is paid or not. The act of your father in-law taking your wife away from you is illegal and unjustified.

In the event your wife is unable to return, you can seek for an order of the Court to compel your father in-law to return your wife in your care.

Religious v customary marriages

I was married under customary law in 1989 and blessed with three children. In 2004, my husband wanted to marry a second wife while still married to me, to which I had no objection. He celebrated a Christian marriage with this new woman and had two more children. We lived in harmony, as all of us were well maintained by my husband. In 2008, my husband died without a Will, and the brother of my husband was appointed as administrator. After the burial ceremony, much to my surprise, the administrator disinherited me, my children. All of my husband's properties were given to the 2nd wife and her children. I was told that my marriage with the deceased was not legally recognised, and the Christian marriage with the 2nd wife was superior to the customary marriage. Is this true? How do I fight for my rights? Am I not a wife of the deceased to whom I have been married longer than the second wife? Please advise.

2nd August 2010

The Law of Marriage Act recognises two types of marriages – polygamous and monogamous. All types of marriages fall under these two categories. The law recognises Christian, Islamic, customary or civil marriages with the same status, and none is superior to the other. Customary, civil and Islamic marriages are presumed to be polygamous, meaning that a man can have more than one wife. Christian marriages are strictly monogamous.

Furthermore, the Law of Marriage Act specifically prohibits a man who is in a polygamous marriage or potentially polygamous marriage to contract a monogamous marriage with another woman to the exclusion of his other wives.

In your case, your husband's 2nd marriage, if it was contracted as a monogamous marriage, was never valid and therefore is of no legal force, because legally he was already in a potentially polygamous marriage, and thus could not contract a monogamous marriage while still married to you. What you can do is object to the distribution of the deceased's assets by the administrator.

Maintenance of pregnancy

I am a 20-year-old woman who had an affair with a man for six months. Two months after separating I found out that I was pregnant. When I approached the man for maintenance for the child he refused, and said that the child is not his. I was also fired from my job as a house girl after my employer found out that I was pregnant. Do I have any legal recourse against the man, considering that I am not legally married to him and the baby is still unborn?

2nd August 2010

Unfortunately, due to the backlog of questions, the answer to this question might be overtaken by events, that is, you may already be a mother.

You have not confirmed whether you believe the child is that of the man with whom you were having an affair. Assuming he is the father, not being lawfully married to him does not legally disentitle an expectant woman from claiming maintenance from the alleged biological father of the child. The law imposes a duty upon such a man to maintain the expectant mother of the child. If it can be proved, which technology can do, that the man is responsible for your pregnancy, you can file an application in Court for maintenance. You are indeed entitled to be maintained.

Another observation is that of being terminated by your employer. Our opinion is that such termination on grounds of getting pregnant is illegal, and you have a good cause of action against the employer.

There is no law in Tanzania that prohibits a woman from getting pregnant, let alone not being allowed to work when she is pregnant.

Helping my neighbour's wife

Next door to me, lives an unemployed woman who has been separated from her husband for the past few years. The children are all below 7-years-old. Out of the goodness of my heart, I have been helping the family with food and school fees. Recently I learned that her husband is very wealthy. After having spent millions of shillings assisting the woman, I decided to approach the husband to refund me for the sums spent. He has flatly refused to refund me anything, saying that I was assisting the lady because I had an interest in her. Is there any way I can recover my costs from this man? Does the law come to my rescue? He is an advocate – does that affect your opinion?

19th July 2010

From the facts you have given us, we are unable to establish whether or not the husband and woman were/are legally married, and if yes, then whether the marriage still exists. However, considering the age of the children and the financial condition of the family, you quite rightly performed your duty of taking care of them. You carried out both legal and moral duties of the husband in his absence, even if there was no contract to that effect.

Your act of assisting the husband's family is known as 'agency of necessity', and therefore you do have a legal cause of action against the husband.

Your attorney can guide you on how to sue this man. The law applies equally to lawyers and non-lawyers alike, and our opinion remains the same, even if he is a fellow legal counsel.

Ambiguity in Will

My father left a Will that has some ambiguity. Two of us have the same first names and surnames but different middle names. There is one property in question that our father has left to one of us, but has not mentioned the middle name, so do not know who should inherit it. This has led to some confusion within our family. What should we do?

5th July 2010

We are not sure how you can have the same first name and surname, but a different middle name. We shall, however, answer your question as you have asked it.

It is imperative that the contents of a Will be very clear and unambiguous. In the event that there is ambiguity, a Will can be interpreted using certain set rules of interpretation, the most appropriate one in this case being the 'arm chair' principle, a principle which was developed by an English Justice of Appeal in the 1800's. This principle allows the admission of extrinsic evidence to explain the meaning of words and expressions in a Will. The Court may, for example, receive evidence of the testator's habits of speech and of her or his family, property, friends and acquaintances in order that it may read the Will from the position of the person making it, as if sitting in the testator's armchair.

In this instance, we suggest that you read the whole Will, understand it and see if the rule would be applicable. You will have to try and make out, from the Will and the actions of the deceased during his lifetime, who he meant.

We do not want to add further confusion, but the deceased perhaps meant that both of you should inherit the property. Your attorneys need to get into the shoes of the Testator to guide you better.

How to prove the child is not mine

I was involved with a woman for several years before we parted last year. A few months ago she contacted me and informed me that she gave birth to a child and claimed I was the biological father. I looked at the child and there is no way in the world that he resembles me. The mother is insisting that I pay maintenance for the child, and has since sent me a notice from a law firm to provide funds for the upkeep of the child and mother. In principle, had the child been mine, I would not have written this question to you. Please advise.

28th June 2010

It is good you wrote to us, as we do not entirely agree with what you have said. To begin with, the most reliable test of whether a child is yours or not, is not by merely looking at the child and seeing if he resembles you. This is an unreliable test that was used in the Victorian days, and has no scientific relevance in today's era.

The most accurate way is to conduct a DNA test, and Tanzania now has the facilities and a law in place to support such tests. As per the DNA Act, there are only a few people and institutions who can initiate DNA testing, including the police for investigation purposes, the Court, a certified medical doctor, or an advocate.

In your case, if the said lady does not object to a DNA test, then you can request your doctor or your advocate to write to the government chemist and request a DNA test. In the event she refuses, you may make an application in Court.

Based on the grounds you state in your application, the Court may or may not order the test. But for now do not be blinded by the resemblance of the child – it is not conclusive.

Executor claiming burial expenses

My younger brother died last year leaving behind a number of properties. Even though he was not married, he was living in his own house with his 12-year-old son. Before his burial, I received money from one of his debtors who wanted to repay his debt. I used the money for the funeral. We did not know of the existence of the Will until recently, when we discovered that he had appointed one of his friends to be an executor. The executor is now coming after me, saying that I should refund the money, otherwise he will proceed to institute legal action against me. Is this fair? Please advise

24th May 2010

Generally the law provides that any person who intermeddles with the estate of the deceased or commits any other act which belongs to the office of executor while there is no rightful executor in existence, makes himself an executor of his own wrong. As such, that makes one to be answerable to the rightful executor/administrator or legatee or creditors of the deceased.

However, going by the facts you have given us, we find that using your brother's money to provide for his funeral was appropriate.

We advise you to explain this to the executor, and show him the receipts of all expenses incurred. If the money was legitimately used for the burial and was not misused elsewhere, we do not see why you should have any trouble. It seems like the executor suspects some mischief in the way you have used the funds.

Executor fails to act

Our father died two years ago. Fortunately, he left a Will in which he named his best friend as an executor. Unfortunately, the executor has failed to file for a probate for the past two years. Instead he has been making us on account payments to keep us under his command. Is there a way we can terminate him as an executor and appoint someone else in his place? Does the law allow this? Please advise.

17ᵗʰ May 2010

It is very interesting you point out the on account payments. It is even more surprising that you have been accepting them without exerting pressure on the executor to file for a probate and distribute the deceased's estate as per the Will.

The Probate and Administration of Estates Act states that in the event that the executor of the estate fails to carry out his duties, he can be terminated and someone else be appointed in his place. Any person who is a beneficiary to the deceased estate or is a creditor of the deceased estate can cause a citation to be issued to the executor calling upon him to step down. If the said executor does not reply to the citation and does not take any initiative to institute probate proceedings in Court, then the person who issued the citation can apply for an order in Court to declare that the said executor is deemed to have renounced his executorship. Once that order is issued by the Court, the family of the deceased can appoint someone else to be an administrator of the deceased's estate.

Collusion and divorce

My wife was in America pursuing her studies and has just come back. She is no longer interested in the relationship, and I have not been able to reconcile her feelings towards me. I have recently discovered that there is another man in her life. As in other countries, can we simply get a divorce by consent, or sign an agreement to divorce and part ways? What other steps do we have to follow to get divorced?

10ᵗʰ May 2010

As per the Law of Marriage Act, married couples cannot collude to end their marriage. The only institution which can grant a divorce is the Court, regardless of the form or type of marriage. The marriage must have broken down irreparably for the Court to grant a divorce, for the state favours families and not broken families. Hence, we answer your question in the negative – you cannot just draft a divorce agreement and get divorced. It is the Court that grants the divorce.

The first step in initiating divorce proceedings is to go for conciliation – depending on the religion both of you practice, your prayer house would normally have such a committee. The Conciliation boards will try to solve your differences and will give you time to reconcile. When the conciliation board sees that the marriage has broken down irreparably, then it will grant you a certificate that the marriage has broken down irreparably.

After this certificate is issued, you can petition to divorce in Court, where you must satisfy the Court that the marriage has broken down irreparably. Based on the Court proceedings, the Court will make an appropriate order as to the custody of children, visiting rights, distribution of matrimonial properties and the like.

Legal definition of separation

I am a girl scared of getting married after reading about the high rates of divorce and separation around the world over. I know about divorce, but do not understand what the legal definition is for separation. Also, when a man and wife are separated, can they cohabit?

10ᵗʰ May 2010

A judicial separation is usually an order by the Court that a husband and wife do not have to cohabit and should live separately. The order does not terminate the marriage but it does free the parties of marital obligations. As to whether they can cohabit, the answer is they can but they are not forced to.

When you are separated, you cannot remarry or engage in adultery, as your contract of marriage persists until you get a divorce. One can look at separation as a starting point while contemplating divorce.

Marriage and Will

I inherited my father's assets about twenty years ago which constituted a number of property and other investments. When I turned 18, I was advised by a close friend of my dad to draft a Will. An English solicitor made the Will for me although I was reluctant to proceed with signing it as I did not know whom to leave the assets to in case I died. I am now getting married and am informed by the same solicitor that my Will will automatically be revoked. Please advise.

26th April 2010

Our recommendation is that anyone above the age of 18 can have a Will. In your case, not knowing whom to leave your assets to means that it is even more important to have a Will. You must understand that Wills are not only made when you have family. Some of the most eligible bachelors around the world have left their assets to charities that continue to benefit from this kind of generosity.

In answering your question, your solicitor is right in that if you get married, your Will will be automatically revoked and hence the need to draw a new one. We do not seem to understand your reluctance. Drawing a Will does not send one earlier to the graveyard!

Not married but living together

I have been living with a woman for the past few years when her former boyfriend came back from overseas and is now threatening me with action. I am not sure what to do. Am I doing anything wrong? What kind of action can be taken when a man and woman, out of their own free will are living together? Do we have to be married to live together and have a relationship? Can only a married couple live together? What should I do?

19th April 2010

We have read your question, which is very interesting. In the absence of knowing who you are or having your number to call you, we are construing your words 'threatening to take action' as meaning threatening to file a law suit against you. In the event that it is a physical threat, our simple response is to report this to the police as it becomes a criminal matter.

Is there a law that bars an unmarried couple to live together? Our answer is in the negative – the law does not disallow such a relationship. There is case law from other countries including the United Kingdom that supports what we are saying.

One of the most recent case laws that we came across, with facts very similar to yours, is an Indian decision in which the Supreme Court had to decide on whether a 'live in relationship' which included pre marital sex was an offence.

The Justices queried on what offence it was for two adult people to live together and the Court concluded that there was no law which prohibits' live in relationships' or pre marital sex. The justices further concluded that living together is a right to life.

You might be confusing morality with legality. Whether it is moral or not to have pre marital sex and live together is not a legal question and we as legal practitioners are least qualified to answer that part.

Our response to your question would be different if you were living with a married woman and the husband decided to take action against you.

No boys in marriage

My husband and I have had three lovely daughters from our marriage. My husband really wanted a male child and we tried our luck again. After I conceived we went to the doctor to determine the sex of the child only to be told that it is a girl again. My husband wants to abort this child. Is that legal? Is this sufficient ground for my husband to divorce me? He has threatened more than once that if I do not bear him a boy, he shall leave me. I am under immense pressure. Please assist.

12th April 2010

Abortion based on the above facts is illegal, a criminal offence and punishable by law. Your husband's wish to have a male child cannot result in you aborting your fourth child. This child is as much yours as it is your husband's. If the reason for abortion was on health grounds in the interest of the mother, it would be legal. Not otherwise.

This is also no ground for a divorce. You might want to educate your husband that the sex of a child is determined by the male sperm and not the female egg.

Mother dating younger man

My parents divorced two years ago and I have been living with my mother ever since. Recently my mother has started dating one of my friends' boyfriends, who is a mature person, and now I hear that they might be getting married. This has caused a strain in the relationship with my friend with whom I have grown up with. Is there a law that disallows such relationships? Can I get a Court injunction?

12th April 2010

We are unsure what you mean by dating. Assuming that it is a sexual relationship, we do not see anything wrong in this relationship as long as your mother is divorced and the man she is dating is above the legal age of marriage. There is no law that can prohibit such a relationship.

On a different note, the Law of Marriage Act has some restrictions on marriage. The law is clear in that no persons shall marry if they have not attained a certain age which for females is 15 years and for males 18 years. The law also clearly states that no person shall marry his or her grandparent, parent, child or grandchild, sister or brother, great aunt or great uncle, aunt or uncle, niece or nephew. The law further states that no person shall marry the grandparent or parent, child or grandchild of his or her spouse or former spouse and no person shall marry a person whom he or she has adopted or by whom he or she was adopted.

Your case does not fall under any of the above. Unfortunately you cannot apply for any Court orders.

Adoption by a foreigner

I am a Kenyan citizen wishing to adopt a child in Tanzania. What are the conditions for this? Why is adoption more difficult here than in other countries?

5th April 2010

Adoption comes under the newly enacted Law of the Child Act of 2009.

The law clearly stipulates several conditions to be fulfilled by whoever wishes to adopt a child in Tanzania.

Being a foreigner, you shall have to satisfy the Court that the child shall be cared for in a manner that shall be in the child's best interest, that you have stayed in Tanzania for at least three consecutive years, that you have fostered the child for at least three months under the supervision of social welfare, that you do not have any criminal record in your country of origin or any other country, that **you have a recommendation concerning your** suitability to adopt a child from your country's social welfare officer and any other competent authority of your permanent country of residence and lastly that you have satisfied the Court that your country of origin respects and recognises such adoption orders.

If you meet the above criteria then you are eligible to make an application in Court for adoption. All in all, the Court's duty is to make sure that the best interests of the child are safeguarded.

As for adoption being more difficult here than in other places, we are unsure as to which places you are referring to. You must bear in mind that the best interests of the child are paramount in any decision from any Court. That is more or less a universal principle that Courts adhere to.

Mother has child after death of father

Our father died in 2007 and was survived by my mother, two brothers and myself. A few years after the death of my father, my mother gave birth to a daughter. Now that my mother has been appointed administratix of the deceased's estate, she has listed this new child as one of the heirs of the deceased's estate despite the fact that the child is not my father's and there is no blood relation between this child and my deceased father. The magistrate handling this issue seems to be supporting this? What does the law say?

29ᵗʰ March 2010

If the matter is in Court pending outcome, you cannot prejudge the matter. However, the way we read your question, is that in your personal opinion it seems like the Magistrate is inclined towards your mother's proposal.

Assuming the father of the child is anonymous, as far as the law is concerned, where the widow of a deceased person conceives the child of such a conception is entitled to inherit the estate of the deceased

even though he or she is not of his blood. Hence this young girl being your half sister, may be entitled. However, this also depends on the customs you follow. Since we are unsure of your customary background, we advise you to seek a second opinion.

Woman bearing too many children

Is there a law that can stop someone from continuing to reproduce? I am a health worker in the interiors of Tanzania and my friend's mother has already given birth to twelve children and is pregnant again. I will not be surprised if after this pregnancy she is impregnated again. How can I get a Court order to stop this from happening? Can someone come to the rescue of this woman?

8ᵗʰ March 2010

We are not sure whether to sympathise with you or not, as we are unsure how the woman herself is taking it. In some societies women do bear many children. Whilst there is a law in some countries like China on the maximum number of children a family can have, in Tanzania, fortunately or unfortunately, there is no such law. We are also reliably informed that there is no such law in the pipeline either.

In Tanzania, some traditional families continue to have many children. Population outburst is detrimental to the development of a poor country; unfortunately the tradition still continues in some parts of the country. In the absence of any such law, we recommend that you ask the couple to contact a family planning counsellor for assistance as you do not stand a chance in Court

Consent to mortgage property in polygamous marriage

I am a man with two wives. I only have one house where each of my wives stays with me for one month on rotation. I intend to borrow money from a bank to start a busi-

ness and wish to mortgage my house. The bank wants my wife to sign on a certain document. My second wife is much more understanding and I want her to sign the document. Is that good enough? What will be the consequences when I fail to repay the loan and the other wife (who did not consent) objects to the sale of the house? Will I face any criminal charges?

15th February 2010

You have a very interesting arrangement with your spouses. When you are intending to mortgage your matrimonial house, your wife's consent is mandatory because of the sensitive nature of the house. As per the Law of Marriage Act, it is stated that all wives, if married to the same man, will have equal status i.e. neither of them is above the other. It is also very clearly stated that when a spouse wishes to mortgage a matrimonial home he should seek consent of the other spouse. The definition of 'matrimonial home', per the Act, is a building within which the husband and wife ordinarily reside, which is the case here.

Since both women live with you though at different times, it is a matrimonial home for both and you need to get consent of both of them. The case would have been different if each of your wives had a separate house.

We do not encourage you to lie to the bank as to the number of wives you have, as per the Mortgage Financing (Special Provisions) Act 2008, it is the duty of the mortgagor to state whether he has a spouse(s) and if you sign a declaration or statement to the bank in relation to the issue of spouse(s) and it turns out to be false you may face criminal charges.

If you fail to pay the bank, which hopefully is not your intention from the onset, and your other wife has not signed the consent, it is likely that the bank will not be able to execute the sale of the mortgaged home. However, the bank may still pursue you for recovery.

Husband married twice

Since 1989 I was living with a man and we were blessed with six children. Six years after we met, my partner contracted another Christian marriage with another woman, with whom we shared the same man until he died due to an illness. During the period he was sick, he went to church, and prayed that in the event of his death, his burial ceremonies should be conducted in accordance with the Christian faith. There, he was, however, sanctioned to leave one wife before his request could be accepted. He chose the second wife with whom he celebrated the Christian marriage. He died a few months later and left no Will. His Christian wife then took all the properties of my partner and distributed them to herself and her children excluding me and my children. She alleged in front of the leaders that I was not the lawful wife and therefore my children could not inherit from the deceased's estate. What are my rights having lived with this man for over two decades?

8th February 2010

The Law of Marriage Act recognises two types of marriages which are polygamous and monogamous marriages. These marriages can be contracted in Christian, Islamic, customary or civil forms but regardless of the form, all these marriages are of the same status before the law, meaning that they do not take ranks over each other. However, while customary marriages, like Islamic marriages, are presumed, unless the contrary is so proved, to be polygamous or potentially polygamous, all Christian marriages are monogamous meaning that no marriage can co-exist with them.

Even though you have not gotten a formal marriage certificate, you have been living with the man for many years and in the eyes of the law, you are recognised as man and wife.

The above being true, the alleged Christian marriage is illegal and void *ab initio*. This is so because your marriage with your late husband came in place first and was still subsisting at the time he contracted the alleged Christian marriage. Secondly the later marriage, being a Christian one, could not be contracted the same being monogamous.

Does that now mean that the second wife has no rights? Since the second wife also lived and had children with your husband, she is also recognised as a wife of the deceased under customary law and hence you, her and all the children are entitled to benefit from the estate. Neither of you can be excluded.

Child not mine

I am a young man aged 24 years and have been in a relationship since 2007. We stopped seeing each other in January 2009 due to a misunderstanding. In March 2009 the girl gave birth to a baby boy; one major reason we broke up was because I was not sure if I was the father of the child as my girl-friend was also quite intimately associated with a close friend of mine. Currently the girl is forcing me to put my name as the father on the birth certificate. What does the law say in a situation like this? How can I make sure that I am not the father?

1st February 2010

The law provides that it is compulsory that every child born alive must be registered and the duty is imposed on the parents of the newly born. The Births and Deaths Registration Act provides that no person shall be bound as a father to register the birth of a child born out of wedlock and no person shall be entered in the register as a father of such a child except at his own request and upon his acknowledging himself to be the father of the child and signing, or affixing, his mark to the register.

In a nut shell we can say that the position of the laws in Tanzania does not compel you to get the birth certificate in your name as a father of that child.

Your last question is very difficult to answer. Science has advanced and gone are the Napoleon days when a father could deny that a child is his or not. In today's era, a simple DNA test will reveal who the biological father is. There is nothing that can be done to 'make sure' that you are not the father – this is not a computer game where you can reset the options.

Changing my Will

I recently got married and wish to consider making a Will. However, there are some large acquisitions I am making that I want to mention in the Will. Should I wait till the transactions are concluded? How often can I change my Will?

8th February 2010

There is a very famous saying which says: there are two certainties in life; death and taxes! Everyone is surely going to die one day and we advise everyone to have a Will. It is one of the single most important instruments that you will ever create that will not help you, but assist your loved ones and beneficiaries. Most people undermine and underplay this fact.

We have noted the transactions you are entering into. We suggest that you immediately create a Will and mention the acquisitions in the Will. Once these transactions are concluded, we suggest you prepare another Will and ensure that these assets, if purchased, are clearly and unambiguously mentioned.

You may change your Will as many times as you wish. When you make a new Will, it automatically revokes the older Will.

Knowledge of the Will

I have made a Will and want to know

whether there is an automatic way for the beneficiaries to be informed that they are beneficiaries after my death. I also wish to know how my executor will know that I have appointed him as my executor. I do not want the contents of my Will to leak out to anyone including my wife and any other beneficiaries. Is there a particular place that I can use to store my Will?

11th January 2010

Neither your beneficiaries nor executor(s) will know that they are mentioned in your Will if you do not inform them. It is as simple as that. There is no authority that informs them automatically.

Our first suggestion is for you to make sure that you ask the executor if he is agreeable to act as the executor. It is wise to also appoint an alternate executor should the first executor fail to act for some reason. Make sure you also inform this alternate executor. Most people forget to appoint an alternate executor.

Secondly, you should make sure that the executor and/or the beneficiaries or someone very trustworthy knows where the Will is stored. The facility you use should only release the Will upon your demise.

Will security is also vital as is ease of access. You may need to make changes, for example to add a new child or grandchild to your Will. Whatever the case may be, it is a good idea to review your Will once every couple of years.

Some people store their Wills at home. Others store them in bank vaults with instructions to their bankers to release it to particular people upon one's demise.

Others use Will storage facilities. We are not aware of specific Will storage facilities but there are many such facilities outside the country.

These facilities normally guarantee that the Will shall not be opened and easily accessible. These are fireproof facilities that hold records

dating over two hundred years.

Advance decision on treatment

I am a high net worth individual and want to make sure that in case there arises a situation where I do not have capacity to make a decision for myself on any health condition that I may be facing, a person appointed by myself should make decisions as per my written instructions. How should I go about this?

21st December 2009

This is an interesting question. To begin with, you do not need to be a high net worth individual to think this way. Many others make such decisions based on religious and other family reasons.

What you are intending to make is called an 'advance decision' which is a decision made by you that at a later time and in circumstances specified by you, and when you are not otherwise able to consent to or refuse the treatment, you do not wish a specified treatment to be carried out or continued. In other words, it is a means for you to communicate in advance your wish to refuse any treatment you might otherwise receive. It can be used to refuse treatment you object to on religious or other grounds.

It is important to be very clear as to precisely what treatment you are specifying and in what circumstances you intend to refuse it. It is worth consulting a doctor for precise definition of the treatment you wish to refuse.

This advance decision will not apply if there are reasonable grounds for believing that there are circumstances which you did not anticipate at the time you made the advance decision and which would have affected your decision had you anticipated them.

Please note that the advance decision can only apply where the person providing your health care is aware of it. You should think carefully about where you keep the decision and how it will be communicated to the relevant professional. It may be necessary to have its existence recorded on your hospital files with a copy of the advance decision. You should also consider making family and friends aware of the existence of the advance decision. We suggest that this advance decision be made in writing and by way of a power of attorney.

We are also unsure why you are thinking on these lines. Are you suffering from a terminal or any other serious disease? If so, we would strongly recommend that you also make a Will.

Unwanted pregnancy and abortion

I got pregnant by a man I never intended to have a baby with. I know abortion is illegal but some of my friends have been telling me that I can abort my unborn child as long as I have valid reasons to do so. Is this true?

26th October 2009

Our answer is not what you want to hear. From your question, you have honestly told us (which we appreciate) that your reason to abort is that you never intended to have a baby with the man who impregnated you. You have also correctly pointed out that abortion is illegal, unless there are reasons for aborting. Your reason is not accepted by our law and hence you cannot abort.

Abortion has been a controversial subject in societies around the world, because of the moral and ethical issues that surround it. It has been regularly banned and otherwise limited, but abortions have continued to be commonplace in many areas where it is illegal. In Tanzania under the Penal Code, performance of abortion is generally prohibited. Any person, who, with intent to procure the miscarriage of a woman, whether she is pregnant or not, unlawfully uses any means upon her is subject to fourteen years of imprisonment. A pregnant woman who undertakes the same act with respect to her own pregnancy or permits it to be undertaken is subject to seven years imprisonment. You can see that if you go ahead and abort, you may end up in jail.

There are, however, exceptions to that effect especially when abortion is performed to save the life of a pregnant woman. Section 230 of the Code provides that a person is not criminally responsible for performing, in good faith and with reasonable care and skill, a surgical operation upon an unborn child for the preservation of the mother's life, if the performance of the operation is reasonable having regard to the patient's state at the time, and to all the circumstances of the case. In addition, section 219 of the Code provides that no person shall be guilty of the offence of causing by willful act a child to die before it has an independent existence from its mother; if the act was carried out in good faith for the purpose of preserving the mother's life.

Wife refusing to have children with me

I have been married to a woman since 2006. Prior to our marriage my wife never raised any objections to having children knowing that I am particularly fond of children. Oddly after the marriage, my wife insisted on the use of contraceptives, which I accepted assuming that she did not want to have children immediately after marriage. It is now over three years and she is refusing to come off the contraceptives. She also avoids discussing the matter and refuses to have sexual intercourse without contraceptives, which is straining our relationship. This is affecting my health. What should I do?

21st September 2009

Most Tanzanians believe that children

bring luck to the family. The law does not, however, say that. The Law of Marriage Act does not make it mandatory for a couple who are married to have children. Children are a natural outcome of the marriage.

You have a few options: you can both go visit a marriage counsellor. This is not a legal solution but we choose to mention it. The second option is for you to petition for a divorce. One ground of divorce that you may be able to use is that of cruelty. Your wife's conduct in insisting on the use of contraceptives and refusing to bear a child is also causing you mental anguish. The test here is a subjective one but you have good chances of succeeding. Your wife's deliberate and consistent refusal to satisfy your natural and legitimate craving to have children can be interpreted as amounting to cruelty.

If the counselling does not work, and your desire to have children outweighs the importance of being married to this woman, then go ahead and file a petition for divorce.

Amendments to my Will

I made a Will ten years ago and wish to change it. My uncle who happens to be my executor advises me that I need not write the whole Will again; I could pass an amendment and attach it to the original Will. What do you suggest?

18th August 2009

A codicil is a written amendment to a person's Will, which must be dated, signed and witnessed just as a Will would be, and must make some reference to the Will it amends. A codicil can add to, subtract from or modify the terms of the original Will. When the person dies, both the original Will and the codicil are submitted in Court for the issuance of a probate and forms the basis for administration of the estate.

Typing out the amendment to your Will is appropriate. However, it seems like you have not reviewed your Will for a very long time. We normally advise our clients to review their Wills every two years if not every year, mainly depending on changes in their asset base.

Whilst the codicil is fine, we would highly recommend you to draft a new Will that shall capture all changes in your asset base over the ten years. Drafting a new Will does not take time and you should seriously consider it.

Should you still decide to draft a codicil make sure that it is clear and unambiguous.

No intercourse after marriage

Two months ago I married a girl from India who has refused to have sexual intercourse with me. She does not give me any reasons. She insisted I get a HIV test which I did. The results came out negative and she still does not want to cooperate. What can I do? Mine was an arranged marriage – my wife looks like a film star and my friends tell me that I might not be as good looking.

10th August 2009

You are in a very difficult position. We are lawyers and not marriage counsellors. We would, however, first advise you to seek the help of a marriage counsellor who may be able to assist.

The law is very clear. Consummation of a marriage is the completion of a marriage by an act of sexual intercourse which is defined as complete penetration with or without a condom. If your spouse is incapable of consummation or refuses without good reason to consummate the marriage, these are good grounds for annulment of the marriage. Annulment of marriage would require a declaration by Court that a marriage was never legally valid i.e. that you were never really married.

The fact that your wife looks like a film star and you being not very attractive does not matter. There is a very famous English case with very similar facts. Your petition for annulment will be successful irrespective of your looks.

No contact from husband

My husband and I had lived in Dar for many years before he was posted to go to the DRC. Since he left in 2002, I only heard from him once in the same year and have no contact from him since. His family is also unsure where he is and it seems everyone has lost touch with him. I have recently found a new man in my life and wish to remarry. Please guide me.

3rd August 2009

In circumstances such as yours, the Law of Marriage Act provides that where a person has not been heard of for five or more years by those who might have expected to have heard from him if he were alive, there shall be a rebuttable presumption that he is dead. Hence in the eyes of the law, it can be assumed that your husband is no more.

Our law provides that in such circumstances you cannot just contract another marriage without obtaining a decree of dissolution of the marriage from the Court on the ground of desertion. You will need to make a formal application in Court for such orders, and until such orders are granted, you should not enter into a contract of marriage with the new man in your life.

Distinction between adultery by wife and husband

I got married to my husband seven years ago with whom I have lived happily until last year when my husband started having an extra marital affair with our former maid. In retaliation and out of anger, I also had a quick affair with a certain man. A few weeks ago, my husband found me kissing that man. He started accusing me of adultery. I responded by telling him about his affair and he ordered me to shut up claiming that he was the man of the house. Is this fair?

13th July 2009

What constitutes an essential fact of adultery is not defined under our Law of Marriage. Nevertheless, one would define adultery to mean any act or acts with effect of violating the marriage tie, which is committed by either of the spouses by copulation, with a third person. Adultery can also be committed by acts other than carnal intercourse which also constitutes violations of marital fidelity, such as libidinous acts and artificial insemination. Commission of adultery therefore does not only require the overt moral infidelities but even simple lascivious acts committed by a wife and vice versa with a person other than a husband or wife suffice.

Coming back to your question, you said that you started to have a 'quick affair' (whatever that means) with a man and hence there is no doubt that the act of you kissing the man constitutes adultery.

Whether there is a distinction between adultery by the wife and/or by the husband, the answer is in the negative. The marriage between spouses is governed by moral and legal equality of the husband and wife, within the limits laid down by the law (in most communities customary law) to safeguard the unity of the family. Notwithstanding, we decline to suggest that a husband has right over the wife about marital fidelities. Considering the current state of affairs, it seems like your marriage is disintegrating and that deliberate steps are required by both of you to salvage the situation. Before you see a lawyer we recommend you meet with a marriage counsellor for guidance.

Dowry not paid for marriage

I was born thirty six years ago in Serengeti

district, Mara Region. In 2000, I impregnated my neighbour's daughter and thereafter lived with her as man and wife. We were also blessed with three children. A month ago, my wife died in a bus accident and her parents took the body and denied me her body for burial claiming I had not paid dowry. So as not to cause any chaos I succumbed to the pressure. Was it proper for them to act that way?

8th June 2009

Since May 1st 1971, the law governing all questions of marriage in Tanzania, are in the Law of Marriage Act 1971. This Act clearly states that a marriage which in all other respects complies with the express requirements of the Act shall be valid notwithstanding any non-compliance with any custom relating to dowry or the giving or exchanging of gifts before or after the marriage. In other words since the coming into the operation of the Law of Marriage Act, payment of dowry or bride wealth is no longer (if it was) necessary for the validity of a marriage. Payment of dowry or bride wealth is a mere customary rite which has no legal significance for a marriage.

The fact that you and your wife lived together in the circumstances led the outside world to believe that you were husband and wife and that was a valid marriage in all eyes of the law. Hence the argument that you were not the husband was wrong and the parents to your deceased wife did not act fairly with you.

Can I change my Will?

I own about five properties in Dar es Salaam and had made a Will where I gave two of the five properties to my wife, and the other three to each of my three children. However, due to the current market conditions, I have had to sell four of the properties and

only remain with one. What should I do with my Will? Could I sell the properties that I had written on the Will?

15th June 2009

People often believe that once they leave property under their Will, they lose the right to sell or otherwise dispose of the property during their life time. This is not so. You retain the right to do whatever you choose with your property, notwithstanding its mention in your Will.

You cannot give what you do not have. Hence the four properties cannot be inherited by your wife or children. The property has changed hands. We suggest you draw a new Will.

Succession by children born out of wedlock

My father died two years ago and left a Will where two thirds of his properties are bequeathed to two children, which my father had out of wedlock. I am not satisfied with the way my father distributed his property. What should I do?

1st June 2009

Every person owning property has the right to enjoy and deal with their property the way they like. A dead person can only deal with their property through a Will.

A Will is a statement in writing signed in accordance with certain formalities by which a person disposes of their estate to take effect after their death.

If someone wants to leave their property to certain named individuals or organisations, they will have to leave a valid Will. A Will is said to be valid if it is in writing, signed, witnessed and it contains unambiguous and clear statements regarding the disposition of the person's property upon death. If someone dies having made a valid Will, he or she has died testate. If no Will was made the person will have died intestate. The validity of a Will is normally proved by the Court.

The process of proving a Will is known as probate. During the probate the Court approves and gives authority to the executor, who is the person appointed to execute the Will. Once a probate is done, the executor will carry out the Will. However, the executor has no power or authority to vary or distribute the deceased's estate contrary to the contents of the Will.

Coming to your question, whilst we do sympathise with your personal position, unless the Will left by your father is not valid, there is nothing you can do. The wishes of your father must be respected and the estate of your father must be distributed according to his Will. However, you might wish to take a copy of the Will and meet your attorney for further guidance, if any.

Mother in law a nightmare

My husband and I live in a house with my mother in law. Over the past six months, I have been having major issues with my mother in law. I do not accept the way she behaves with me. Everything I do is an issue for her. She asks me personal questions and is not allowing me to live in peace. I want to a divorce. How do I go about this?

11th May 2009

The contract of marriage is like any other contract – built on mutual consent and understanding of the two parties. You are married to your husband and not to your mother in law. The contract is between you and your husband and not between you and your mother in law.

The fact that your mother in law is behaving weirdly with you does not mean you divorce your husband. Your question does not say that your husband is misbehaving. You are

specifically mentioning your mother in law. Answering your question strictly, the reasons adduced above are not grounds for you to divorce your husband.

However, if your husband is taking sides with your mother in law, which he very well may be, and you have no peace of mind or are being treated cruelly by your husband, you may petition for divorce. However, prior to filing your petition, the law requires you to refer the dispute to the Marriage Conciliation Board which will summon you and your husband and try to resolve the said dispute. If the Marriage Conciliation Board fails to resolve the dispute, it will issue a certificate setting out its findings and you can proceed to Court.

In order for the Court to pass a decree for divorce, it should be satisfied that the following grounds, which show that the marriage has broken down irreparably, exist. Some of these grounds are adultery, sexual perversion, cruelty, wilful neglect, imprisonment for life or for a period of not less than five years, mental illness certified by at least two doctors or change of religion by either party.

In your petition, you may also pray for other reliefs such as child custody, if any, and maintenance for yourself and the child.

Breach of promise to marry

I am a 26-year-old girl and had a relationship with a married man with whom I have a child aged 5. The man had promised to marry me but has now changed his mind. He no longer wants to see me or maintain our child. What should I do?

20th April 2009

There being a subsisting marriage that man cannot marry you. Under the Law of Marriage Act a married man cannot contract to marry another woman unless the subsisting marriage is polygamous. You have not told us the kind of marriage the man has, whether it is monogamous or polygamous. You have also not told us the reasons for him avoiding you or refusing to support the child. However, taking facts as they are, it seems that the man has cheated you – it is a breach of promise to marry.

Under the law, a breach of a promise to marry is actionable. Though you cannot sue for an order for specific performance of the promise to marry i.e. for him to be forced to marry you, it is allowed to sue for damages provided the claim is presented in Court within the period of one year from the date of the breach. Suing for damages is the only available remedy available to you, for Courts cannot force one to marry another.

With regard to the issue of maintenance for the child, you should remember that the child is, as far as the man is concerned, an illegitimate child. He is a child born out of wedlock and as such, under the Law of Marriage Act, has no direct right of maintenance from the man. However, this should not discourage you. You can still file a petition in Court and get an order against the man for maintenance of the child.

Under the Affiliation Act Cap 278 you are allowed to petition against the man for orders of maintenance of the child if you can prove that the man is the biological father of the child and that the man paid some maintenance for the child within twelve months after the birth of the child.

Administration of our senile father

Our father is 92-years-old and has become incapable of managing his affairs. Our step mother is taking the chance to transfer his properties into her own name and dispose some of the properties without the consent of the rest of the family. What should we do?

28th April 2009

Even though your father has become incapable to manage his affairs including his properties, that does not mean that he has lost his interests and rights over the same. Your step mother cannot deal with his properties the way she is purporting to, for lack of authority. The law, the Mental Diseases Act, has provided a procedure of managing affairs of persons having problems, like that of your father. The law allows any relative of the person facing the problem to apply to the High Court for an order to manage and administer the estate of such a person. The application in that respect is made in the way of chamber summons supported by an affidavit.

The affidavit must state in detail the grounds upon which it is made and particulars as to the properties and kindred of the person to whom it relates. We therefore advise you to organise a family or clan meeting in which you will nominate a person suitable for the charge. A person appointed by the Court under this procedure will discharge his duties under directions of the Court.

Caught red handed in adultery

I have, for quite some time suspected my neighbour of having an affair with my wife. I arranged a trap and caught them red handed. The event was witnessed amongst others by two policemen. Very surprisingly the police have refused to take my offender to Court urging me to finish the matter at home. Is this correct? Advise me.

20th April 2009

Police do not open case files for every complaint made to them except those which are supported with some evidence of the commission of the offence. Under our law, an act of adultery is not a criminal offence. It is a tortuous liability atoned by damages. It is a civil wrong committed by the adulterer. Being a civil wrong, adultery does not fall within the ambit of the duties of the police.

The job of the police is to enforce law i.e. make people obey the law, prevent and solve crime. Since adultery is a tort and not a crime, the police have nothing to do with it unless on the eventful date there was a commotion resulting in bodily injuries, which is not the case here. We therefore subscribe to the way the police dealt with your case. As said above, you can sue the adulterer for damages because his acts amount to an enticement.

Husband having an affair

My husband is definitely having an affair. I obviously cannot prove it but I found many intimate messages on his phone. Can I get a divorce? What should I do?

13th April 2009

Having an extra marital relationship is one of the factors upon which Courts can dissolve a marriage. The problem is proving adultery. This is so because those engaged in adulterous affairs do so in secret. However, this should not discourage you to file for a divorce, if you so wish, because the Court can still grant a decree for divorce after taking into consideration all relevant evidence regarding the conduct and circumstances of the parties involved in the alleged adulterous association.

In your case you say you cannot prove that he is involved in an adulterous affair. Yet you have said that you have seen such evidence that makes you believe he is involved with someone else.

Such evidence with any other independent evidence can be used in a Court of Law. You have not told us when you contracted your marriage with your husband. Assuming two years have passed since you were married, the procedure to follow is to refer the dispute to a Marriage Conciliatory Board for reconciliation. In the event the reconciliation fails, the board will issue you with a certificate to that effect and you can then petition for a decree of

divorce, in any competent Court. You are also allowed to include in your petition, prayers for custody of children of the marriage, if any, maintenance of the children and yourself, and division of matrimonial assets you have jointly acquired during the subsistence of the marriage. Your last question 'what should I do?' cannot be answered by us. It is entirely your decision on how you want to approach the issue.

Foreign divorce

I got my divorce in the UK a few months ago. I am a Tanzanian national and wish to know if I need to get my divorce decree registered here. My first marriage was blessed in Dar es Salaam six years ago.

6th April 2009

Our Law of Marriage Act recognises decrees' passed by any Court of competent jurisdiction in foreign countries. The foreign divorce decree is effective and can be registered in Tanzania regardless of where the contract of marriage arose.

There is a standard procedure to follow for such registration. Application for registration of foreign decrees for divorce is made to the offices of the Registrar-General in the administrator general's offices known as RITA. It is advisable that you register the decree at the soonest possible.

Dying early if I make a Will

Our family believes that if you make a Will you die early. A close friend of mine advises me that it is important for me to have a Will. What do you suggest?

30th March 2009

We cannot comment on whether one dies early or not if he prepares a Will. What we can tell you is that preparing a valid Will is important. Without a Will you cannot control who will inherit your property after your death. If you die without a Will, you die intestate and the management of your assets is placed in the hands of administrators appointed by the Court. We have noticed that this leads to major conflicts, enough to split entire families.

Your friend has advised you correctly. In today's fast changing world, it is important that anyone above the age of 18 prepares a Will. If you are married, both you and your wife should prepare a Will. This is true even if marital assets are primarily in the name of one spouse.

Usually you will wish to make your spouse as your main beneficiary and include an alternative gift to take effect if he or she predeceases you.

Before preparing your Will, make sure that you have a list of your assets and decide how you want such assets to be distributed. You will also have to name an executor in the Will, who shall have the responsibility of managing your property after your death and distributing the property according to the terms of your Will. Once a Will is prepared, it is valid until it is revoked. We advise that you review your Will once every year.

We have noticed that many people do not prepare a Will because they are poor or in the middle income group. However, poor you are, you must have a Will. Preparing a Will is normally inexpensive and quick.

New administrator challenging old sale

In 2004, I bought a house in Turiani township from the administrator of an estate. The sale was conducted at the office of the primary Court magistrate and one of the witnesses was the magistrate. Three months later, one of the family members challenged the process leading to his appointment. The administrator of the estate was changed following the case. I had already demolished the old house and am building a new house on the plot. The new administrator of the estate now threatens my workmen at the site that I am an illegal owner of the property and that by being appointed administrator of the estate, he has rights over all properties, including the ones sold. What do I do?

9th March 2009

An administrator is a person appointed by the Court to manage the properties of the estate of the deceased; his main duty is among others to collect the assets of the deceased person, payments of the debts, if any and distribution of the surplus to the beneficiaries of the estate of the deceased.

In administration of the estate of the deceased, change or removal of the administrator is a common thing. The change of the administrator can occur for different reasons including death of the administrator, failure to perform duties due to health reasons, negligence or fraudulent and/or unfaithful acts. When one of these is established, the Court can order for removal of the administrator.

However, the important issue here is what will be the fate or rights of the third parties who might have dealt with him/her during his/her tenure of office as an administrator. To put it differently what would be the status of all the transactions done between the 3rd parties and the outgoing administrator after the removal of the administrator? Will the removal of the administrator affect his/her previous transactions as far as the 3rd parties are concerned? The answers to the above question must be in the negative. The removal of the administrator does not invalidate any acts or transactions done by him/her during his/her tenure of office as administrator of the deceased's estate. This is because in dealing with the administrator, 3rd parties were faithfully in all reasonable circumstances, dealing with the right person. There are of course few exceptional circumstances where the removal of an administrator will adversely affect the status of his previous transactions. One of these includes a situation where after assuming the office, the administrator involves himself in unfaithful or fraudulent transaction to the detriment of the deceased's estate and its beneficiaries. For example where the administrator assigns the properties of the assets to his own relatives or where he keeps proceeds of the assets of the estate for his own use. Under such circumstances the change of the administrator will definitely affect the previous transactions in the event it is established that the 3rd parties participated in the mischief that led to the removal of the administrator. In your case you are a bonafide purchaser of the house in question as long as you did not take part in any mischief. If the new administrator is threatening you or your workmen, you can take legal action against him including filing a suit for a perpetual injunction to restrain the new administrator from trespassing or interfering with your joyous ownership of the house.

Parents dead, administrator cheating us

I am the eldest son in our family. Our parents passed away last year and our paternal uncle was appointed, by the High Court, as an administrator of the estate of our deceased parents. We now do not benefit from our parents' properties and want to remove the administrator of the estates for dishonesty. How do we go about this?

16th February 2009

This has happened to many people in many parts of the world. Some of the appointed administrators look at their own selfish interests and are not honest and transparent in discharging their duties as administrators or executors.

In order to remove or revoke the grant

of the letters of administration to the administrator (your uncle), you will have to prove that he is not faithful or honest in his dealings related to the estate. You will have to file an application in the High Court, the same Court that appointed your uncle, for revocation of the letters of administration and you will have to prove the allegations made. The application must be filed by way of a chamber summons supported by an affidavit. If the issue is urgent, then you may also attach a certificate of urgency to expedite the hearing of your application. Make sure you are well prepared to support your allegations.

Mother unaware of marriage of 16-year-old

My husband consented to a marriage proposal for our 16-year-old daughter while I was away on a business trip. I was shocked to find my daughter married when I got back. Is this legal?

23rd February 2009

Marriage is a voluntary union of a man and a woman intended to last for their joint lives. A marriage is contracted if there is free and voluntary consent given by the parties who are purporting to get married. Under our law, the Law of Marriage Act 1971, a person is not allowed to get married to a girl who has not attained the age of 15 years unless there are special reasons. Your daughter, however, is 16 years which is the age that the Act allows a girl to get married at. However, to marry a girl who is 16 years or above but has yet to reach the age of 18, the law provides that you have to also get consent of the father of the child. If the father is dead then the consent of the mother, and if the mother is also dead you can get consent of the guardian of the said child.

If your daughter consented to the marriage freely and voluntarily, and since the father also consented, the contract of marriage cannot be challenged.

If your daughter has been forced into marriage and hence the consent was either obtained fraudulently or by coercion, then the contract of marriage is challengeable.

You need to speak to your daughter immediately and find out if she had agreed to the marriage. If she was forced into the marriage, you can file an application for annulment of the marriage.

Husband beating wife

I am married and living with my husband here in Kigoma. Since our marriage in June 2007, my husband has been beating me severely and I feel that I cannot live with him anymore. Can I divorce him?

19th January 2009

Beating one's wife is termed under the law as cruelty and a good ground for divorce. However, the Law of Marriage Act does not allow a couple to divorce if the marriage has not existed for at least two years. The option that you have is to apply in Court for leave to divorce before the two years of marriage have elapsed. Based on the information, that you are suffering exceptional hardship, it is likely that leave to petition for divorce shall be granted although two years have not elapsed. However, prior to going to Court for leave, the law requires you to refer the dispute to the Marriage Conciliation Board which will summon you and your husband and try and resolve the said dispute. If the Marriage Conciliation Board fails to resolve the dispute, it will issue a certificate setting out its findings.

When leave is granted you will have to file a petition for divorce to Court attaching the certificate from the Marriage Conciliation Board. The petition can be filed in any Court be it a District Court, Resident Magistrate's Court or High Court.

In order for the Court to pass a decree for divorce, it should be satisfied that the following grounds, which show that the marriage has broken down irreparably, exist. Some of these grounds are adultery, sexual perversion, cruelty, wilful neglect, imprisonment for life or for a period of not less than five years, mental illness certified by at least two doctors or change of religion by either party.

In your petition, you may also pray for other reliefs such as child custody, if any, and maintenance for yourself and the child.

Child custody battle

What factors does a Court consider before deciding in whose custody an infant should be placed? My boy is 12 months old.

26th January 2009

The underlying principle is the welfare of the child. According to the Law of Marriage Act, before deciding on the custody of the child, the Court considers several factors some of which are the age of the child, character of the parents (example one is not involved in prostitution or an alcoholic), wishes of the infant where he or she is of an age to express an independent opinion, income of the parents and the wishes of the parents. If you are of sound mind, good character, have the means of supporting the child, and since the child is below the age of seven years, it is very likely that the Court shall grant you custody of the child as the Law of Marriage Act clearly states that it is good for an infant below the age of seven years to be with his or her mother.

Employment Disputes

The way you treat your employees is the way they will treat you.

Understanding Employment Law is challenging at the best of times. Misconceptions, misinterpretations and simple ambiguity often find us seeking advice and clarification both from the employee and employer. This chapter provides some clarity on employment issues and labour laws. Such laws may or may not be implemented at the work place; however if there is a labour dispute the Labour Law will come into play and more often than not, the law will be in favour of the employee. Ignorance is not an excuse. Know your legal rights; know the rights of an employee and know the rights of an employer. It will save you and your company a lot of time and money.

Pay as an expat

I was born in Tanzania but have lived in Norway for the past fifteen years. I came to visit Tanzania after ten years and loved the place. I decided to reapply for my Tanzanian passport, which I got in a record seven days. I have now secured a job with a consultancy company and want to apply for a work permit so that I get paid as an expatriate. What should I do?

7th April 2011

Under our laws your action of applying for a second passport is illegal and you are liable to be prosecuted. As of now, Tanzania disallows citizens to have dual citizenship. Applying for a work permit when you are a citizen of Tanzania is also illegal. Your lawyer can guide you further.

Exemption from NSSF

I am an expatriate staff employee by a holding company in the UK. Presently I am working in Tanzania and being paid here. I have a pension scheme back home but the National Social Security Fund (NSSF) wants my company to pay the statutory pension contributions. What should I do?

7th May 2011

NSSF is governed by the NSSF Act. In this Act, the employee is defined as a person who has a contract of employment and is employed in mainland Tanzania.

The normal principle of insurance that the insured, in this case the pensioner, should not benefit twice is also applicable here. You must remember that the pension amounts are your funds entrusted by statute on the NSSF for you to enjoy upon retirement. Since you are already enrolled in a pension scheme back in your country, you can apply to the NSSF for an exemption. If the scheme back home is similar with the NSSF scheme, you may be allowed an exemption. Otherwise you will have to contribute to NSSF locally, failure of which your company may face criminal prosecution.

Termination because of Facebook

I was a secretary in a bank in Dar es Salaam. A few months ago there was a memo sent by the management that we were not allowed to visit any social networking sites such as Facebook and Twitter. After some weeks, I happened to be logged onto Facebook and my boss saw me and warned me verbally. A few weeks later my head of department also saw me logged in to one of these sites, and reported it to HR. The HR Manager called me in and held a disciplinary hearing. Three days later I was fired. One of the reasons was the comments I posted about my employer and work place. Was this legal? I feel this was unfair because I just sneaked into Facebook and my performance was not bad at all in the work place.

21st February 2011

We do sympathise with you on the loss of your job. We are, however, not as sympathetic with you on the termination.

The Employment Laws of Tanzania stipulate that the termination of an employee is judged to be fair or unfair after examining the reason for termination and the procedure used for termination. This test is in most cases subjective.

It appears that you had once been warned about logging onto Facebook during office hours. Furthermore, your employer gave you an opportunity to be heard before termination, and hence used the correct procedure.

Even though social networking sites like Facebook are fairly new in Tanzania, whenever they are incompatible with job activities, termination can be effected. The issue of you posting comments about your work place and employer on your Facebook page may also be grounds for termination.

Most employers disallow use of Facebook in the workplace because Facebook is addictive and affects one's concentration, resulting in inefficiencies. While it is a subjective test, we personally think that the termination was fair. However, you should consult your attorneys, who can review all of the facts and guide you further.

Types of work permits

I intend to invest in Tanzania and wish to know how difficult it is to get an immigration permit. What types of permits are there and where does one start? If I want to be employed as an expatriate, what do I do?

7th February 2011

There are three types of residence permits which are issued to anyone intending to reside in Tanzania for business, work, or any other acceptable purpose. These are Class A, for self-employed foreigners (investors), Class B, for foreigners having secured jobs in Tanzania, and Class C, for other classes of foreigner such as missionaries, students or volunteers.

The power to issue a residence permit is held by the Director of Immigration Services. Applicants who are not satisfied by the director's decision may appeal to the Minister for Home Affairs.

As a prospective investor, you must apply for a Class A permit, and will be required to submit, a certificate from the Tanzania Investment Centre (TIC), a cover letter, a curriculum vitae, educational certificates (if appropriate), company registration, memorandum and articles of association, evidence of business premises, sectoral approval from any relevant ministry (if applicable), share certificates, and a copy of passport pages authenticating nationality and validity of passport.

Director in a company

I was appointed as a director in an agriculture company. For the past ten years all of the profits have been retained and reinvested in the business. In January 2010, the company declared dividends, but I was not paid my dividends as a director. What should I do?

10th January 2011

As a director you are entitled to directors' remuneration as agreed upon. You are not a shareholder of the company and hence not entitled to dividends. We believe you are confusing being a director of a company and being a shareholder. However, in some companies the directors are also shareholders.

In your case, perhaps because of your professional qualifications or relations with other members or directors of the company, you were appointed as a director of the company and do not own any shares. We do not see anything wrong in what the company has done to you.

Not to work 'elsewhere' clause

I recruited, trained and promoted a pilot with the understanding that he would not work with any other airline for the duration of five years. He has now served me with a notice of three months intending to quit. I am unable to convince him not to leave. Can I stop him from working in any other airline?

30th November 2010

This depends on the exact wording of your clause. However, a 'not to work for any other airline' clause for five years is very unreasonable. If this would go to Court, your employee's argument would be 'what do you expect him to earn for the duration of the five years when he is unemployed?' Put yourself in his shoes – don't you think your clause is very restrictive and unreasonable? You cannot expect a pilot to stop flying and start driving a *daladala* just because he entered, very foolishly and perhaps out of desperation, into this weird contract with you.

If you have a loan agreement with him to finance his studies and he is to repay through his salary, you may be able to pursue him on the loan agreement for the loan amount. You will not be able to stop him from working elsewhere. Your clause is in restraint of trade and our opinion is that no Court will entertain your suit.

Labour laws very unfair

I am a foreign investor finalising my manufacturing plant in western Tanzania. I have been informed by my lawyers that in Tanzania you cannot just terminate an employee. Does that mean my employees have life time contracts? Is it also true that there is extensive litigation in labour Courts?

15th November 2010

It is not true that employees have life time contracts in Tanzania. With the coming of the Employment and Labour Relations Act, there is a procedure to terminate your employees.

You cannot just wake up one fine day and, without cause or justification, terminate your employees.

It is best to have a fixed term contract with your employees with a termination clause which would also automatically apply as soon as the term of the contract expires. You can, at your will, renew it and this should protect your interest.

There are clearly set guidelines on how an employee can and should be terminated. If the employee has committed an act of gross misconduct, this is a ground for termination, but you have to follow a laid down procedure which includes giving the employee a chance to defend his position. If the procedure is not followed, it becomes a ground for the

employee to raise unfair termination issues at a later stage.

You sound like you would become a slave if you employ a Tanzanian. This is not the case – whilst many claim that the law is in favour of the employee, it is also true that there is adequate protection for the employer. The key is to make sure that when you terminate you follow the right procedure.

On the litigation front, yes it is true that there are many cases in the Labour Courts including the Commission for Mediation and Arbitration. Employees have realised their rights whilst employers, sadly, continue to flout the termination rules. Sometimes it seems to us that employers have either not understood the Act or have just not read it.

Legal effect of omitting part of claim

In 2008, I was unlawfully terminated by my employer and filed an employment case. After a long hearing, the Commission for Mediation and Arbitration decided in my favour and granted payments in lieu of notice, leave payment, severance allowance, etc. The total amount came to TZS 3.5M. The employer complied with the order and I was accordingly paid. Recently I discovered that I'd not claimed against the employer for overtime, which is worth TZS 800,000. What procedures should I use to get my overtime payment? Please advise me accordingly.

8th November 2010

Essentially, it is in the interest of justice that disputes should one day come to an end. Claimants should always claim the entire sum and/or reliefs unless completely relinquished. In your case, you ought to have claimed the overtime in your original suit because it involved substantially the same matter. The law is very clear that once a party elects to sue for part of their claim at the time when other parts of their lawful claims arising out of the same parties and cause of action are fully matured, then the omission or part so relinquished cannot usually be claimed afterwards. It is likely that the remaining part of your claim will be barred under the law under a principle of law known as 'res judicata'.

Boss makes ten times my salary

I came back from Europe two years ago and have been working as a secretary in a mining company in Mwanza. A few weeks ago I managed to get access to the payroll of the company and found that my boss, who is not as smart as he thinks, gets paid ten times my salary. Is that not discriminatory? How can one person be paid so much? How can I institute a suit against the company?

4th October 2010

There is no law in Tanzania that limits the amount of executive pay in the private sector. You claim to have lived in Europe and should know about this. Whether your boss is as smart as he thinks, or looks, does not matter. As long as you are being paid above the minimum salary, the mining company is not in breach of any law.

We must mention one more thing – your action of illicitly viewing the payroll could lead to your dismissal. Please take note of that.

Employment for person with disability

I have been disabled since childhood, having fallen victim to polio. I was brought up in Kigoma, moved to Moshi and then to Dar. During my lifetime, there has been no facility for the disabled. In Kigoma and Moshi, I would have to be physically carried into schools and offices, as none of these buildings had access points for persons with disabilities. Dar es Salaam, even though it has newer buildings, is no better. Is there no law that forces developers to build facilities for persons with disabilities? My

second question concerns on the job discrimination against people like myself. We are underpaid, mistreated and many a times unemployed. Who comes to our protection?

30th August 2010

You have raised some very pertinent questions. Unfortunately, the older buildings still do not have easy access points for persons with disabilities.

A new law has been passed by parliament – the Persons with Disabilities Act 2010. This has addressed some of your concerns.

The law is clear in that all persons with disabilities shall be entitled to a barrier-free and disability-friendly environment with social amenities to assist and promote their mobility, thus enabling them access to public premises and facilities for public use, roads, and communications. The law further adds that architects, engineers and other people who are involved in the design and construction of the physical premises shall observe and comply with accessibility requirements to ensure that all new buildings, roads, playgrounds, transport facilities and renovation of the old ones, conforms to designs aimed at creating access for people with disabilities. Under the law, it is an offence for a person with disabilities to be denied access to such public buildings.

As for the discrimination towards employment of a person with disabilities, the law states that this is illegal and an offence punishable by fine, imprisonment, or both. In short, any employer or potential employer who discriminates against a person because of his disability may end up in prison.

Working without a contract

I have been employed in a locally registered company in the agriculture sector. Since I started working here, I have never signed a contract of employment. This is my seventh year in the company, and when I recently went to ask for my contract I was looked at very suspiciously. Please advise.

24th May 2010

You have a very interesting question – are you employed by the company that you have worked for? The answer is in the affirmative. Just because you have no contract, does not mean that you do not work there or have no rights against your employer. The law looks at you as an employee, and you should receive the same treatment as a colleague who has a contract. Should you be fired, you will be entitled to whatever the law provides.

Employee transfer

I am employed in a private company with branches in different regions of Tanzania. My superiors have transferred me to the southern part of Tanzania. I have not objected, but I want my wife and children to come with me. The problem I face is that if my wife is to join me, she will lose her current job. Does my employer also have to look for a job for my wife?

3rd May 2010

Although we sympathise with the consequences of your transfer to a new working station, we are of a settled opinion that your employer is not under any legal obligation to look for employment for your wife. It would also not make business sense for the law to require employers to do so.

In view of you agreeing to the transfer, your wife's job loss is a family matter that needs to be sorted internally. The employer should, however, pay for the cost of transferring you to this new area.

Coming late to work

My company is one of the largest players in the agriculture sector in Tanzania. I have not-

ed a lot of my workers do not come to work on time or are absent claiming they are sick. The employees who come late, claim that they rely on unreliable transport services and hence come late to work. I fired a few of these workers who have now taken me to Court. Is this allowed? Does the law not allow me to fire those who come late or are absent?

15th March 2010

It does not matter whether you are a large player or small player. The law applies to all and you cannot stop one from going to Court. We do sympathise with you on the absenteeism – however, in order to fire an employee there is a procedure that the law clearly states must be followed.

Those employees, who are coming late, must be warned of their behaviour and if this does not stop, you should issue them with an official warning letter, clearly stating your concerns. If the behaviour does not change, you are to call a disciplinary committee meeting, giving the employee a minimum of forty eight hours to prepare themselves for such a meeting. In the meeting, the employee can come with a representative of the union or a fellow employee. Minutes of the meeting should be taken, and based on giving the employee a chance to be heard, you may terminate the employee if the reasons adduced in the meeting are not to your satisfaction and amount to misconduct on the part of the employee. Please note that you cannot just fire employees without conducting this meeting and following the above mentioned procedure.

As for the sick leave, please be advised that the employee claiming sick leave must produce a medical certificate from a medical practitioner, whom you may choose to appoint or is acceptable to you. Without a medical certificate, an employee cannot claim sick leave and you can proceed to follow termination procedures as mentioned above.

Sick employee

I had a back injury and was away from work for three months. I was told to bed rest and take no stress. My employer insisted that since I am a computer programmer, I could work from my hospital bed and get pending work out of the way. I refused based on medical advice. After my release from hospital, I reported to work only to find that I was terminated. My desk had been cleared and the receptionist had instructions not to allow me in. It was very embarrassing for me. What should I do?

22nd February 2010

The Employment and Labour Relations Act 2004 is very clear on sick leave – an employee who produces a medical certificate from a registered practitioner acceptable to the employer, is entitled to sick leave that is paid in full for the first sixty three days and half pay for the subsequent sixty three days. In your instance, you are entitled to full pay whilst you were in hospital – you need not work for this pay as you are on sick leave, unless your employer was not notified. On the termination front, assuming that your employer knew of your sickness, be advised that you cannot be terminated on the grounds that have been mentioned in your question and can pursue it.

Fallout with my boss

I have been working for a company for many years. Recently, my relationship with my boss has deteriorated and he insists in giving me the toughest assignments. In view of this, my performance has dropped and I was forced to resign. What are my rights? A few months ago the same company also conducted a health check where they also tested employees for HIV/AIDS. One of them tested positive and was quietly removed. How does the law protect this person?

15th February 2010

The Employment and Labour Relations (Code of Good practice) GN 42 clearly states that where an employer makes an employment intolerable, which may result in the resignation of the employee, that resignation amounts to forced resignation or constructive termination. Unless there is something you have not told us, your case falls under this category and you have good grounds to lodge a complaint with the Commission for Mediation and Arbitration. You stand very high chances of success.

The same regulation comes to the protection of the person who has tested positive with HIV/AIDS by stating that no employment shall be terminated merely on the basis of HIV/AIDS status. It goes further and says that HIV/AIDS infected employees shall continue to work under normal conditions in their current employment for as long as they are medically fit to do so. The employer has illegally terminated the infected HIV/AIDS employee, who can take a similar action as what we recommended to you.

Terminated because of HIV

I work in a company that manufacturer shoes. Recently, the company has started testing its workers for HIV/AIDS and then has silently released some employees. I believe it is because they have tested positive. Is this sacking legal?

14th December 2009

One's employment cannot be terminated merely on the basis of their HIV/AIDS status. As a HIV/AIDS infected employee, one is like any other ill employee entitled to continue to work under normal conditions, as long as he or she is medically fit to do so. When the condition becomes critical and one cannot continue with employment, then there are grounds upon which the employer can apply to determine the employees' fate. To terminate one's employment merely on the basis of HIV/AIDS status amounts to discrimination against an employee at his/her work place and is illegal and a criminal offence under the law.

Both the Employment and Labour Relations Act, No.6 of 2004 and the HIV and AIDS (Prevention and Control) Act, No.28 of 2008 prohibit any acts, policy and any behaviour on the part of the employer which stigmatises or discriminates in any manner against the employee on the grounds of such employee's actual, perceived or suspected HIV/AIDS status.

Under the HIV and AIDS (Prevention and Control) Act, for example it is particularly stated that any person who stigmatises or discriminates in any manner against any other person on the grounds of such other person's HIV/AIDS status commits an offence and is liable to a fine of not less than TZS 2M or to imprisonment for a term not exceeding one year or both.

In the case you mentioned, should your fellow employees be fired because of their HIV/AIDS status, they can report the matter to the police and to the Legal and Human Rights Centre for help and guidance. As stated in law, it is an offence for which your employer can be imprisoned.

Employing a 14-year-old house girl

I have a house girl who is 14-years-old. One of my friends came to my family home and told me that it is against the law to employ a child of that age. I know many other people who have house girls younger than mine. Am I breaking the law?

19th October 2009

Child labour is a human rights issue of immense sensitivity. Child labour refers to the employment of children, under a certain age, at regular and sustained labour. This practice is considered exploitative by the United Nations and other international organisations and is illegal in many countries including Tanzania.

UNICEF estimates that about 158 million children aged 5-14 are engaged in child labour – one in six children in the world. Millions of children are engaged in hazardous situations or conditions, such as working in mines, working with chemicals and pesticides in agriculture or working with dangerous machinery. They are everywhere but invisible, toiling as domestic servants in homes, labouring behind the walls of workshops, hidden from view in plantations. In Sub-Saharan Africa around one in three children are engaged in child labour, representing sixty nine million children.

The minimum age at which a human can be put to work differs from country to country. In Tanzania under the Employment and Labour Relations Act, 2004, a child is a person under the age of 14 and for the employment in hazardous sectors, child means a person under the age of 18 years. Under this law, no person shall employ a child under the age of 14 years and that a child of 14 years of age, like your house girl, may only be employed to do light work, which is not likely to be harmful to the child's health and development; and does not prejudice the child's attendance at school, participation in vocational orientation or training programs approved by a competent authority. To employ a child in contravention of the above stated law is an offence.

Hence, if your house girl is not attending school, which she most likely is not, your employing her is illegal.

Retirement age in private sector

My company wishes to retire a senior level

officer who has been working with us for the past twenty five years. Is there a retirement age that I need to follow? I am informed that I cannot remove him from employment purely because of age?

5th October 2009

You effectively want to terminate the employee because of age. We assume that you are in the private sector which does not have a statutory retirement age. There is also no law that states that you cannot retire a worker – the information you have is therefore incorrect.

If your contract has a retirement age, that becomes the retirement age for that particular employee. Assuming there is no retirement age stipulated in your contract of employment, you would adopt the normal retirement age or policy of your company. For example, if past practice of retirement in your company is 65-years-old, that will, by default become the retirement age for the employee. If your company does not have a retirement age, then the industry norm for retirement would apply. This would then depend on the industry that you are in.

Termination because of breast feeding

I delivered a child six months ago and resumed work after ten weeks of delivery. I need to feed my child every one hour and go home for about fifteen minutes every hour. Initially my employer did not object but four weeks ago I was informed that this would not be allowed any longer and that if I do not stop breastfeeding, I would be terminated. Please advise?

27th July 2009

The hourly breast feeding schedule is very hard to understand and believe, unless you meant every few hours. However, for the purposes of answering your question, we will assume that it is an hourly feed that you are

referring to.

Your employer cannot ask you to stop breastfeeding. However, from what we can make of your situation, your employer is perhaps informing you that the hourly feeding is not acceptable. This might not be the answer you want, but we find it very hard to understand how you can go feed your child at home, on the hour, and still be working. You would hardly be working three to four hours a day and no employer would accept this. Think about it from the employer's point of view as well.

Whilst we sympathise with you, we wish to alert you to the Employment and Labour Relations Act, which states that where an employee is breast feeding a child, the employer shall allow the employee to feed the child during working hours up to a maximum of two hours per day. In your case, you are spending more than two hours breastfeeding and if you do not change, this would be a good ground for termination.

Forceful HIV/AIDS test

I have applied for a job as a secretary in a shipping line and am being forced to undergo a HIV/AIDS test. Is this allowed? How will such results be treated? Can my doctor just forward the results to a prospective employer?

6th July 2009

The HIV and AIDS (Prevention and Control) Act of 2008 is very clear on this. No person can be compelled to undergo HIV testing unless there is an order of the Court or the person is a donor of human organs and tissues. No consent is required on testing sexual offenders for HIV.

The Act also allows a medical practitioner to undertake a HIV test for a person without the consent of that person if the person is unconscious and unable to give consent and if the medical practitioner reasonably believes that such a test is clinically necessary or desirable in the interest of that person.

In your case, none of the above applies and hence you cannot be forced to undergo the test.

As for the release of HIV results, the Act also stipulates that all results of an HIV test shall be treated confidentially and shall only be released to the person tested. However, such results may also be released to a guardian of a child in the case of testing a child, a spouse or sexual partner of an HIV tested person or the Court. A doctor cannot send results to your employer without your consent and breach of confidentiality is an imprisonable offence.

Stealing to recover salary

I had a house girl who worked with me for a period of three years. Unfortunately, I did not pay her salary for the last seven months. She decided to steal my radio and run away. Is she liable for that act?

6th April 2009

The house girl could be charged with theft under the Penal Code. Under the law, dishonestly appropriating property belonging to another with the intention of permanently depriving the other of it is an offence of stealing punishable with imprisonment for a term of three years.

In your case you have not paid salaries for seven months the girl could argue that she was not dishonest as she believed she took the radio to compensate her unpaid salaries.

It is a general rule that a person is not criminally liable in respect of an offence relating to property if the act done by him or her was done in the exercise of an honest claim of right and without intention to defraud.

Considering the unpaid salaries, your house girl, if charged in the Court of Law, is most likely to leave the Court room as a free person if she proves that she had a claim of right and that she had not been paid her salaries. It is a good defence for her. To avoid such happenings, you should perhaps pay your people on time.

Salary not what was promised

I have been employed with a certain organisation and was promised a salary as indicated in their advertisement in the newspaper. Unfortunately, when I was employed, they gave me a salary below that which was published. They are claiming that I will be paid the published salary if I perform. How do I get my rights?

2nd March 2009

As a general rule a newspaper advertisement is an invitation to treat rather than an offer unless such an advertisement can be interpreted otherwise, which in your situation does not seem to be the case. The terms of contract of employment as stipulated were not final that is why we assume that when you responded to the advertisement, there was an interview that you attended based on which you were given an offer.

In Tanzania, there is specific regulation which regulates employment contracts in an effort to provide a measure of protection to employees. The Employment and Labour Relations Act provides that at the commencement of employment, the employer must provide an employee, in writing, the remuneration and its method of calculation and details of any benefits or payments in kind.

If you signed a contract with your employer, then the terms of contract are the ones that appear on the documents you signed and not what appeared in the advertisement. You were at liberty to elect not to sign the papers; however, since you did sign the contract, you cannot deny that you were not aware of the salary offered. If the salary is below what is in the contract, you have a good case against your employer and should pursue it.

We have answered this with a few assumptions and without having seen the advert that you are referring to. We suggest you also get advice from an employment consultant.

Trade union at workplace

A trade union approached us and wants to sign our employees as their members. I do not want a trade union. What should I do?
9th February 2009

The law gives a right to any authorised and registered trade union to enter into an employer's premises for the purposes of recruiting and communicating with members, meet members in dealings with the employer, to hold meetings of employees on the premises and vote in any ballot under the union constitution. Therefore the union has a right to recruit your employees and you are also required by the law to provide such union with any reasonable and necessary facilities required for it to conduct its activities at the workplace. Apart from that, the law also allows a trade union to establish a field branch at any workplace where ten or more of its members are employed.

This means the trade union has a right to open a field branch at your company only if ten of your employees are members of such a trade union. If such terms are fulfilled you cannot stop the establishment of a trade union at your workplace as it is a right provided by law. However, the trade union cannot forcefully sign up members at your premises. If your employees do not want to join the union, then the union cannot compel them to become members.

Termination from work

I have been terminated from work after having worked for a period of seven years. I was paid only a month's salary in lieu of notice. What other benefits do I deserve and how can I get them?
2nd February 2009

Assuming you are not objecting to your termination, your entitlements will depend on the contract of employment between yourself and your employer. Otherwise your statutory terminal benefits apart from one month's salary in lieu of notice include remuneration for work done before termination, any annual leave pay if not taken, severance allowance, transport allowance (which shall include subsistence allowance) if termination is done at a place other than where the employee was recruited. You are also entitled to a certificate of service. Should your employer ignore you regarding your rightful terminal benefits you are advised to refer the matter to the Commission for Mediation and Arbitration within thirty days from the date of termination.

Consumer and Claimant Rights

The law has realised that consumers do not read contracts. The law is evolving to ensure consumers are automatically protected by it.

Most business agreements have formal official contracts drawn up-and this is how it should be. However, contracts are long and tedious to read so many of us skim over the content and sign them. How many of us read the fine print? This chapter presents examples of what happens when you do not read contracts in their entirety. The chapter also covers various disputes with service providers whether it be with the insurance company, mobile company, financial institution or healthcare provider as well as disputes over tenancy agreements. You are within your right to seek clarity – so our advice to you is to read, ask questions and read again. Before you sign formal documents or enter into an agreement ask questions if you are unclear or if something does not seem right to you. You have nothing to lose by asking questions but perhaps a lot to lose if you do not.

Land grabbing in Bagamoyo

In 2006, I bought a piece of land from my neighbour adjoining my farm in Bagamoyo Township. There was no formal contract for the sale except the letter that I wrote to the seller upon which the seller acknowledged the receipt of the purchase price of the land in question. Subsequently, the seller re-sold the land to another person without my knowledge and consent. I was advised to sue both the seller and the buyer to recover my land, but to my surprise, the Chairman at the Land Tribunal has ruled against me. What should I do? What about the money I paid the seller?

25th April 2011

We do not have the Tribunal's proceedings with us in order to appreciate the Tribunal's reasons for ruling against you, nor do we have a copy of the letter that you executed between yourself and the seller to conclude the land transaction. It would have also been helpful for us if we knew what defence was brought by the parties you sued. From our past experience, we strongly suspect that you might have lost the case because the letter (contract) did not satisfy the necessary conditions of the law connected with the performance of the contract of sale of land. Under the Land Act, disposition of land must be in writing, which can take the form of a contract, memorandum or a note, provided it clearly defines essential terms such as identity of parties, the price and the description of the property being sold. With regards to your money, this will also depend on what claims your lawyer presented at the tribunal and reasons of the decision of the tribunal. Should you still believe that the decision of the tribunal is improper, we advise you to appeal to the High Court for further consideration. Your lawyer can guide you further.

Factory owners colluding in price

There are certain factories owned by some big shot owners that have developed monopolistic behaviour. They have colluded to fix prices of the product and are creating an artificial shortage. These are all signs of practices that are anti-competitive. Is there a law that can protect consumers in such a scenario?

25th April 2011

The Fair Competition Act will protect you. This Act established the Fair Competition Commission (FCC) which oversees such activities and protects the interests of consumers. The Act incorporates the Fair Competition Rules, Under the said rules there are provisions on how complaints are handled. As a consumer, you can complain by submitting information to the FCC in any manner, or using a standard form that the FCC Rules provide. Thereafter, the investigation department of the FCC will review the complaint and determine if those you have complained against have a case to answer or not. The Commission can use its discretion whether to entertain your complaint or not and if not, reasons must be provided. We suggest that you take the route above and fight for your rights through the FCC.

Injury in boxing ring

I fought a Tanzanian boxer who hit me very seriously below the jaw. I had a critical injury and the police are not allowing me to file a complaint. Can I sue for damages?

18th April 2011

In Law there is a famous doctrine – *volenti non fit injuria* i.e. that to which a man consents cannot be considered an injury. No act is actionable as a tort at the suit of any person who has expressly or impliedly assented to it and no one can enforce a right which he has voluntarily waived or abandoned.

This applies to intentional acts which would otherwise be tortuous. It seems like your injuries are as a result of the boxing match and hence the refusal by the police to file the complaint.

With the knowledge we have about boxing, a punch below the jaw is legal as far as boxing is concerned and hence, in our opinion, there is very little chance of you succeeding in any case that you intend to bring. Your lawyers can guide you further.

Fooled by cyber criminals

I am a job seeker, and while searching for a job, I came across an advertisement on a website. One of the requirements was to take an English proficiency test offered by an institute overseas. I had two options – either to pay by credit card, which I do not have, or remit the funds to a certain bank account, which I obediently did. Unfortunately, to date I have not been contacted on where to do the exam. I went to investigate and the website is also no longer active. E-mails to the address that I was communicating with remain unanswered. All my phone calls go into voice mail, and no one bothers reply-ing. I went to the police, only to be informed that I was one of the many hundreds of peo-ple who have reported this to them, and that they do not have the means or skills to trace these fraudsters. Do you think I have a chance of recovery?

4th April 2011

It is very unlikely that you will be successful in tracing the fraudsters. A website, be it Tanzanian or foreign, can be run remotely from any part of the world and it is difficult to find out who is running it and whether or not it is a genuine website. We sympathise with you and the police who are also caught unaware and ill equipped to fight this. It must be pointed out that according to various criminal law columnists, one of the biggest threats to our security are cyber criminals, who are unknown and can move without been seen. Other common scams on the internet include messages to e-mail users to give out their password so that they could store it for backup – typically these messages purportedly come from your service provider. Once you give your password, the fraudster sends out e-mails to everyone on your mailing list that you are stranded and require a few hundred dollars. They also provide a bank account for remittance, and proceed to take the cash from whoever remits the funds. Coming back to your query, yes you have been conned, it is a criminal offence, and you have done the right thing alerting the police. On the recovery front, you will need to consult IT specialists who may be able to trace the whereabouts of the website. You also have a chance tracing the owners of the website through the bank account they used. A banker needs to do due diligence before opening an account.

Courier company standard terms

I used a leading courier company to send my passport to an embassy outside of Tanzania. The courier package got lost and I was delayed in applying for my student visa and as a result lost a year of studies. I subsequently applied for a new pass-port and am reapplying for my visa. The courier company manager told me that their standard carriage terms limit their liability to refunding me the amount I paid. He showed me the document which is very tightly worded. What can I do?

28th March 2011

The courier company cannot limit its liability the way it seems to be indicating. You entered into a contract with it to deliver your passport to the embassy. The express term of the contract was for delivery to take place, for which you paid an amount. And since the delivery did not take place, the courier company is in breach of its obligations. It seems like you never saw the standard carriage terms when you couriered your pack; and even if you did, there is a breach and you do have a cause of action to proceed against the courier company. Unfortunately, many people think that anything nicely typed and printed is 'mistake free' and standard procedure. That is not the case. You need not give up; your attorney can guide you further after reading the standard trading terms and understanding the entire matter.

Non-payment of insurance premium

My motor vehicle insurance was automatically cancelled by my broker. There was, however, no intimation that the premium had not been paid. Now that I have a claim, the insurance company is refusing to pay it, as I have not paid the premium, although I have a sticker. The premium amount is less than TZS 1M, whereas the claim is for nearly TZS 20M. I came to an agreement with the insurance company that they would pay me the difference, but to my utmost surprise they have refused. What should I do?

28th May 2011

The simplest answer to your question is to always make sure you pay your insurance premiums on time. Global insurance principles and the law here are clear – non-payment of premium renders the insurance void. It does not matter that you have a sticker. The sticker does not automatically mean you have a valid contract of insurance. Thus, we agree with the insurance company: no claim is payable to you. On a different note, if insurance companies were to offset premiums with claims the way you suggested, it would defeat the principles of insurance. Simply put, insurance companies

collect premiums in advance, and hope to pay less to the claimant than the amounts they collect. This is called an 'underwriting surplus'. The other way insurance companies make money is by investing the premium in various ventures; this is called 'investment income'. Your proposal of the offset actually cuts out one of the fundamental income streams of insurance companies. Unless the insurance company pays you on an ex *gratia* basis, this claim is not payable .

Withholding of information by doctor

About twenty weeks ago, a mother who was expecting was referred to me by a junior doctor. After examining her and ordering some tests, I found something seriously wrong with the unborn child. The lady's information card had the phone number of her husband, whom she had given us consent to consult in case of any such matters. I found the expectant mother to be a person who would not have been able to absorb the information. After deliberating for two days, I asked the lady to come see me. During this time, I called the husband who unfortunately was travelling. I found it difficult to discuss the matter over the phone and insisted that he come see me immediately. He appeared the next day and I informed him of the issue. I then did not hear from the couple until recently, when their lawyer has sent me a notice stating the couple intended to sue me for not informing the lady that very day. Apparently the lady was treated in Nairobi, and the child passed away. The doctors in Nairobi wrote in their report that had she been treated earlier, the child would have survived. What should I do?

21st March 2011

Therapeutic privilege is the right of a doctor to withhold information from a patient when it is feared that the disclosure could cause immediate and serious harm to the patient. For example, if he or she is suffering from severe depression. In exceptional cases, the need to withhold information may be considered to override the requirement to obtain informed consent before proceeding with treatment. In your case, we do not have all the facts. However, you do seem to have a plausible defence and should contact your lawyers.

Refund of debt by heirs

I am a Tanzanian residing in a European capital and working in the Tanzanian Embassy. While on leave about five years ago, I concluded a contract of purchase of land located in Dar es Salaam. Due to my office commitments, I could not process the transfer of the purchased land into my name. In 2008, I commenced the transfer process, but was unsuccessful due to lack of consent of the Commissioner for Lands. Upon refusal, the lawyer who dealt with it informed me that the whole transaction was inoperative and that I should claim my money back. Upon approaching the seller, I was informed by his wife that he had died in an accident a year earlier and that all the deceased assets were administered by an administrator and distributed to the heirs. The amount I paid as advance is substantial. What should I do?

28th May 2011

You have not told us the reason for the refusal of the consent by the Commissioner for Lands. If we knew this, we might advise you to continue pursuing the consent. Requirement of consent is a mere formality which does not invalidate a contract between you and the seller. Your specific question is – can you recover the funds paid in advance? The fact that the seller is dead and his estate has been completely distributed among his heirs does not change the answer. If you have

opted not to follow up the consent, we advise you to approach the administrator who will, upon going through the documents, call upon each heir to refund in proportion the funds you paid in advance. In case the administrator does not cooperate, you are legally allowed to institute recovery proceedings against the administrator and all the heirs. We advise you to consult your lawyer for further details.

Substandard cosmetics damaged skin

I bought a lotion to lighten my skin from a shop in Kariakoo. The lotion was manufactured in South Africa and has resulted in my skin peeling off. This has caused me serious skin conditions. Who controls the importation of such lotions? What should I do? How do I go about this?

21st February 2011

In Tanzania there is a body called Tanzania Food and Drugs Authority (TFDA). This body is empowered to control all drugs and cosmetics imported into Tanzania, and has the power to visit any shop or go down and inspect drugs and cosmetics being sold or stored. The authority has the power to declare any cosmetics or drugs to be harmful and ban the importation or selling of such products. If the trader refuses to stop selling the banned product, he can be fined or imprisoned.

The first step is for you to inform the TFDA about the product, where you bought it, and what happened. The TFDA in Tanzania is known to be quite aggressive and we suggest you do approach them immediately.

As for suing the trader, you do have a cause of action against him and can proceed to sue. Another option is for you to join the seller and jointly sue the manufacturer, based on a very famous English case, Donogue v Stevenson. This eighty year old case established the principle of extended liability, setting out principles of what the Justice called the 'neighbour' principle, which was derived from the Holy Bible, of 'loving your neighbour', found in the parable of the Good Samaritan. We recommend you sue the manufacturer since he has a lot to lose. Not only will the lotion that he or she has supplied you be banned from the market, but the manufacturer may have all of his other products also banned.

It must be pointed out that the liability of the manufacturer will depend on whether or not there was interference or alteration of the original product after the product left the manufacturer. There are many intermediaries who are involved: the distributor, the importer, and trader. Any modification by one of these intermediaries will absolve the manufacturer of liability.

Lastly, we do not want to behave as if we are doctors, which we are not, but it is a known fact that skin lightening lotions contain chemicals like Lead and Mercury, which kill certain pigments in the skin and make you look fairer, though not younger. Such chemicals are associated with skin cancer, and it is highly recommended that you not use such products. Being fair does not make you any prettier, after all beauty is in eyes of the beholder.

Smoking by *daladala* conductors

I am visiting Dar es Salaam and use the buses commonly known as *daladalas*. On a recent journey from town to Gongo la Mboto the conductor started smoking, which sparked a heated debate between the passengers and the conductor, who said he was the boss and the bus was his property. The conductor also used abusive language towards the passengers. Is smoking in buses legal? What appropriate legal steps could we have taken against the conductor?

31st January 2011

The conduct of bus conductors is regulated

by the Traffic (Motor Omnibuses) (Conduct of Drivers, Conductors and Passengers) Rules. Under the said rules, the conductor is prohibited from smoking in or on a motor omnibus during a journey or, if not en route, when there are passengers on board. The conductor is obligated to take all reasonable precautions to ensure the safety of passengers in, entering, or alighting from the motor omnibus. The conductor is also not allowed to use obscene or offensive language, and he should conduct himself in a civil and orderly manner.

The quickest step to take is to report the incident to a police officer, who after investigation may take the matter to Court. Upon conviction, the accused would either have to pay a fine or be imprisoned for a period not exceeding one month, or both.

Mobile companies steal credit

I know for certain that my mobile phone company is debiting my postpaid account a few cents every day. They also purposely disconnect you when you are on the line so that you redial and they make more money. What can I do?

24th January 2011

As a customer of the mobile operator, you have a contractual relationship with the company. Your allegations against the cellular operator might be true and you can sue them, but the hardest part is to prove these allegations.

We did research the subject and found that some operators in other parts of the world have been found guilty of different kinds of mischief. Your operator may not be a saint after all, and should you have evidence against it, you have a good cause of action. It might also lead to an investigation of the company, for if they are improperly debiting your account, they could be doing the same to many other people.

We suggest you collect evidence and go see your attorneys.

Car tyre bursting causes an accident

I was driving from Morogoro to Mbeya when one of my tyres burst, resulting in a head on collision with a bus. Several people were seriously injured, and the police blamed the accident on a burst tyre. Can I sue the tyre manufacturer? Who else can I sue?

10th January 2011

You can sue anyone, who, in your opinion caused the accident. It could be a pedestrian, it could be another car, it could be a passenger in your car who distracted you, it could be the car manufacturer. It can be absolutely anyone you can think of who could conceivably have caused the accident. However, you must sue the party against whom you can prove the allegations you are making. There is no law that stops you from suing anyone; however, remember that a party that you sue unsuccessfully can claim costs from you after the case is over.

You claim that the police confirmed that the accident was caused by a burst tyre. From what we read here, the police have not confirmed that the accident was due to a faulty tyre supplied by the manufacturer, but merely due to a tyre bursting. The burst tyre might not have been the manufacturers fault, although we have not ruled that out. But it could have been caused by too much or too little pressure in the tyre, lack of tyre maintenance, or any number of reasons. In this case, it is very difficult for us to guide you on whether you should sue the tyre manufacturer or not. You will need to investigate and understand the actual cause that led to the collision, and then make an informed decision. The police are not experts when it comes to understanding tyre quality, and if you sue the tyre manufacturer,

he or she will bring in their experts to disprove whatever you are trying to prove. You need tyre experts to guide you before you embark on any litigation.

Identity theft on google.com

I find that my picture, my full name and personal details, including where I live and work, are all on Facebook. What beats it all is that the information is correct, but the person is not me, it is someone pretending to be me. The person is connecting with my friends and talking all sorts of rubbish. I am not a member of Facebook and have a good reputation. The Facebook page shows that I am a single woman desperately seeking short term sexual relationships. I came to know this as over the last few weeks. I have been receiving phone calls from unknown men who are showing an interest in me. Initially I thought I was being complimented, only to find that the men think I am some sort of call girl. This is causing me great embarrassment. I am also at the verge of losing my fiancé who has somehow started to believe all this. What can I do? My friends tell me it is impossible to locate or sue Facebook because they are way too big.

27th December 2010

Technology comes with many advantages, but clearly you have spotted a down. Identity theft is the next big challenge in the cyber world. It is said that some websites are more powerful than governments, as they can spread information efficiently, aggressively, and at the speed of light. Yes, this is a serious concern, not only for you, but for a citizen of any country. Cybercrime is on the rise and has caught many people off-guard.

To answer your question, you do have a cause of action against Facebook, the person who is impersonating you, and any other service provider who is disseminating this information to the world at large.

While you can open multiple law suits and sue for defamation, the fastest way to salvage the current situation is to write to Facebook and get them to investigate the matter. We are informed that Facebook takes identity theft very seriously, and after doing quick investigation, they will block the user from impersonating you. You are not the first one who has had this issue on Facebook.

As for not being able to locate or sue Facebook, please be informed that Facebook is a well-known company in the US, and a summons can be served upon them from Tanzania. The fact that they are big does not mean you cannot sue them – there is no law that stops you from suing them.

We also wish to mention that in our experience, it is always close friends, or former friends, who tend to impersonate. After all, they have access to all your information. I would not trust 'the not being able to sue' advice from your 'friends'. On the contrary, we would be suspicious of these friends and investigate which of them might be involved in this identity theft. When you find out, you can sue them as well.

Lastly, Facebook has been sued many times for various reasons. We are informed that it has been sued before for breach of privacy, breach of confidentiality, defamation and unlawful transfer of data. What you have experienced is indeed actionable and you should contact your attorneys for further guidance.

Chicken stinks, life miserable

I am a retired man living alone in a two bedroom flat in Dar. I have been living peacefully in my residence for the past thirty years until a few months ago when a restaurant opened next to my house. The restaurant grills chicken at night. While I do not mind the mess they create outside with all the parked cars, the smell of the chicken makes my entire house smell of the masala they use. It has made my life miserable. When I contacted the city authorities, they came, ate some chicken with the owner and left. I wrote letters to everyone I could think of, including the mayor, but to date no action has been taken. I see big shots including ministers coming to enjoy the chicken, which I admit is very good and fresh, but the smell of it in my house every day is making me depressed. What should I do? Because I do not have a contract with the owner of the chicken place, I am told that I cannot sue him.

20th December 2010

Just because Ministers come to eat chicken does not turn a wrong into a right. In any case, we are sure neither the Ministers nor the other customers of the chicken place appreciate the difficulty it is causing for you. In a very famous English case it was said by one of the Lordships that 'every man... has a natural right to enjoy the air pure and free from noxious smells or vapours, and anyone who sends into his neighbour's land that which makes the air there impure, is guilty of nuisance'.

The act of the chicken place owner is actionable under tortuous liability and you need not have a contract with him to sue him. You have a very solid case and should manage to get injunctive relief should you take the appropriate actions in Court. You need not think twice if this is causing you so much trouble – contact your attorney.

Everything on demand

I entered into a loan agreement with a bank, whereby everything the bank wants is on demand. Money due shall be paid on demand, interest on demand and additional security, if required, on demand. This sounds like a life sentence to me. How can I get around this?

13th December 2010

From the tone in your question, it seems

you signed the loan documentation and then started reading the documents. In the many years that we have practiced, we have noted that this is what most of the borrowers do – get the money from the bank, and then start reading the documentation when there is a default or any other problem!

Covenants to pay in bank security documents are usually to pay on demand. This has the advantage for the bank in that time does not start running under the Limitations Act until demand is made. Quite obviously a valid demand can only be made in respect of moneys which are due. This does not mean that a term loan becomes a demand loan. The normal covenant that we have come across requires payment on demand of all moneys obligations and liabilities when the same shall become due. If that is the clause that is causing you this irritation then it is a very standard clause.

We must point out that the 'on demand' clause to provide additional security is very strange. We would have to read the entire document to understand how it is to be construed. From reading it in isolation, it is a very strict condition and does indeed sound like a life sentence. Since we have not seen the entire document, we advise you to contact your attorneys to guide you further.

Tenancy in common v joint tenancy

My wife and I have lived all our lives in a National Housing Corporation flat. We have now finally bought a house and have been given the choice of either owning it as joint tenants or as tenants in common. What is the main difference and what do you recommend us to do?

13th December 2010

The 'joint tenancy' and 'tenancy in common' are the two types of joint ownership. Under a 'joint tenancy' agreement, the joint owners together own the whole property and do not have a particular share in it. If one of the owners dies the other automatically becomes the sole owner. This would be the case even if a Will had been made leaving the deceased owner's 'share' to someone other than the co-owner. On the other hand 'tenancy in common' is the opposite of joint tenancy in that the tenants in common each have a definite share in the property. For example you and your wife could own the property in equal shares. This would be the most appropriate agreement where people want to own a property in separate pre-determined shares. Under 'tenancy in common' if one of the owners dies, his share of the property will pass on to whoever he specifies in a Will, or if a Will is not made, in accordance with the rules of intestacy.

We normally recommend couples that get along well to adopt a 'joint tenancy' as there is perceived to be no advantage in defining separate shares in the property, and it would be the intention that upon the first death of one spouse, the property would automatically pass to the surviving spouse.

Variable interest rate applicability

I borrowed TZS 550M from a bank and am in dispute with it over the way they have charged me interest in my loan account. The bank has shockingly varied the interest according to the way the treasury bills have moved over the years. Can this be done? What remedy do I have?

29th November 2010

The law that applies here is the Mortgage Finance (Special Provisions) Act, which is clear in section 10 that an interest rate may be varied periodically in accordance with a formula set forth in the terms of the Mortgage Agreement. If, according to the Mortgage Agreement, the interest rate can be changed by a written notice from the lender to the borrower, then the bank can change the rate. Generally in cases where there is a variable interest rate, the Mortgage Agreement states that the bank must state clearly and in a manner likely to be understood by the borrower what the new interest rate is, the date of change, any change to the amount of the payment due, and the first date on which the new payment is due and any alternatives to the new rate, if provided in the mortgage agreement.

So, the law does allow a change of interest rate if that is what has been agreed. However, because you claim that you were shocked to see that the interest rate was changed, we assume that you were not given proper notice of such a change. If that is the case, you have a good case of challenging this interest rate change.

One word of caution. Do check your statement, as we believe that the interest rate differential might work in your favour. In that case the bank may be able to challenge you on the reduction!

Demand notice from bank

I borrowed money from a bank and pledged my property as security over which there is a registered mortgage. My business has not been doing very well and I am behind in remitting payments for only six months. The bank has sent me a strongly worded demand notice regarding this default, stating that they will take further action if I do not pay. What is the legal bearing of such a letter? Do I have recourse against the bank? What should I do?

29th November 2010

There are certain indisputable facts. You have borrowed money and have not paid. There is a mortgage and the bank has security against you in case you default. In the eyes of

a banker it is not 'only six months'. Six months in banking is a long period, as the depositors of funds in banks do not wait or accept such reasons.

The legal bearing of such a letter is that it may follow a statutory notice under section 127 of the Land Act, which will then give you sixty days to pay the loan or face a sale of the mortgaged property. We are unsure what reasons you will give in Court to get an order restraining the bank from selling your property, since you have admitted that you have not paid. Timely payment is a key ingredient of a loan agreement and you are in default of this.

Our advice is for you to either pay the outstanding amount or try and reschedule the loan with a new business plan, or look for another bank that is willing to take over your mortgage. Failure of all of the above may result in the mortgaged property being sold. Unfortunately there is no free money out there, least of all from banks.

Peeping into my apartment

I have been living in a National Housing (NHC) property for the past fifteen years in the city centre. Recently a ten storey hotel has cropped up right next door to our block. There is one particular room in the hotel that is occupied by the hotel manager and his family, and whose windows are always open. They can see me through my window when I am changing. Is this not illegal? How can I stop them from doing this? What are my rights?

15th November 2010

First and foremost there is no law that can prevent the hotel manager from opening and keeping open his window. We are not sure if you are asking about the legality of the hotel managers' family looking through your window or the hotel being constructed next to your building. Either way it is very unlikely that a Court will support you in an application to stop the manager from keeping his window open. The building was surely constructed with a valid building permit and all factors, including the distance between buildings, are taken into account when granting a building permit. You need to consult your attorneys to see if there are any other grounds that you've not mentioned that you can use against the hotel owner and/or management of the hotel.

We wish to also point out that normally when changing, one would close their curtains. You might want to consider doing likewise.

Bank pursuing under personal guarantee

Several years ago a friend of mine was final-ising a loan with a bank in Mwanza. The bank manager who knew me at the time, asked the borrower to get my guarantee, as I was well known to the bank. I signed the guar-antee without really looking at it. My friend has defaulted, and the bank is now after me. Even the bank manager's tone has changed when he speaks to me. I did not borrow the money, nor did I use the amount. My friend genuinely lost money in a gold deal and the bank is pursuing me. In fact, a few weeks ago, the bank even tried to block me from with-drawing money from my company account, although they later allowed us to do so. This situation is worrying me. What should I do? Can they come after my matrimonial home?

8th November 2010

It is a well-known fact that bank managers' tones change when there is a default! We need to read the guarantee to understand what you have guaranteed and to what amount. However, one thing is clear, under your personal guarantee, the bank cannot and should not try and offset the loan amount from your company account, which we assume is a limited liability company. In the eyes of the law, your company and you are two distinct personalities. Should they try this again, you can sue the bank and claim damages.

Most personal guarantees hold you personally liable for amounts unpaid by the borrower. At the time of signing, you should have read the guarantee. It is very difficult to disown the guarantee at this point.

As for the bank coming after your matrimonial home, it all depends on the wording of the guarantee. The matrimonial home is a very sensitive asset and its seizure affects many people, including your children. While the bank may try to go for your dearest asset, your home, it will not be an easy task for the bank, as your wife might not have consented. Either way you need to contact your attorney.

Bank demanding life insurance

I am about to borrow USD 8M from a bank in Dar es Salaam. The bank is demanding that I also provide them with a life insurance policy for the same amount. I fail to under-stand why they require this, as the mortgage we have created is over USD 11M. Is this life policy necessary? What should I do?

8th November 2010

The bank is obviously trying to protect its interests. Your company may be a one-man show or you may be the key person in the company, and in the event of your demise, the bank feels that there might still be exposure that they may not be able to recover.

There are a couple of things we wish to bring to your attention. First, the amount of the policy need not be the full amount of the loan. The bank has adequate cover on the property you have pledged, and in view of that, you can negotiate for a lower sum insured on the life policy.

Second, you can negotiate with the bank on who pays the premium for the policy. If the bank is willing to contribute, which some banks do agree to, you may get some relief there. A life insurance policy is not a bad idea – what you need to look into is how you offload the premium you pay under the policy. It ultimately depends on how you negotiate with the bank. This practice is not uncommon in the market, especially for big loans, and we are not surprised that the bank has asked for such a policy.

Delayed caesarean, child dead

My wife was in the delivery room at a large and new hospital in Dar es Salaam. We entered the delivery room at 6:25pm on a Saturday and were attended to by a midwife. My wife was immediately taken to the delivery room. At about 9pm the foetus' heart beat started to drop and the nurse in charge used her phone to beep the doctor on call as she had no credit. The doctor did not call her back. At 9:05 pm the nurse used my phone to call the doctor, who responded that he was far away and that the nurse should call another doctor, who was not on call. The other doctor did not pick up the phone despite us frantically calling him. We then again tried calling the doctor on call, who had switched off his mobile. All this time my wife was put in a special position while awaiting a surgeon. Meanwhile the foetus' heartbeat continued to drop. At about 9:45pm, the nurse decided to call the general surgeon on call who instructed that my wife be immediately transferred to theatre and that he would arrive in twenty minutes. As it was a Saturday night, and not many nurses or attendants were on duty, we had to assist the midwife to push the bed to the theatre. Just after 10pm, the general surgeon appeared, rushed to the theatre and performed a 'C' section on my wife. A beautiful baby girl was born. The Apgar score at

one minute was two; the Apgar score at five minutes was one. The surgeon came out and informed us that the baby was not normal and that we would have to keep her under oxygen for the night. The baby girl died at 4:45am the next day. I did some research on the net and found out some facts. First, the emergency was because the umbilical cord prolapsed and had the doctor on call come on time, it would have saved my daughter's life. Second, the position that my wife was put in while waiting for the doctor, is called the Trendelenburg position, and confirms that there indeed was a prolapsed umbilical cord. The midwife and doctors tried to convince us that it was the will of God and that it was likely the child would have died anyways, but I am now convinced that the hospital is responsible for this. It also turns out that the doctor who refused to come does not live far from the hospital and was supposed to be on call that day. I have lost my daughter because of the hospital's negligence – I will never get her back. I want to take the hospital to task to make sure this never happens to anyone again. What should I do?

25th October 2010

We are glad to hear that you are not subscribing to the hospital's baseless argument that this would have happened anyways. The nurse and doctor who told you this should have perhaps trained as fortune tellers rather than medical practitioners.

It is apparent that the hospital and/or the medical practitioners have been negligent in the way they handled the delivery as a whole. While child birth has great risks to both the mother and baby, that is the reason one goes to hospitals and does not stay at home.

In your case, and from the description you have given us in your question, it is quite apparent that the hospital and doctor(s) are liable for the death of your new born baby.

FB

You must ask yourself three questions: Did the hospital owe your wife a duty of care? The answer is yes. Secondly, were the doctors and/or hospital in breach of this duty? The answer seems to be in the affirmative – a hospital dealing in maternity should have a surgeon on call, and such surgeon must timely respond to such a call. Lastly, did this negligence lead to the death of the newborn? The answer again is yes.

We believe you have a good chance of success and should sue not only the hospital but also the doctor who did not show up. You should also include any other people you feel were responsible

Supplier changed sample

I am the procurement manager of a school and came to Dar to buy various equipment for our science labs. One of the items to purchase was a dozen weighing scales, samples of which I had seen and approved. The shopkeeper promised to deliver the items to the school in Lushoto. Ten days later, when the goods came, the weighing scales were totally different from what he had shown me. Is this not an offence?

13th December 2010

The Fair Competition Act is very clear in that when there is a contract for the supply of goods to a consumer, there is also a term in the contract, expressed or implied, to the effect that the goods are supplied by reference to a sample. Furthermore, there is an implied condition that the bulk will correspond with the sample in quality, that the consumer will have a reasonable opportunity to compare the bulk with the sample and the goods will be free from any defect that renders them unmerchantable, that would not be apparent on reasonable examination of the sample.

You can hence pursue the supplier under this particular provision of the law.

Barber cut all my hair

What can I do to a barber who accidentally cut off my moustache that I have been growing for the past ten years? What if he has a notice saying that one cuts hair at his or her own risk? Does that change your position?

25th October 2010

We are not sure if this barber actually cut your moustache or if you are asking this question for general interest. We have all been to barbers in Tanzania and have not seen such signs saying 'you cut your hair at your own risk!'

Where a contract for supply of services exists, there are certain terms implied into the contract. The relevant implied term in the contract to cut your hair or moustache, is that of reasonable care and skill. Where the supplier is acting in the course of a business, an implied term exists that the supplier will carry out the service with reasonable care and skill.

In this case, the barber has not used reasonable care and skill, and hence you would have a cause of action against him. This now brings us to the second part of the question – does the notice exempt the barber from acting with such reasonable care and skill. Our answer is in the negative.

Wrong medication from pharmacist

I was prescribed medication by my physician only to be given the wrong drugs by the pharmacist. It resulted in my sugar level remaining out of control, long periods of absenteeism from work and a lot of distress. The pharmacy owner personally apologised to me. Should I accept the apologies?

18th October 2010

We are not sure how one 'accepts' apologies and what qualifies us to guide you on this. As lawyers, we are certain about one thing –

you have a good cause of action against the pharmacist and the pharmacy, and should jointly sue them. You can claim for various damages – case law on this in Tanzania is not as developed as it is in other countries, but you do have a good case. You should not feel bad about suing professionals; you will actually be making the system more efficient.

Lease ending with husband's death

I am a widow with three children. My husband recently passed away leaving us in a rented house belonging to a certain parastatal. We have occupied the house for the last twenty years and have always paid the rent on time. Surprisingly, now that my husband has died, the landlord wants us out, alleging that the person with whom he signed a lease agreement is no more, and therefore the lease is terminated. Is this demand from the landlord legally justified? What should I do?

18th October 2010

From the facts of your case, and under the eyes of the law, and unless the lease had expired or the deceased had defaulted payment of rent, the landlord's move is illegal. Death cannot terminate the existing lease agreement – we doubt that the lease would have such a clause, and even if it did, you could likely challenge it. Normally, as the wife of the deceased, you are able assume the tenancy if you were residing in the house before the death of your husband, as long as after the death of your husband you remain in compliance with tenancy terms and conditions, including prompt payment of rent. The landlord's move should be condemned. You should, however, read the lease in its entirety to make sure that there are no other defaults that could lead the lease to be terminated. If the landlord does not understand this position, you will have to file an application in Court. We advise you to consult your lawyer.

New landlord not renewing lease

I have been living in a bungalow in Oyster Bay for three years. My landlord sold the property to a developer who is not willing to renew my lease on grounds that he wants to demolish and develop the property. Does my lease apply to the developer? Should I have not been offered this property before my landlord offered it to this developer? What should I do? Isn't this against public policy?

18th October 2010

Our answer to this question is not likely to please you.

From your letter, it appears the developer bought the property subject to the lease, and is hence bound by it; he becomes your new landlord. And if the lease is expiring, and he does not wish to renew it, there is nothing you can do.

There is also no law that makes it mandatory for the landlord to offer the property to you, unless it was specifically agreed upon, which does not seem to be the case here.

Nor do we see any public policy issue that will come to your rescue. The law encourages new development to alleviate the shortage in housing. If anything, the opposite is true – blocking the development may be against public policy.

We advise you to consult a lawyer to discuss any options you may have in this matter.

Loan be paid on demand

I am in the final stages of borrowing USD 2M from a large bank in Tanzania. In one of the documents, it clearly states that if called upon, I shall have to pay the loan on demand. I spoke to the bank and they said this is standard wording and that everyone in town has signed such a document, even those who have borrowed tens of millions, and that I, being a small 'fish' cannot now start getting the bank to redraft its documents. Is this normal?

11th October 2010

This term 'loan' that you are negotiating sounds like a demand loan! In bank security documents, agreements to pay are usually to pay 'on demand'. This has the advantage for the banks that the clock does not begin ticking under the Limitation Act until demand is made. However, demands can only be made in respect of moneys that are due. Otherwise, term loans would not make sense, as your investment is long term. The correct form of wording that you should insist on is 'demand of all moneys when the same shall become due.'

The bank's comment that others have signed such documents has no legs to stand on. Equally worrying is the 'big fish small fish' theorem that the bank has put forward. All loan documents have to be read, understood, negotiated, renegotiated, and only then signed and sealed by you. Your desire to kick start your project with the borrowed funds should not induce you to sign anything that comes your way – you may come to regret this in the future.

Gambling 'karatatatu'

A police post refused to register and work on my complaint against a player of a game popularly known as '*Karatatatu*' who fraudulently took my TZS 10,000 during a game. The police refused to take action even after I insisted that my offender was still at the play site, alleging that I lost the money out of my sheer foolishness. Was the police's response acceptable? Is this game legal?

11th October 2010

You were probably playing the game at an unlicensed location, making this type of gaming illegal. The police should have taken action against the 'offender', but they could have also taken action against you. Both you and the offender are lucky you got away with this, as both of you should have been arrested. Sometimes people who go to the police to complain get arrested themselves – the police have powers to do that. Merely being the first to report to the police does not make you any less guilty.

Defence procedure in summary suit

I bought a car and issued a post-dated cheque for TZS 20M. Upon giving the cheque, I was given the vehicle, which I started using. The seller presented the cheque and it bounced as the bank had no funds to pay. The seller, being aggrieved, filed a summary suit against me, claiming amongst others payment of the sell price and damages. I am not legally trained and do not know if this is an offence. Please give me the best advice.

4th October 2010

In answering this we assume that when you said the bank did not have money to pay, it was your personal account on which the cheque was drawn that had no funds available?

Summary proceedings are ordinarily available for cases that require prompt action and generally involve a small number of clear-cut issues, for example non-payment of utility bill, default in mortgages and bounced cheques, as is the case here. Defence under summary suit is not automatic – the Defendant must apply to the respective Court within the time frame indicated in the summons, in order to appear and defend his case. The application must be accompanied by an affidavit indicating which facts the Defendant requires the Plaintiff to prove before he is entitled to the summary judgment. In short the affidavit should disclose triable issues to the satisfaction of the Court.

In your question, you have not mentioned why the cheque bounced. Should you not have sufficient grounds to defend your position, it may be difficult to satisfy the Court if there are triable issues, and the Court may reject your application. If your application to defend the suit is rejected, you may find judgment being entered against you.

Our 'best piece of advice' is not what you perhaps want to hear – pay the funds to the seller immediately and pray that he waives the damages.

You do not need to be legally trained to know the consequences of issuing a cheque when your account does not have sufficient funds – this is also a criminal offence commonly called 'kite flying' and is imprisonable.

Excluded to participate in Miss Tanzania

I am a 23-year-old married woman who wanted to participate in the Miss Tanzania competition last year, but my application was refused, as I am not single. I have all the qualities to become Miss Tanzania and would not let down the country like all the former Miss Tanzania's. Isn't this regulation not to allow married woman to participate discriminatory? I want to participate in such competitions – what do you advise?

20th September 2010

Much as we sympathise with you on the rejection to participate, we do not see anything discriminatory. It is true that failure to treat all persons equally, when no reasonable distinction can be found between those favoured and those not favoured, is against the law; in your case we do not see existence of such discrimination.

Just like other contests or competitions, the organisers of Miss Tanzania are free to pass their regulations and rules for eligibility

in their beauty pageant. Yes, you might be beautiful and might perform better than all the other former Miss Tanzania's, but the organisers cannot bend the rules just for you. The rejection to participate could be looked at differently had the rules allowed married woman and you were rejected.

If your interest in participating in such contests still exists, you might want to check if there are any beauty contests for married women, perhaps Mrs. Tanzania. Our response to you should not be construed as saying married women are any less beautiful than single women. After all, as the 3rd century Greek saying goes, beauty is in the eyes of the beholder.

Terms of contract at back of receipt

I boarded a bus from Morogoro to Mwanza. Upon reaching my destination, I found that the contents of one of my five suitcases were totally destroyed by water. Most of the items were electronic and very valuable. I informed the office of the bus company, but was informed that it was clearly stated at the back of the receipt that I travelled at my own risk and that the bus company was not responsible for any damages or loss of baggage. However, I never received a receipt; I was only given a ticket for the journey. Can the bus company limit its liability by putting in just one line such as this? I had not even seen the back of the ticket? Is there anything I can do?

9th August 2010

The law specifically requires that if a person or a company wishes to exempt itself from liability, it should specifically inform the party with whom it is entering into a contract of that exemption. In your case, you cannot be considered to have been put on notice of such exemption, as you were not informed prior to travel. Further to that, the terms were written on the receipt, not the ticket, and by then it is very likely that you had concluded the contract of transport. We are convinced that you can recover the loss that you have suffered by instituting a civil suit against the bus company.

Purchase of car over the internet

I want to buy a car over the internet because it is cheaper. I found a web site which sells cars, but they want full payment before delivery of the vehicle. Are there any other ways of paying? Should I buy the car?

26th July 2010

Whether or not you buy a car is not a legal question. What you probably want to know is if it is safe to buy a car over the internet.

The quick answer to this question is no. There are many things that can go wrong – the description of the car on the internet may not match what you get delivered, or you may not get delivery of the car at all. We know of a few people who have gotten excellent car deals over the internet; we have also come across individuals who have paid on the internet and have never received the goods. It is very hard to verify the authenticity of the company you are dealing with over the internet. Ultimately it is a commercial decision that you have to take. We must caution you that the recovery process for sums paid on the internet is very difficult, especially when you do not know the physical address or identity of the party you are dealing with.

A safer mode of payment that offers more protection is a Letter of Credit (LC). If you are still very passionate about buying this car on the internet, we recommend you contact your bankers and open a LC.

Prior to opening the LC, you should determine whether the website accepts such forms of payment or not.

Medical negligence causing death

My father was taken to the emergency wing of a hospital after which he had to undergo surgery. His blood group was type A and by mistake the medical staff gave him type B. When they were at the blood bank, I kept on insisting to the nurse that the hospital was making a mistake, but the nurse was confident of results of the blood group obtained from the laboratory. We later discovered that the laboratory was using reagents that had not been properly stored. Due to the hospital's negligence my father died a few hours after surgery. Can I claim against the hospital?

19th July 2010

Medical malpractice involves more than an undesirable outcome to medical treatment. If you want to sue and win on a malpractice claim, you will need to prove several elements to be successful.

Your healthcare provider owes you a legal duty by virtue of the doctor-patient relationship. Part of this duty is to provide you with care that is in line with professional standards. To win a medical malpractice claim, you will need to prove that the doctor did not provide the standard of care required.

While it is not easy to prove medical malpractice, it seems like you have enough evidence for a strong case against the hospital, doctors and nurses. Your lawsuit against the hospital or the doctor in charge will not bring back your father, but will surely help improve the efficiency in hospitals.

Life insurance claim rejected

For the past seven years, my husband had a life insurance policy with a private insurer. He died in September of last year when he jumped out of a moving car. The insurance company initially paid for the funeral and gave all indications that they would pay under the policy within ninety days. I have now been informed that they will not pay. What should I do? Can I sue the insurance company?

28th June 2010

You have not given the reasons for repudiation of the claim, but there is something we have spotted in your question. Why did your husband jump out of a moving car? What caused such an action? If it was suicide, the claim will not be paid. There is a very clear suicide clause in all life insurance policies that exclude suicide as a covered risk or limits the insurer's liability, in the event of a suicide, to the total premiums paid. The fact that the insurer paid for the funeral expenses cannot be held against the insurer as an admission of a claim. We suggest you meet your attorney, who can guide you step by step before you blindly institute a law suit.

I want my money back

I booked a room in a hotel in Mbeya where I was to attend a seven day seminar. However, due to unexplained reasons, the organiser postponed the seminar, and as a result I did not travel to Mbeya. The owner of the hotel does not want to refund my money paid in advance. What should I do to recover my funds, as I have not made use of the services?

14th June 2010

Yours was a contract for the purchase of service of a room. Normally, when a consumer makes a contract for the purchase of service, he or she is under a basic obligation to pay the contract price. Therefore, if you booked a room at the hotel you cannot simply cancel your booking, and as a matter of strict law, the hotel owner has a right to forfeit your deposit and can even sue you for damages if he can prove that he suffered additional loss due to your cancellation. In your case, it depends how quickly you informed the hotel owner of the cancellation and what the terms of the booking were. From the facts, it is unlikely that you will succeed in your suit against the hotel owner. You might want to consider suing the organiser, but that again would depend on the terms and conditions.

Goods warranty not honoured

I am a tailor operating a tailoring mart within Tabora municipality. In September 2009, I bought four sewing machines from a shop in Dar es Salaam and was issued with a valid receipt and a six month warranty. About a month later I found that several of the machines were defective. Because of the unexpired warranty, I contacted the seller for repair or replacement. The seller simply replied that that particular model had been discontinued! Is this not a breach of contract? Will I be compensated under the warranty for transport costs if I return the machines back to Dar? Can I get compensation for loss of business?

21st June 2010

The dictionary definition of a warranty is a legally binding assurance that a good or service is, among other things, fit for use as represented, free from defective material and workmanship, and if relevant, meets statutory specifications. A warranty normally describes the conditions under and period during which the seller will repair, replace or compensate the buyer for the defective item without cost to the buyer.

In your case, you are definitely within the time limit of the warranty. You need to further read the fine print of the warranty to see what you are covered for. In principle, the reason given to you by the seller of the machines being discontinued is irrelevant and easily challengeable. You have a good cause of action and may pursue this.

Whether the warranty covers you for transport back to the place you bought the goods from will largely depend upon the wording of the warranty. Loss of business is normally not covered under a warranty, but may be claimable depending on your attorney's understanding the entire facts of this matter.

Hire purchase agreement

In January 2009, I hired a tricycle commonly known as *bajaj* from a company in Dar es Salaam, on the understanding that I would pay hiring charges in six equal instalments, and upon payment of the last instalment, the *bajaj* would become mine. I have paid five instalments and the last instalment was supposed to be paid at the end of November 2009. However, I found out that the *bajaj* is defective. The company has ignored my claims, saying that the claims are afterthoughts, for I had an opportunity to inspect the *bajaj* before it was delivered to me. The company insists that I must pay the balance immediately, otherwise they will sue me for recovery. What are my rights in these circumstances? I intend to return the *bajaj* to the company and claim my money back.

7th June 2010

Yours was a contract of hire with an option to purchase, in which the company lets the *bajaj* out on hire and transfers ownership to you after receiving certain payments. The law puts the company under obligation to determine that the tricycle is reasonably fit and suitable for the purpose for which it is expressly let out. If the damage or loss is caused to you due to some defect in the fitness or adaptability of the tricycle which the company should have been aware, the company is liable not only for the immediate results of its lack of care. The company may

also be liable for other damages incurred by you due to the defect of the *bajaj*.

Unfortunately, we cannot answer the question any more clearly than this, as we do not know what kind of defect you are talking about. If it is normal wear and tear, or due to your own negligence, then it will be a tough battle to fight. On the other hand, if the tricycle was not of the required merchantable quality, the company's defence that you were given an opportunity to conduct a preliminary inspection of the tricycle before delivery cannot stand. Since you know the facts better than we do, you can decide which of the above two scenarios you fall under.

Cancellation of insurance

I wish to cancel my insurance policy, but my broker insists that it is not possible and I must wait until it automatically expires. Is this the norm in Tanzania?

14th June 2010

Your insurance policy is similar to any other contract, where normally there is a termination clause. From the standard policies that we have come across in the market, an insurance policy is terminable, and normally there is no restriction. In your case, it will depend on the wording of the insurance policy, which we advise you to read thoroughly.

When one terminates an insurance policy, you may not be able to get back, the premiums paid, even on a prorated basis. And towards the end of the policy you may not be able to recover any premium at all. Your broker's reluctance may be as a result of this, but you should check with him or her.

Livestock damaging my compound

My neighbour does not put his livestock (goats) in a proper compound. As a result, his goats stray into my garden and destroy and damage vegetables causing a loss to me. I have complained to him, but he does not co-operate. I have reported the matter to the relevant authorities (police and local government), but it seems that the neighbour is very well connected and actually gets sympathy from the police. Do I have any recourse against this neighbour? Please advise.

21st June 2010

Generally the law imposes duty upon owners of livestock to keep them in a proper pound, so that their livestock does not damage or destroy others' properties or injure neighbours. Failure or omission of this duty renders owners of livestock liable, and this is so regardless of whether the release of livestock is done deliberately or negligently.

In your situation, you have a good case against your neighbour for damages caused to your garden and any other property. You may also retain those stray goats, but if you decide to do so, you must make sure that you keep them in reasonable care and supply them with adequate food and water. In case you retain them and the owner does not take any steps immediately to recover them, you may proceed to sell the goats and apply the proceeds of sale to recover the value of your damaged garden and other costs, including the expenses incurred in retaining the goats.

Price and legality of contract

In 2003, I bought a lorry at a price of TZS 5.6M from my employer with whom I worked for fifteen years as a driver. My employer died in 2009, and the deceased's family is now trying to avoid the agreement for the sale of the lorry, alleging that the value of the lorry is higher than the price it was sold to me for. The family has reported the matter to the police, who have also alleged that I have forged the deceased's signature. What should I do?

24th May 2010

The sale being a contract, we assume that both of you got what you contracted for. A Court of Law cannot bargain for parties on the price they wish to sell their assets for, otherwise we would have queues outside Courts! What is important is that the lorry belonged to the deceased, and the same was lawfully sold to you by him at an agreed price. In our view that price, as far as parties to the sale agreement are concerned, was the value (consideration) of the lorry, and therefore sufficient in the eyes of the law. In contracts for the sale of goods, the consideration need not be adequate, but it must be made with free consent of both parties. Unless there are details you are withholding from us, we do not see how the family can void this agreement.

As to the police case, the law does not disallow anyone from reporting to the police an issue which, in their opinion, has some elements of criminality. Let the police conduct their investigation.

Unregistered pharmacists

In Morogoro half the employees of pharmacies are not qualified to be pharmacists, although they present themselves as such. Is this not very risky? Is there no law that can stop these technicians from acting like pharmacists? Are they not misrepresenting themselves?

10th May 2010

The Pharmacy Act establishes a pharmacy council which is the sole body that registers pharmacists in Tanzania. This council also regulates and sets the standards of conduct of pharmacists, maintains a list of pharmacists across the country and evaluates the education level of pharmacists. So there is a law in place.

The Pharmacy Act states that no person other than a qualified pharmacist may use this title, or any emblem or description to suggest that he or she is a pharmacist. The law further states that any person who does represent himself as a pharmacist, while not a pharmacist contravenes the law and is liable to a fine of TZS 2M or imprisonment for a period not exceeding two years, or to both.

You can report this serious issue to the pharmacy board to look into. The law also requires that all pharmaceutical technicians be registered with the board.

Gambling in Tanzania

I am an expatriate and have lived in Mwanza for the past year. A few months ago, for the first time ever, I travelled to Mwanza from Dar by road and was disgusted to note how heavily and passionately the poor men played the slot machines at various places on the main road. There was no shortage of slot machines and people were lining up to play on them. Does the law allow such activity? Is there no age restriction, as I saw young people gambling? I also observed a young man arguing with the owner on the amount that he was to be paid. I am certain that the owners are reaping benefits from the winners as well. Taking into consideration that Tanzania is one of the world's poorest countries; don't you think that gambling should be made illegal?

10th May 2010

Gambling comes under the Gaming Act, which regulates slot machines. Subject to the provisions of the Act, gambling in Tanzania is not illegal. All slot machines must be licensed by the gaming board, which is established under the Act. There are also various licenses that the board issues based on the type of activity and game.

As for your observation on the young playing the slot machines, the Gaming Act is very clear about the age of the participants – the minimum age is 18. The Act makes it an offence for the owner to allow people under this age to linger in the gaming area, to be present when the game is being played, or to play any of these games. The law states that any person who is found contravening this may be fined TZS 500,000 or imprisonment for three months, or both.

The law also prohibits cheating a winner and has provided a fine of TZS 1M or imprisonment for one year, or both. Other provisions of the Act that may interest you include license forfeiture by the gaming board in cases where there has been a contravention of the Act, penalties and imprisonment for participants who attempt to cheat, and exemptions allowing charitable institutions who run lotteries to raise funds, as long as the entire amount of funds raised are used for the charity.

We are unfortunately not qualified to answer the last part of your question.

Liability of a bank to joint account holder

My husband opened an account with a bank in Dar es Salaam in 1998. It was a joint account that I was also a signatory to. Although I never went to the bank, my husband used to deposit funds in the account for our joint use. My husband passed away eight months ago and the bank refuses to release the funds to me on the grounds that some steps in the account opening forms were skipped, although the statements came in our joint names till date. The bank is not responding positively, and is showing all signs of trying to stop me from accessing these funds. Please assist.

3rd May 2010

It will normally be clear from the account mandate form that the bank is in privities of contract with each joint account holder. You say that you are a signatory of the account.

That means you are known to the bank and we fail to understand why the bank is not releasing the said funds. Unless there is information that you are concealing, we wish to answer your question below.

In a similar case within the Commonwealth, it was held the fact that one of the holders of a joint account does not contribute to or draw upon the joint account does not prevent that person from having a beneficial interest. Nor does it matter if such a person does not even know of the existence of such a joint account. Moreover, the fact that a joint account holder was never intended to use the account while the other was still alive would not prevent the former from succeeding to the whole account by survivorship. In law, a joint account is simply debt owed to the account holders jointly.

Based on the above Case Law and the facts as presented to us, we believe that the bank is illegally withholding your funds and you have a good case. We recommend you contact your attorneys.

Landlord's wife a nightmare

My landlord (and especially his wife) frequently come to the house that I have leased from them despite me observing the tenancy conditions. The landlord actually just walks in and at no specific time. She never calls – she walks in any day at a time that suits her. This is very disturbing for our family. I have told her on more than one occasion that she should at least call before she comes. Don't I have my rights as well? She claims that the law allows the landlord to enter the leased premises. She also has very good lawyers to back her up. What should I do?

26th April 2010

The landlord is correct in that she has the right to come and inspect the leased premises. As a tenant in the house, although you have exclusive use of it, you are not in exclusive occupation because the landlord in the case of tenancy, retains to herself the legal occupation to the house though she has agreed to give the exclusive enjoyment of the occupation to you, the tenant. In your case, you have not stated the terms and conditions of the tenancy agreement but as a general law principle, the landlord is allowed to come and inspect the leased premises.

However, the fact that she comes in at any time, does not give notice and comes as frequently as she does, is in breach of the law. The law protects you here in that whilst the landlord has a right to enter the leased premises, there has to be reasonable notice before such inspection. From the tone in your question, we assume that the landlord comes every other day or every week that also without notice. Perhaps she has nothing else to do and is 'attached' to her property!

In any case, if this continues, you can stop her from entering without notice and sue her for nuisance. Your landlord has to be reasonable on when she can come and for what purpose. For the duration of the lease, you are entitled to your privacy and quiet and peaceful enjoyment of the property.

The fact that she has a good team of lawyers means nothing – lawyers cannot change the law. We all live within the law. You may also need to consult your attorney.

Doctor withheld information from me

I have been visiting a Dar hospital for the past three months and as a matter of convenience I have been accompanied by my mother. The cause of my illness was unknown and the doctors continued performing various tests. A few months ago I went back to visit the Doctor who told me that he needed to speak to my mother, who had not accompanied me on that particular day. Does a doctor have the right to withhold information like this? Why should my mother

be informed and not me?

19th April 2010

Normally, a doctor cannot withhold information from a patient. However, there are circumstances where a doctor has the right to withhold information and the withholding of such information is a defence in case the doctor is sued. This is called therapeutic privilege.

Therapeutic privilege is the right of a doctor to withhold information from a patient when it is feared that disclosure could cause immediate and serious harm to the patient. The therapeutic privilege is an exception to the general rule of informed consent and only applies when disclosure of the information itself could pose serious and immediate harm to the patient, such as prompting suicidal behaviour. The exception of therapeutic privilege does not apply when disclosure will merely lead to refusal of care that the physician thinks beneficial.

You have to understand why the doctor refused to inform you. If it falls under the above, you have no cause of action against the doctor. If it does not, you may consider suing the doctor for non disclosure of medical information.

Tenant in property, first right of refusal

I have been a tenant in a property for many years. Three months ago I was served with a notice to vacate the premises on grounds that the property had been sold. Is there no law that the landlord should have offered it to me before selling it in the market?

19th April 2010

As per the Land Laws in Tanzania, there is no legal provision which puts the landlord under obligation to sell his/her property to the existing tenant unless it has been specifically provided for in the tenancy agreement, which

is rare. If your tenancy agreement has a right to buy, or right to refusal clause, then depending on the wording of the clause, you may be able to challenge the sale of the property and not otherwise.

If your landlord is a public body, the requirements of advertising and tendering must be met. If that condition has not been met, you may also challenge the sale. Furthermore, though the property has been sold, your right to stay remains as per the terms and conditions in the tenancy agreement. You should read the termination clause of the tenancy agreement for further guidance.

Affected but not a party to contract

My landlord has signed a contract with some people who are creating havoc around the premises we are residing in. He had written to us about this contract but we had not agreed to it. Our lawyer says since we are not a party to the contract, there is nothing much we can do. What do you suggest? This disturbance is affecting our health.

26th April 2010

Unfortunately, you are being misguided. From the facts, we are of the opinion that you still have a good cause of action against your landlord. So long as you have observed the terms and conditions of your lease, you are entitled to peaceful and quiet possession of the property and to enjoy the premises without interruption. This is a mandatory covenant imposed by the law to regulate landlord tenant relationship.

Although you have not specifically stated the contents of the contract the landlord has entered into or what precisely the problem is, our opinion is that as long as the disturbance is affecting your health you may file a suit against both the landlord and the party causing the problem in any Court with competent jurisdiction and obtain injunctory relief to restrain the mischief that is causing your ill health. You need to contact your attorney for further guidance.

Buying stolen goods

A boy employed by a large store in Mbeya was found guilty of stealing about one thousand pieces of roof sheets ('*mabatis*') from his employer. The same '*mabatis*' were innocently sold to me at market price by the boy. The magistrate not only convicted the boy but also ordered that the seven hundred pieces lying at the police station be returned to the owner. I am aggrieved by the order as I bought the said goods in good faith not knowing that these were stolen goods. Is the order of the Court justifiable?

29th March 2010

We are unsure what you mean by 'buying the goods innocently' at market price. There is some camouflaging that we believe you have done when you were writing to us! For example Mbeya is a small town and a boy 'just' appearing and selling you roof sheets is very suspicious. You have probably never dealt with this 'boy' yet you claim that you bought the goods in good faith.

From the facts you have given us, it is unlikely that the goods belonged to the boy and without the authority of the owner, the title of the goods could not, and cannot be passed to you. The law is clear that where goods have been sold and the offender is prosecuted and convicted, the property reverts in the person who was the owner of the goods and the Court can issue an order for restitution of goods. In your case, the goods are traceable and we do not see anything wrong with the Court order. We are curious to know why the Court only ordered that the goods at the police station be returned to the original owner, as three hundred pieces seem to still be in your custody.

As to the fate of the money you paid to purchase the sheets, you may proceed for recovery against the boy by filing a civil suit. Before filing this case your attorneys should do a quick analysis of the costs involved vis a vis the recovery expected, otherwise you shall end 'deeper in the red'.

Lost cheque at bank

I deposited a cheque of USD 220,000 in a bank. The amount was credited to my account and utilised. Six months after the deposit, the bank, without informing me, debited my account for the same amount after 'timing' another large cheque that I deposited. I approached the bank and an expatriate manager very rudely told me that the initial cheque was not to be found and that I should get the cheque reissued. I did not want issues with the bank and decided to approach my client, a company that provides services to mining companies. They strictly told me that the entire management had changed and it would be very difficult to get a cheque reissued. Can the bank just debit my account like that? I am starving for cash flow and the bank does not want to bulge.

15th March 2010

There is a very similar case in Tanzania where it was held by the Court of Appeal that where a customer deposits a cheque with a collecting bank and the cheque gets lost, the bank owes a duty of care to the customer to inform him promptly of such loss so that the customer may take appropriate steps that might be open to him or her to avert any or further consequences resulting from such loss; it was also held that such duty exists whether the cheque was lost by the bank itself or a third party in possession of the cheque for the bank.

In the above mentioned case, the Court of

Appeal agreed with the decision of the High Court that had awarded the client the amount claimed and compensation. In your case, the time in which the bank got back to you, is in our opinion, very unreasonable. You have a very good chance of succeeding to recover the funds that have been debited and may also claim damages.

Sub standard product claim

For over fifty years our company has been in the confectionary business. Our manufacturing plants use world class technology to ensure that we produce quality products within international hygiene standards. Six months ago, a customer unknown to us, sent us a demand notice that his child fell sick after eating one of our products. Now the same person has filed a case against us claiming TZS 400M. Is this not outrageous? How can the law allow people to file such cases which have no basis? Does insurance normally cover this?

1st March 2010

There is nothing outrageous about the case. The plaintiff, in his capacity, believes that your company has wronged him by supplying sub standard products in the market. Even if you have been in business for five decades, there is always a chance of quality going wrong somewhere. It has happened recently to giants like Toyota and it can happen to anyone including your company.

What you need to understand is that the plaintiff has to prove his case in Court. He has to prove how he or his son suffered, and how he came to the figure of TZS 400M. This might be a large amount for Tanzania, but internationally claimants in product liability suits claim billions.

The law does not stop people from filing suits in which they genuinely believe they have a claim. It would be against public policy

and would cause a lot of injustice. It is for the Court to adjudicate the matter and decide whether there is a basis for the claim or not, and what amounts, if any, should be awarded.

On the insurance front, your normal insurance policies do not usually cover this. If you have product liability insurance or an industrial policy with a product liability cover, then your insurance policy can be triggered. Such policies usually also cover for reasonable attorney fees.

Mobile phone companies cheating users

I have been in Tanzania for many years and have seen the mobile industry grow. The competition has increased and so has the cheating. Just to give you a few examples, many of our very poor villagers sms to join the daily unlimited talk service and their funds would be debited immediately but they would only be connected to the free service in the afternoon! This happens every other day. Most recently I have noted that a customer who tried to subscribe to this free service, had his whole TZS 5,000 credit debited. Our NGO works with some of the poorest people in the world and it is a shame that this mobile company steals from such people. If the mobile company is inclined towards stealing, they should steal from the rich people in the cities and leave these poor farmers alone. What can we do about this injustice?

8th March 2010

Your comment on whom the mobile companies should start stealing from reminds us of Robin Hood. The law in Tanzania does not discriminate between the rich and poor and hence if you steal from the rich, the law does not look at you differently. Your recommendation cannot hold as it is illegal. You also assume that such incidents are only happening in your region. If they exist, which many people claim they do, then the occurrences must be happening in other parts of Tanzania as well, both the rich and poor parts.

The best way to proceed is to send a demand note to the mobile company with an explanation on what happened and when it happened. Unfortunately, pre paid customers do not get a monthly printed bill and it might be wise for the claimant to ask for his or her statement before sending out the demand notice.

If there is no response to your letter, or the response is not to the claimant's satisfaction, he or she can proceed to file a suit against the mobile company. Remember that one who claims has to prove. The claimant needs to be prepared with proper evidence to substantiate the claims, which might be difficult. However, whether the mobile companies are intentionally cheating or have system failures to the detriment of their users is something that the Court will have to decide upon.

Bank breaches confidentiality to wife

I have an account in a bank in Dar es Salaam. This is my personal account and I do not share any details of this account with any-one including my wife. A few months back, whilst I was overseas on an assignment, my wife saw an old bank statement in one of my drawers. Since she knows a few staff at the bank, she managed to convince them to give her my latest bank balance and other details of my account and the bank released them without my consent. The reason I am upset is because my wife and I were at the verge of separation and this has exacerbated the matter even further. My wife is now making demands that she would have never dreamt of making had she not seen the bank state-ment. What do I do?

22nd February 2010

When you ask 'what do I do', we assume that you want us to advise you on the breach of confidentiality as related to the bank and not what to do with the demands your wife is making.

The bank has a legal and moral duty not to disclose details of your account to any third party, unless the law compels the bank to do so or where the interests of the bank require disclosure or where the account holder has consented to such disclosure. Though you and your wife are married, in the eyes of the law, you two are distinct and separate individuals. Just because the lady is your wife, does not entitle her to access your bank account.

The bank is in breach of this duty and you can sue the bank for damages. Please be advised that you may also be able to sue your wife depending on the particular circumstances under which she managed to get the information.

Aircraft tyre on my car

I am a taxi driver working at the Mwalimu J. K. Nyerere International Airport. Recently, whilst my car was parked at the airport, an object from an aircraft which looks like a tyre, fell from an aircraft and damaged my car's windscreen. I lost business for two weeks repairing the dam-age. How can I recover this loss? Please advise me.

8th February 2010

This is a very strange occurrence. If it was a tyre, we wonder how the aircraft landed! We have not read of any aircraft crash landing around the region recently and wonder what the 'object' really was. In any case, we choose to answer your question whether there really was an object or not.

The law in Tanzania imposes liability for damages caused by an air craft. A person who suffered that loss may recover it if he can prove that the loss was caused by an air craft. The Civil Aviation Act provides that where a material loss or damage is caused to any person or property on land or water by a person in, or an article or person falling from an air craft while in flight, taking off or landing, then unless the loss or damage was caused or contributed to by the negligence of the person who suffered, damages in respect of the loss or damage shall be recoverable without proof of negligence or intention or other cause of action, as if the loss or damage had been caused by the wilful act, neglect, or default of the owner of the air craft.

The law does come to your protection but you will have to prove that the tyre or object actually fell from the aircraft. You can also seek recovery from your insurer if you have comprehensive insurance. However, do check if your comprehensive insurer covers you for damage to your windscreen. Many insurers do not as it is a separate cover for which you pay a separate premium.

Forgery in my account

I have a personal account with a bank in Musoma. On the day I was supposed to travel to Dar, I looked at my bank statement only to find that a large sum of money was debited fraudulently from my account. Upon my return from Dar, I went to see the bank only to be told that I had delayed in reporting the matter and that I would not be refunded. I demanded to see the cheque leaf used and the signature on the cheque is 100% different from mine. Even a blind man could have spotted the difference. The bank is not cooperating. Do I have any recourse?

4th January 2010

What surprises us is the fact that there has been a forgery and you did not report the matter to the bank until you came back from Dar. If the amount was as large as you claim,

we are quite shocked at how slowly you have moved to sort the matter.

In banking, the customer owes a duty to inform his bank of any forged payment as soon as one becomes aware of it. This is often referred to as the Greenwood duty, after a famous English case. If he does not, and the bank's position is thereby prejudiced, he adopts the cheque and is stopped from asserting the forgery.

The obligation and duty require that a person must not knowingly allow another to be prejudiced by the fraudulent use of a forged instrument to which he has set, or appears to have set, his hand.

All said and done, we feel you still do have a case but your chances of full recovery are reduced to a certain degree because of the Greenwood principle. We suggest you meet your lawyers and explain the entire case before suing the bank.

Banker did not Inform me

For the past fifteen years, I have been banking with a bank in Tanzania. I am also one of their large borrowers having invested in various industries in the country. Over the past two years, I have been travelling and spending most of my time overseas for medical reasons and have just returned. On my return, I have realised that the bank has not alerted me on various new products and offers that they launched which would have saved me millions in interest and other bank fees. My competitors took advantage of these offers and have done very well. Does the bank not have a duty to inform me? Does the bank not owe a duty of care to its customers?

28th December 2009

There are many implied duties that a bank has towards its customers including protecting the customer from fraud of agents (including directors), various statutory protection and at times in giving financial and investment advice. It is impossible to give an exhaustive list of the duties of care owed by banker to customer, because in any given case the Court is concerned with the particular contract or, in the case of an alleged duty of care in tort, the proximity of the parties, reasonableness and justice on the particular facts.

Your question is whether the bank should have informed you of the better offers they were providing that you could have taken advantage of and saved millions.

This would depend on the type of agreements you have signed with the bank. In our experience, it is very uncommon for the bank to provide in any agreement, a term requiring the bank to inform you of such products. Ultimately, whether you choose the product or not is your decision. It is very similar to the case where you walk into a department store, buy a television set for a price, and find out that it is on 50% off the next day.

In a famous English case of Suriya & Douglas v Midland Bank, the Court of Appeal rejected the argument of the claimant's firm of solicitors that there should be implied into the contract between banker and customer a term requiring the bank to inform its customers of the introduction by the bank of new and more advantageous forms of accounts.

Your case falls very close to the above and it is unlikely that you will be able to successfully sue your bank. We suggest you contact your lawyers for further advice.

Staying as a paying guest

I am a student from Singida currently studying A levels in Dodoma. I stay with a family as a paying guest. I was provided with a room to be shared with two other students. A few weeks back, the family squeezed into the room a further four students, totalling seven in one room. The room size is not more than fifteen square metres. There is hardly any room to breathe when we are all in there. It is tighter than being in jail. What should I do?
21st December 2009

The family you are staying with is in breach of the contract that you have with them. However, for such an issue is it really worth suing on breach? Perhaps not. The family is also contravening section 63 of the Public Health Act 2008 which states: A person shall not at any time receive and accommodate into a lodging house, room, dwelling house, school, institution, hostel, vehicle, train or vessel in a greater number of persons as to cause overcrowding. Any person who contravenes the above commits an offence and on conviction is liable to a fine not exceeding TZS 200,000 or to imprisonment for a term of three months or both.

In your case, the seven students in a fifteen square metres room is very likely overcrowding. You may want to inform this to the family you are staying with, as a custodial sentence applies in the event that the family is found guilty of contravening the Public Health Act.

Cheeky insurance company

A few months ago my factory was gutted down by fire. I did all I could to rescue the items in there including the most expensive asset of all – my machine. My employees risked their lives and assisted in removing the expensive machine in addition to other items. However, in removing the machine, because of the speed with which we had to remove it, the machine was damaged and whose cost of repair is only 30% of the cost of its replacement had it burned down. The insurance company now comes back and tells me that I have fire cover but because I moved my machine, the machine is not covered since it did not burn. I wish I had left my machine to burn as it would have been covered. I am really frustrated, please assist.

23rd November 2009

We can imagine your frustration. Your good actions have actually landed you in a soup and you probably wish you had let the machine to burn.

Your action to reduce the loss is a condition of any insurance policy. It is also not unusual for an insured person to take action which, although aimed at reducing the loss, leads to damage. This does not necessarily break the chain of causation. Indeed the consequence of finding that it did might not suit insurers since it could discourage action to reduce loss.

The issue in your question is whether the damage to your machine is covered under the fire insurance policy. Interpreting it strictly, as the insurance company is probably reading it, the machine is not covered.

However, since the damage has been caused as a result of the 'rescue efforts' the scope of cover in fire policies is extended to cover this. Additionally you may also claim the expenses you incurred in trying to fight the fire.

As a way forward, you should send in a notice to pay to your insurance company and also inform them that the more they delay the claims settlement, the more you are losing in your business. If they do not budge do not think twice, go ahead and sue; you have an excellent suit.

Building in a common area

There are six different owners with a common pathway round the block of apartments that I live in. One of the residents in the back has started building on this pathway and hence removed access for the other tenants' tanks including free movement of the other tenants. What are the rights of the tenants?

19th October 2009

From your question it seems like the area your neighbour is building on or obstructing is a common area which is to be used by all the six owners in the block of apartments you have mentioned.

There is no doubt that the tenants on the upper floors need access to the tanks; from the facts you have availed to us, this building and/or blocking is illegal. It also amounts to nuisance. You can petition in Court to have such nuisance removed and/or get an order for entry or demolition as the case may be.

You may also want to check with the municipal council to see if such construction is legal and whether they have issued a permit. If no permit has been issued, the municipal council has the right to intervene and demolish any such illegal construction.

Bank not crediting my cheque

I opened an account with a bank and have been regularly operating it. I deposited a significantly large cheque in the bank over nine months back, and to date the cheque has not been credited to my account. The manager keeps on giving me lame excuses which include that the cheque has gone for international clearing. He recently told me that my account cannot carry such amounts of money as the cheque amount is five times my annual turnover. My business is suffering because of this. Can the bank sit on my money like this?

12th October 2009

If all that you are telling us is true, then you have a very good case, unless of course the cheque has not been honoured or the cheque is forged, neither of which you have mentioned. Either way the bank should give you reasons for the delay. To have a cause of action, you need to establish that you have a customer banker relationship based on the following ingredients: you must have an account in the bank – which you do have; relationship of a banker and customer begins as soon as money or a cheque is paid and the bank accepts it – this is true in your case; the duration is not of the essence to establish a relationship, meaning, that it is not necessary for the account to have been operated for some time to merit a person to be a customer of the bank. Since we have answered the above in the affirmative, you do have a customer banker relationship.

The bank is thus bound to use reasonable skill and diligence in presenting and securing payment of the cheque and placing the proceeds to your account. It does not take nine months to clear an international cheque and this is indeed a very lame reason. The duration in most banks is four to six weeks.

The manager has told you that the amount is large and that it cannot be 'carried' in your account. Please note that a bank has thousands of accounts and each account does not have its own safe from which amounts are deposited or withdrawn! What he most likely means is that looking at the normal operations of your account, the amount you have deposited looks 'fishy' as to the source of the funds. Normally banks would refer such transactions to the Bank of Tanzania for investigation but again it cannot take nine months to investigate.

You are being taken around the mulberry bush without being given reasons. You have the right to demand reasons, and should do so in writing. The bank cannot just sit on your cheque like this. You can write to the bank informing them of the circumstances and the inconvenience they are causing and if they continue giving reasons that do not make sense, you should sue the bank. In your suit, you should also ask for damages.

Please note that our advice is based on the information you have provided us. A bank not crediting an amount and not providing reasons for over nine months raises a lot of other questions in our minds. If there is anything you are hiding from us, ignore the advice we have given you and seek the services of your lawyers.

Third party claim due to accident

My car was involved in an accident with a cyclist in Dodoma. The cyclist was injured and taken to hospital and treated. I paid for the treatment. I have been held to be responsible for the accident as I did not know that it was a one way street. The cyclist has several other claims against me. I passed them on to my insurance company in Dar es Salaam. The cyclist travelled all the way to Dar es Salaam and the insurance company 'meanly' offered him TZS 50,000 to settle the matter. That amount would not even cover the poor man's travel expenses to Dar and thus he declined. The cyclist has now opened a suit against me. What should I do?

28th September 2009

Insurance companies have a bad reputation world over for delaying or denying paying claims, especially on third party claims. Your case is no different. We are also equally shocked at the amount the insurance company offered to pay – it shows the 'meanness' you have referred to. There is a common joke about insurers that they will not realise the amount they should pay to third party victims until the claims managers are one day the third party victims. In this case you need not wait that long!

We suggest that in your defence, you bring in the insurance company to be part of the suit, by way of following the third party procedure. Where a defendant in a suit (such as you) claims against any party (such as the insurance company) not a party to the suit any contribution or indemnity, such defendant may apply to the Court for leave to present to the Court what is called a third party notice. You will effectively be bringing the insurance company into the law suit that will then have to defend itself.

Apart from this, you should also file a written statement of defence within twenty one days of receiving the plaint.

Removal of graves for mining

My parents recently informed me that an area which is commonly used for burial purposes in our village is about to be given away to a foreign investor, whose plan is to establish a mine. It is believed that the area is very rich in diamonds. What should we do?

21st September 2009

The issue at hand is a very sensitive one. On the one hand you have the graves of the villagers which do not generate any revenues for the government but acts as a memorial. On the other hand you have our government trying to allow an investor to develop a mine that will hopefully benefit the villagers and Tanzanians.

A strict economist's view would be that a mine is more beneficial than a graveyard. Religious leaders will likely say that we need to respect the dead and should not let our materialistic values take over our spiritual being.

The law governing such cases – The Graves (Removal) Act provides that the Minister responsible for lands may cause a grave and any dead body buried therein to be removed from the land if such grave is situated on land which is required for public purposes. The meaning of the term public purpose is that provided under the Land Acquisition Act which among other things provides that land shall be deemed to be required for a public purpose where it is for or in connection with

mining for minerals or oil.

The procedure to follow is for the Minister to give a twenty one day notice for the removal of the graves. Within the twenty one days you may object to the proposal citing your reasons. The fact that there are lucrative diamonds beneath the land reduces your chances of succeeding.

Cash for death on Yemen Airways

A few months back a Yemen Airways flight crashed off the coast of Comoros killing all but one passenger. My husband was on board that fateful flight. His body was recovered off the coast of Tanzania and I was flown here by Yemen Airways to identify the body. I have now been offered USD 20,000 by the airline, as compensation for the death they caused. They have given me some documents to sign before I get the money. I am also in need of the funds and am not sure if I should accept this kind gesture. I was not even expecting it. Are they trying to trick me? Should I take the money?

14th September 2009

This is not a kind gesture. As a wife of the deceased, you have every right to claim over the airline. Remember that you have lost a loved one and that no amount of compensation will bring him back.

The amount that an airline is liable to pay is governed by various international conventions some of which are the Vienna Convention and the Montreal Convention. These international conventions regulate liability for international carriage of persons, luggage or goods.

We will answer your questions one after the other: Should you sign the documents? It is very likely that the documents will enable the airline to limit its liability to the amount they intend to pay you and hence you will not get more than the USD 20,000 that has been offered to you. Is the USD 20,000 enough? This amount is below the amount mentioned in the conventions. Depending on where you are, your domicile and the like, the amount varies but it is definitely much higher than the amount that has been offered to you. You seem to have shown desperation for cash and hence a lower offer has been made to you.

Are they trying to trick you? The airline or its insurance company is trying to minimise its loss. Whether you call that tricking or otherwise, is up to how one looks at the equation. In our opinion, the airline and/or its insurers are taking advantage of you and underpaying you. Whether you should take the money or not is entirely your decision but we recommend you seek legal assistance from an aviation lawyer immediately.

We also wish to point out that families of victims of the recent Air France crash were given a compensation of Euros 17,500 just as an advance. This was given by the airlines insurers without any strings attached. The final settlement for these victims is expected to run into the hundreds of thousands of dollars per passenger.

Insurance for mortgage

For the first time I have taken a loan of TZS 800M from a bank in Dar having kept my house as a security. The bank has insisted that I alter my insurance policy to reflect that they are the insured. I do not seem to understand why I should change my policy to reflect this? Am I being tricked? Why does the bank have an eye on the insurance and why should they be concerned? Who should pay the insurance premium?

31st August 2009

The fact that you have taken the mortgage for the first time is irrelevant in the eyes of the law, at least as far as insurance is concerned. The house belongs to you as we speak.

However, if you default in making your scheduled loan repayments, the bank will take over the house to settle the loan.

We are unsure if the bank is asking you to change the policy to entirely reflect its own name or it wants to appear as an insured beside your name. If it wants to take over the policy then that is exposing you to risk which in our opinion is not acceptable. However, if the bank wants its interest to be reflected in the policy beside you, then this is standard practice and we do not see you being tricked by the request.

The bank is concerned about the insurance as it has an insurable interest in your property.

In the Law of Insurance, the insured must have an interest in the subject matter of his or her policy, or such policy will be void and unenforceable since it will be regarded as a form of gambling.

An individual ordinarily has an insurable interest when he or she will obtain some type of financial benefit from the preservation of the subject matter, or will sustain pecuniary loss from its destruction or impairment when the risk insured against occurs.

If for example your property is gutted down by fire, the bank will be fully exposed with no security if it is not one of the insured.

You are also asking who should pay the premium. The standard market practice in Tanzania is for the borrower to pay the premium. You can, however, negotiate this with the bank as we have seen in some transactions where banks pay part of the premium.

Suing restaurant for food poisoning

Our family went out for dinner to a very popular restaurant in Dar and all four of us had severe cramps two hours after we had our meal. The food tasted delicious but the treating doctor said that we had very likely been exposed to bacteria from the

food that resulted in the pains. Can we sue the restaurant?

24th August 2009

You can sue anyone for just about anything. Whether it is worth your time and resources is another matter – after all it is your personal decision.

Though it might be difficult to prove that it was this particular restaurant that caused the problem, you can go ahead an institute a law suit. However, you might want to first try and do an off Court settlement and to get that started you should send a legal notice to the restaurant.

If that fails you should charge the restaurant owners with negligent conduct for manufacturing food unfit for human consumption. But in the absence of conclusive evidence, you may also charge the restaurant owners with negligent business practices for poor selection of food suppliers and failure to adequately supervise employees who may have transmitted the disease by failing to wash their hands properly with soap.

The success in your suit will depend on the evidence you produce. You might not have been the only guest who suffered such pain – look for other people who have had similar issues. You will also be shocked how much information the waiters have on the hygiene status of the restaurant. Gather as much information as possible to prove your case. Be assured that the restaurant owners will also put up a fight – be prepared.

Serious injury at the gym

I was working out at a gym in Dar when one of the machines failed and caused me a very serious shoulder injury. The wire snapped and the whole weight came on me. Luckily I was on medium weights and survived but the injury could have been fatal. The gym has a tendency not to service its machines. When I approached the manager, he rudely pointed out a notice that read – all customers exercise at their own risk. Does that allow them to get off the hook? They have involved their lawyer. I mistrust lawyers as they are always out to get you.

17th August 2009

Just because the gym has a notice, does not mean you cannot sue them. The gym has a duty to care for its members and the snapping is proof of breach of that duty, as long as you were not involved in any way in the snapping. The severity of the injury makes us believe that you can really take the gym owners and managers to task for failing to discharge their duties.

Unfortunately, we have not seen many litigations of this type in Tanzania but elsewhere suing a gym or your trainer is very common.

The involvement of their lawyer also sends a message that they are concerned on the action you might take. Whether you mistrust a lawyer is irrelevant. On the contrary because of lawyers and the way they think, the world has become a more efficient place. All lawyers are not saints but neither are they as bad as you make them sound in your question.

Do not think twice – sue the gym.

Insurance company after me

My truck was involved in a head on collision with a bus and a passenger vehicle at the same time. My driver was held to be at fault by the Court and fined. I now have the insurance company that insured the bus and vehicle after me. They are claiming over TZS 200M for the loss occurred. I fail to understand how this is possible. Is it not illegal?

6th July 2009

This is called subrogation and is legal. Subrogation arises as a consequence of the indemnity principle and refers to the right of an insurer, who has paid for a loss, to pursue the wrongdoer in the name of the insured. It enables liability for loss to be fixed to the person responsible without allowing the insured to recover from both that person and the insured, which would violate the principle of indemnity.

You should have had third party insurance which is mandatory. If not, than that in itself is a criminal offence. Assuming you did have third party insurance (or comprehensive insurance), then the insurer to the bus and vehicle should (and can) pursue it with your insurer. It is standard practice.

What surprises us is why the insurer is pursuing recovery from you. It is possible that you did not have insurance or the insurance that you did have (the insurance sticker) had expired or that the third party insurance sticker was one that was stolen. You need to contact your insurance broker or agent and also an attorney for further guidance.

Insurance claim repudiated

In July last year, I had insured my shop against theft with a local insurance company. They issued me with a cover note and subsequently a policy. My shop was robbed recently and the insurance company has declined to entertain my claim because the premium was not paid. I had the money ready but the company did not come to collect it. Why should I suffer? Is this the company's conspiracy against me? In any case I sent them the cheque by registered post.

15ᵗʰ June 2009

A contract of insurance is one in which one party (the insurer) agrees for a payment of a consideration (the premium) to make monetary provision for the other (the insured) upon the occurrence of some event or against some risk.

Whilst we sympathise with you, unless your policy clearly mentioned that the insurance company will collect the premium, it is very unlikely you will be paid. The norm is for you to remit the payment.

In your case you have not paid the premium which is the consideration, and without consideration there is no contract and hence no insurance cover. Unless there are other things that we do not know, we do not see how the insurance company will pay you. You will only get a refund of the premium you posted by registered mail. We also do not see any conspiracy against you.

We also wish to point out that this is the second or third time we have received questions where an insurance premium has not been paid!

Injury at factory

My uncle works as an engineer for a certain factory. He uses a ladder for his work which is given to him by the storekeeper. Recently he fell off a ladder by stepping on a faulty rung. He was seriously injured and taken to hospital. The employer denies any liability claiming that my uncle was negligent in the way he used the ladder. Is the employer liable? Please advise.

8ᵗʰ June 2009

An employer owes a duty of care for his employees' safety. In particular the employer in a factory has a duty to ensure that his factory is safe and to provide properly maintained plant and equipment. For example, under the Occupational Health and Safety Act, 2003 the employer has a duty to make sure that none of his employees operates a machine unless such an employee is sufficiently trained to work on such a machine and is also fully aware of the dangers involved in the operations of the machine. Many factory owners are either not aware of this law or neglect it.

From the facts you have provided above,

it looks like the ladder was defective and perhaps poorly maintained, especially if a rung collapsed. The fact that the ladder was provided to your uncle by the storekeeper will also not avail any help to the company. And even if the storekeeper should have checked the ladder for its safety (which he did not), the company is still liable for the storekeeper's negligence. Unless there is something more to this, we do not see how your uncle's employer is not liable.

If there is no proof that the personal injuries were attributable to wilful misconduct of your uncle, he is entitled to not only his statutory compensation but any other compensation that he can justify claiming which may include damages arising out or, or consequential to, the incident.

Insurance company cheated me

My godown was totally burnt in a fire. I had insurance with a local company which deducted 5% of the claim amount that I agreed to. I feel I have been cheated. I was surfing the net and have noticed that insurance companies have a solid reputation of cheating their clients. What should I do?

23rd March 2009

What the company has deducted from your claim is called a policy excess. A policy excess is an amount that you have to bear in any claim and is as per the contract of insurance (policy). It is a standard clause in such contracts. The excess is also priced into the premium you pay and is meant to reduce the number of small claims you can make. Processing claims for insurance companies is expensive. Sometimes the insurance companies spend more resources processing a claim than the claim amount itself and hence inclusion of such a clause.

Answering your question, we are unsure as to what the excess clause is in your policy.

If it is 5% of the claim amount the insurance company has certainly not cheated you. However, the standard clauses are 5% of the claim payable or a certain fixed amount, whichever is less. If that is the clause, then do some quick math and see if the insurance company has deducted the lower amount of the two. As for your reading on the net, please note that insurance companies worldwide are strict when it comes to payment of claims. We are not trying to defend insurance companies, but at times the insured unnecessarily and unjustifiably complain without having a thorough knowledge of the contract of insurance they have entered into.

Difference between general and special damages

One of our customers has sued our company not only for the particular breach of the contract, which I have admitted to, but also for general and special damages. He has come with creative ways of increasing the amounts. What are these general and special damages? Can I stop him from claiming these ridiculous amounts?

30th March 2009

By definition, general damages are those elements of loss or damage that need not be claimed or mentioned in the complaint in order to be the subject matter of proof and recovery. Special damages are those which must be specifically claimed and described if recovery for them is to be allowed. The distinction between these two types of damages confuses many. The distinction can also be made another way. General damages are those that the law presumes follow from the type of wrong complained of whilst special damages are those that are alleged to have been sustained in the particular circumstances of the particular wrong, and must be specifically claimed and proved to be sustained.

General damages may also mean damages given for a loss that is incapable of precise estimation, such as pain and suffering or loss of reputation. And in the same context special damages are damages for losses that can be quantified such as out of pocket expenses or earnings lost.

You cannot stop him from claiming these 'creative' amounts. What you can do is prepare a solid defence against the claims. The onus is on him to prove that he deserves to be awarded such damages.

Passenger claiming damages for accident

My car was involved in an accident in Tanga and one of the passengers was severely injured and consequently my driver was prosecuted and fined for causing the accident. Now I have been sued by the said passenger claiming for damages. What should I do?

9th March 2009

Without necessarily saying that you are already liable, in principal, the suit brought against you is under the circumstances narrated, maintainable. You are being sued under the principle known as vicarious liability. The principle imposes liability on persons as a result of action of some other persons e.g. that of the master for the actions of his servants. It normally applies in the cases of negligence and recklessness. The law generally requires us to act, in our day to day undertakings, with due care towards each other. For example the owner of a *daladala* is duty bound to employ a licensed and careful driver. If an accident occurs causing injuries to the passengers as a result of the driver's negligence, depending on the facts, the owner may also be liable. It is not entirely a valid defence, in a suit for damages, for the owner to say that the driver acted against the owner's express directions.

In your case the injured passenger has a right to sue you, your driver and your insurer, if he so wishes.

We advise you to engage an attorney. And if the suit has been filed against you, and if you have a valid insurance, your lawyer can look at joining your insurer in the suit. Your lawyer will have to seek leave of the Court under a procedure known as third party notice. Depending on the terms and conditions of your policy, you may or may not be covered.

Insurance refusing to pay my claim

My building burnt down and my insurance company says I will not be paid because I have not remitted the premium. I told the company they can deduct the premium from the claim or I could pay the premium now, but they have refused. Can I sue?

23rd February 2009

Insurance is a contract in which the insurer (insurance company) agrees for payment of a premium, to take risk on behalf of the insured upon the occurrence of some event. Generally for such contracts to be enforceable there must be some element of uncertainty about the events insured against and the insured must have an interest in the subject matter (insurable interest).

Assuming that the building is indeed yours and that you have an insurable interest, the payment of premium, as per the terms of the Insurance policy is a critical factor for the insurance contract to hold. Unless you had agreed with your insurance company that you will pay premium within a certain period, and you are within that credit period, it is very unlikely that your claim will be paid.

Insurance companies survive on premium being paid in advance, usually yearly, and invested by the company to meet future claims. If all insured, like yourself, fail to pay premiums, insurance companies would cease to exist. Your case is a very tricky one and if you had not negotiated payment terms with the insurance company, your claim will not be honoured as there will be no contract between you and your insurance company.

Jail for smoking in public

I see people smoking in public places with no regard to others. Is this allowed?

9th February 2009

Smoking in public places is strictly prohibited by the law. Our law, The Tobacco Products (Regulation) Act, 2003, whose main objective is to reduce tobacco use and its consequences to the people, restricts manufacture, distribution and use of tobacco products which includes cigarette smoking in a public place. A public place includes a heath care establishment, library, place of worship, enclosed premises intended for social-cultural meetings, sporting or recreational activities, public eating places, office buildings, public transport on air, land or sea, pavilions, enclosed environment such as markets, malls, and any other enclosed place to which the public has admittance. It is a criminal offence to smoke in a public place and he or she who does so commits an offence punishable by a fine not exceeding TZS 500,000 or to imprisonment for a term not exceeding one year. As a good law abiding citizen you are encouraged to report any incidence of a person smoking cigarettes in a public place, to the nearest police station. Many people are also not aware of this law.

Bank harassing wife

I am a married woman. Our marriage has subsisted for a period of three years. My husband has mortgaged our matrimonial house without my knowledge and obtained money from the bank. He has failed to repay the bank's debt and the bank has issued a notice to auction our house. What do I do?

2nd February 2009

Mortgage is an interest in the right of

occupancy or lease or other property for the purpose of securing repayment of a debt or fulfilment of a condition of the debt. The person (borrower) who mortgages his property as security for the mortgage is known as the mortgagor. The person (lender) to whom property is mortgaged is known as mortgagee and the instrument creating a mortgage is known as Mortgage Deed.

The house where you have been residing with your husband is a matrimonial home. Matrimonial home means the building or part of the building in which the husband and wife ordinarily reside together. The law dealing with mortgages in Tanzania recognises rights of the spouse when dealing with the matrimonial house. A mortgage over the matrimonial home does not become effectively operational unless the document used to grant the mortgage is signed by or there is the evidence it has been assented to by the mortgagor and the spouse or spouses living in that matrimonial home. Therefore for the mortgage of the matrimonial home to be valid the wife or spouse must consent and sign the document (Mortgage deed). The law obliges the mortgagee to take reasonable steps to ascertain whether the applicant for a mortgage has a spouse or spouses.

In light of the above, the purported mortgage deed executed between the bank and your husband is not valid for failure to fulfil the above condition. Since you have been served with the notice for auction of the house, you have to expeditiously file an application to the Land Court for an injunctive order to restrain the bank or its agents from auctioning the said house. From the facts given, you have a good case and should pursue it.

Loud music, I cannot sleep

Is there any law that prohibits loud music from being played in residential areas? In Kinondoni there is a club that frequently holds public concerts and parties with very

loud music that disturb residents of the area. Please advise.

9nd February 2009

The act of holding public concerts with very loud music that disturbs residents within a specific area is a wrong. It is a tortuous wrong which in law is commonly known as a nuisance. Nuisance is an activity or state of affairs that interferes with the use or enjoyment of land or rights over land (private nuisance) or with the health, safety, comfort or property of the public at large (public nuisance).

A person is guilty of a public nuisance when he does any act of an illegal omission, which causes any common injury, danger or annoyance to the public or to the people in general who dwell or occupy property. It is an act affecting the public at large or some considerable portion of it and it must interfere with rights of comfort of members of the community or convenience of the public generally e.g. carrying trades which cause offensive smells or intolerable noises like in your case.

Jail for smoking

I have just found out that my 16-year-old son is smoking. I am shocked at the number of cigarette adverts in Tanzania. Is that not illegal? In the UK where I've lived, there are strict controls. Why does not Tanzania have such controls? I have also noticed that restaurants here do not have separate smoking bays.

12th January 2009

Smoking and selling of tobacco products is regulated in Tanzania by the Tobacco Industry Act 2001 and the Tobacco Products (Regulation) Act 2003 (TPRA 2003). Very few people either know of the Act or follow it. To begin with it is illegal for your 16-year-old son to be smoking as per section 7(1) of the TPRA 2003 which is very clear and states 'no person under the age of 18 shall smoke or famish a tobacco product.' A Cigarette is a tobacco product. If one is found and convicted in contravention of this section, as is your son, as per section 33(2) of the same Act, he can be sentenced to up to two years imprisonment or fined up to TZS 2M. There is a similar penalty for those found selling products to those below the age of eighteen. Answering the second part of your question, cigarette advertising in Tanzania is regulated as per section 26 of the TPRA 2003. One of the important aspects of this section is that no person shall advertise tobacco products trying to show as if the tobacco product resulted in sporting or athletic success, professional success, sexual success, that most people are smokers and that smoking brings success in life generally. Hence if you find adverts depicting any of the above, the company or manufacturer advertising the products commits an offence which is also imprisonable. It is also not illegal for cigarette companies to advertise as long as they stick to the advertising guidelines. In response to the last part of your question, as per section 13 of the TPRA 2003, it is clearly mentioned that 'any person being in charge of a higher educational establishment, an office building, a hotel, bar or restaurant, and any other entertainment facility, shall set aside rooms for smoking and non smoking.' The owner is also supposed to make sure that a separate room for smoking is set aside with proper ventilation and that such rooms should provide maximum protection to non smokers, with proper signage of areas where smoking is and is not permitted. The restaurant owners who contravene the above are liable to a fine of between TZS 5M and 20M, or to imprisonment for a period not exceeding three years, or both.

Commercial Disputes & Queries

 Signing a contract is like putting the last nail on your coffin. Read it before signing it.

The last chapter covers questions on consumer related contractual issues. This chapter focuses on commercial contracts, contracts for provision of goods and services to a business, partnership agreements, trade agreements, lease agreements and the like. It also goes into detail on drawing up various contracts, tips on signing contracts, penalty clauses, wording used in contracts and more. Drawing up contracts and getting the wording just right is tricky but simple to do – attention to detail is required. Taking the time to get it right in the first instance is always advised.

Neighbour shop competing with me

I have a shop on a main road in Arusha. For the past twenty years, my neighbour and I stuck to our agreement that he shall not sell products similar to mine. He recently migrated and sold his shop. The new owner signed a similar contract but has started selling goods exactly like mine. I intend to take action against him – please advise.

28th March 2011

Much as we would like to side with you, we find the contract with your new neighbour to be in restraint of trade. Contracts in restraint of trade are contracts where one of the parties restricts his or her future freedom to carry on his or her trade or business with others, usually by way of a covenant. This contract of yours may also be held to be anti-competitive and in breach of the Fair Competition Act in Tanzania. Other similar contracts that we have seen in the market place are between employers and employees, particularly expatriate employees, where the employee signs a contract with the employer that he will not work for any competitor as long as his current employer is in business. This again has been held to be in restraint of trade. Unfortunately, we do not see how you will get this contract enforced. It is likely that your contract will be held to be illegal. Of course, you may wish to seek further legal advice.

Bank taken to Court

Our bank lent money to a company and secured the amount by way of a third party mortgage. We sent a demand notice to the borrower, he failed to pay, and subsequently defaulted. Just as we were preparing to exercise our rights under the mortgage, we were sued by the borrower on grounds that we demanded the wrong amount. While it is true that the amount we demanded was overstated, the overstatement is less than

TZS 1M. What should we do?

21st March 2011

There are conflicting decisions of various Courts on the validity and effectiveness of a demand that is made with an error in the amount. In your case, it seems like the borrower has admitted that he has borrowed and there is an amount payable by him. The only contentious issue is the difference between what he claims to be the amount payable and what you claimed in the demand. It also appears to us that you have accepted there was a mistake in the amount demanded. If that is the case, he is right but that does not mean he does not have to pay! His own admission that he has borrowed and not paid should work for you – capitalise on that and finalize the suit by accepting the amount he has pleaded.

Lack of board resolution

I am the main shareholder and one of the three directors of a renowned manufacturing company in Dar. When I travelled overseas the operations were being handled by one of the other directors. I have come to know that this director forged a board resolution and other signatures and obtained a TZS 1B loan from a multinational bank. The director has mortgaged one of the key yards of the company and the bank is now pressuring us to pay. Can the bank make such a demand?

21st May 2011

The bank can surely make such a demand; in its opinion it has lent your company funds. The main question is whether the bank will have recourse in the event you fail or refuse to pay. There are many factors that will play a role in this matter. For example, did the bank check the signatures and do proper due diligence? Did the bank know of the mischief? Has a mortgage been created?

What other signals did the bank have that should have alerted it to this mischief? Who in your company do the banks usually deal with? Is there any abnormality in the speed in which this loan was approved? You will have to weigh in all these and decide whether or not you have a case against the bank. Your position could then be that the bank did not follow appropriate procedures when granting the loan. It might be a rough journey, and we suggest you disclose all the facts to your lawyers who can guide you further.

Tanzanite sold in error

For the last twenty years I have been trading in precious stones in Arusha. About twelve weeks ago, I sold some stones, believing them to be Tanzanite. The buyer also checked the stones and paid me USD 22,000 for the transaction. It now turns out that the stones were not Tanzanite. I have dealt with this buyer for at least ten years and this mishap is causing me a lot of problems. He wants to cancel the sale. What should I do?

7th April 2011

In your lengthy question with all the details you provided (we have only reproduced the main question) you described the relationship between you and the buyer. You indicated that you wanted to refund the purchase price of the stones. It is by all means your decision. However, when you, or anyone else, writes to us, we give you the legal position, as it has stood in similar circumstances. The commercial decision is for you to take. Before you continue reading, please be warned that our opinion is exactly opposite of what you suggested you wanted to do.

The settled position of the law, since the early 19th century, is that in the absence of explicit contractual statements, the seller assumes the risk that he may have under-charged for an item, and the buyer assumes

the risk that he might have over-paid for an item. The issue in your transaction is whether the buyer can rescind the sale because he was ignorant as to the 'hypothetical fair market value' of the stone.

Our response is that in the absence of fraud or warranty, the hypothetical value of the property sold, as compared with the price paid, is not grounds for rescission of the sale. Neither of you had any knowledge that the stone was not a Tanzanite, so there was no fraud. In addition, there was no agreement of warranty, either stated or implied. Therefore, the risk was equally borne by both of you, and the buyer cannot 'cancel' the sale.

A general comment that we cannot resist making – your approach to this is truly admirable and only heard about in the scriptures. As said in your letter to us, your relationship with the buyer is far more important than the USD 22,000, and on these premises you can proceed and refund the amount.

Why should I sign a personal guarantee?

What is the difference between a corporate and personal guarantee and can a bank ask for both? Is asking for a personal guarantee against the principles of veil of incorporation? I am an appointed director in a company but not a shareholder. Why should I sign such a guarantee when I do not receive any dividends or financial benefit from the company?

28th February 2011

A guarantee in loan matters means that the person is promising something and giving an assurance for the repayment of a loan. In law there are several types of guarantees, including the ones you have mentioned – corporate and personal guarantees.

A corporate guarantee is when one company gives a guarantee for another company for the repayment of whole or part of a loan which remains unpaid in the event that the debtor fails to repay the loan. In Tanzania, a corporate guarantee is frequently given by either the holding company of a borrowing subsidiary company, or by a sister company that has some elements of common shareholding in the borrowing company. Such corporate guarantee is only enforceable if the corporate guarantee has been properly approved by the company's board of directors and the Memorandum and Articles of Association (MEMARTS) allow the company to give such guarantees. We have often noted that banks, in a attempting to disburse loans, do not get proper board resolutions from the company guaranteeing the loan, or do not take the time to read the MEMARTS to check if the board is acting within its powers. This has serious repercussions for the lender when trying to enforce guarantee. Banks blame the Courts for not ruling in their favour!

On the other hand, a personal guarantee is a guarantee given by an individual that he/she will repay the whole or part of the loan in the event that the borrowing company fails to repay it.

The main difference between the two is that corporate guarantee is given by a corporate body, while a personal guarantee is given by an individual.

We now turn to your question on the veil of incorporation, which we believe is a very important question that most directors and shareholders ignore. The veil of incorporation is a principle of Company Law that ensures that a company is a separate legal entity from its directors and shareholders, thus protecting the personal assets of owners and investors from lawsuits. When a director or shareholder signs a personal guarantee, he is exposing himself to the risk of being personally liable for the debts of the company. This is standard practice in a number of countries,

as banks want to minimise risks. However, in some countries, the banks charge higher interest rates when there is no one to sign such a personal guarantee. This option is unfortunately not available here.

Your question is why should you risk your personal assets for a company in which you are merely a director and not a shareholder? We agree with you. Why should you? On these premises, you can refuse to expose your personal assets for the benefit of a company loan, and should not sign the personal guarantee.

Partnership with public sector

We are an Australian company currently negotiating a joint venture with a government ministry to develop large scale farming in the country. The project span is at least three decades and we want to ensure that the documentation is correct. We do realise that the project is much needed in the country but want to be sure about the contract before we commit over USD 300M to the project. What are the procedures to follow? We want to avoid any problems later on.

14th February 2011

Your project falls under the Public Private Partnership Act, which is a new Act that has recently come into existence. Under the Act, a Coordination Unit is established, and a coordinator is appointed to head it. The Coordination Unit coordinates all public private partnership projects (PPP), assesses them, investigates whether they provide value for money, promotes PPP's and, most importantly, determines whether the project is affordable to the relevant ministry.

From your letter, it is not clear whether or not a coordinator has been recruited, and if the coordination unit is functional – though we very much doubt it, and advise you to contact the Tanzania Investment Centre (TIC),

FB

under which the unit is established.

Also under the Act, there is finance unit that is to be established to reviews the PPP feasibilities and ensure that they make economic sense. It is for the Minister of Finance to finally approve. Note that the Attorney General must also provide his legal opinion prior to the signing of any agreement.

After reading your question, it seems like you are only negotiating with the relevant ministry and not yet following the process detailed above. We would also like to add that if you have submitted the proposal, it falls under the ambit of unsolicited bids under the Act Regulations for such unsolicited bids are, to the best of our knowledge, yet to be published. All in all, since this is a much needed agriculture project for Tanzania, you should contact the TIC who can assist in fast tracking this entire process. It is important that in the process you, or the Ministry, do not break the law.

Can a foreigner own land?

We are a foreign company and wish to own land in Tanzania. My accountant tells me that we can do so, but my lawyer informs us we cannot. I am totally confused – should we proceed and purchase the land? If we are not allowed to own land, we will be very disappointed. In this era it is very weird for such a law to exist. Please advise.

7th February 2011

Much as we would like to please you, we have no choice but to disappoint. The Land Act of 1999 states in section 20(1) that a non-citizen shall not be allocated or granted land, unless it is for investment purposes under the Tanzania Investment Act, 1997. Section 20(4) further states that for the purposes of this Act, any corporate body with majority ownership by non-citizens shall be deemed to be non-citizen or foreign company.

Your accountant is referring to section 435(2) of the Companies Act of 2002, which states that from the date of registration and so long as it is registered, a foreign company shall have the same power to hold land in Tanzania as if it were a company incorporated under this Act.

The confusion is caused by the Companies Act allowing land ownership by foreign companies and the Land Act disallowing ownership. However, the Land Act further states that on and after the commencement of this Act, notwithstanding any other written law to the contrary, this Act shall apply to all land in Mainland Tanzania and any provisions of any other written law applicable to land which conflict, or are inconsistent with, any of the provisions of this Act shall to the extent of that conflict or that inconsistency cease to be applicable to land or any matter connected with land in Mainland Tanzania.

If you have the stamina to read the above, you will note that the Land Act prevails over the Companies Act, and you cannot own land as a foreign company in Tanzania unless you are registered under the Tanzania Investment Act of 1997.

Regarding what you call the 'weirdness' of the law, every country has its policies, and the current land policy in Tanzania does not allow companies who come into Tanzania to seize land for speculative purposes. There is nothing weird about it. If you require land for your project, you can easily approach the Tanzania Investment Centre (TIC) in Dar and get a certificate of incentives processed. There is a process to follow which is quite streamlined. The TIC is known for its efficiency and you should not hesitate to contact them.

TRA not respecting the law

I have entered into an agreement with an agency of the government for a project of

national importance running across Tanzania. I was given certain exemptions for the project that I cannot disclose to you because of a confidentiality agreement. For the first two years, the Tanzania Revenue Authority (TRA) accepted the exemptions and granted the waivers. Since July 2010, the TRA has refused to recognise the agreement, saying that the exemptions are not valid anymore, although the contract is still running. The TRA claim that there is a new law that overrides the contract. How can the same arms of the government not be on the same page? What should I do? We are a large company and came to Tanzania because of the incentives we were offered. How can these just be taken away from us? It makes the whole project calculation redundant.

17th January 2011

Normally exemptions by the government are not secretively held and this confidentiality clause specifically related to the exemptions is quite surprising. If we knew what the exact exemption was, we could specifically guide you, as you are not the first to be affected by a disconnect between the TRA and a government agency.

First and foremost, what prevails over any contract is the law. The law is supreme and no contract, no matter how sweetly drafted, can override the law. Your situation from a legal perspective is that you have a contract that says one thing, and there is a law in force contradicting the contract. According to the TRA, the law prevails which is the general principle that applies and is correct. You cannot just freeze the law; it is ever changing.

If your entire project depended on the exemptions that you have mentioned, then you have acted in reliance of these and have a cause of action against the agency that signed the contract and can sue the agency. However, this might turn out to be time consuming and costly.

In our experience, if the project is of national importance as you claim, a quick meeting between the TRA, the agency and its parent ministry will be useful. If you are under the Tanzania Investment Centre (TIC) Incentives, then you can also involve the TIC. Of course, if there is a discrepancy between the law and the contract, you cannot out rightly blame TRA, as they are following the law.

To give you a background on the misuse of exemptions, there are reports that a large portion of the exemptions are misused, and the government and TRA are facing intense pressure to address this. It is also claimed that Tanzania gives the highest number of unnecessary exemptions that are not adding real value to the economy at large, and are in fact hindering tax collection. Obviously such unscrupulous behaviour by some investors tends to hurt the performance of genuine players like yourself.

All in all, should this meeting not succeed, you have a cause of action against the agency with whom you entered into a contract, and should proceed to sue them. We would recommend you sue them in the High Court, Commercial Division.

Who has to prove a tax appeal?

Sadly, TRA blindly issued an assessment and I have had to fight it at the Tax Revenue Appeals Board. I was surprised to be informed by my tax consultant that we are to present our calculation to the board first and we have to disprove the TRA, as opposed to other parts of the world where the tax authority would have to prove its case first. Is this a fact or is it a ploy by my consultant to make some easy money from me?

17th January 2011

The Tax Revenue Appeals Act is very clear in that the onus of proving that an assessment or other decision is excessive or erroneous shall be on the appellant. Since you are the appellant, your tax consultant is correct. We have never heard of a judicial system, even in these so called 'other countries', where the respondent presents its case first. We must also warn you that these are government revenue matters and the Tax Revenue Appeals Board is a no-nonsense body and cases are all fast tracked there.

I do not trust signatures

I am entering into a contract and am worried that the party entering into it may end up disowning its own signatures. I mistrust signatures. What if they just scribble their signatures? How do I protect myself?

10th January 2011

This is a very interesting question. The foolproof way of doing this is to get them to stamp their thumbprints. Unless they cut off both their thumbs, you should be reasonably covered. We are sure the parties to the contract will value their thumbs more than the contract they have entered into.

You are right in that signatures can lead to problems – signatories can disown them. However, there are other ways to prove that there indeed was a valid contract. For example, the contract should have a company seal. Again, you can argue that the company seal can be forged. Other factors include the payments made and performance under the contract. All of these can be used against a party that denies their signature is on a contract. You can also confirm their signatures with signatures in their passports and keep copies of the passport. If you are still worried, do contact your attorney, who can also draft some affidavits in support of the contract.

Suit filed in error

I sued a company in Dar for breach of contract, only to discover, after instituting the suit, that the breach was not the fault of the party I sued. What happened is that I discovered that one of my fellow directors, who had been overseas for a year for medical treatment, approved the delay in delivery under the contract, which is the subject matter of the suit. I was unaware of this communication and proceeded to sue the company. What do you suggest I do now? Did my fellow director act beyond his powers?

3rd January 2011

Under our law, after a suit has been instituted, a plaintiff may at any time, withdraw the suit. In your case you are at liberty to do so, although the defendant may claim costs. You also should be very sure you wish to withdraw the case, because once you do so, the law will bar you from reinstituting the suit again. In answering this question, we assume you are the only plaintiff in the suit.

Unfortunately we are not in a position to answer the second part of your question, as we do not have enough details. We must, however, point out to you that it is quite surprising to note how you two, as directors, are not communicating. It can be costly to your company in the future, not only pertaining to this case but in other business matters. You should remedy this lack of communication immediately.

Old owner after my land

I moved with my family from my home village to Dar es Salaam sixteen years ago, and settled in a place called Tegeta. When I moved here, there were very few people in this area. About two years ago, a man who seems to be well off, came to my plot and said I should leave, since that plot belonged to him. He even showed me an old contract and Certificate of Right of Occupancy showing that he had been allocated/sold the plot even before I moved in. A few months ago, the same man came with the police to try and forcefully evict me. What does the land law say? Can he interfere with my rights just like this?

27th December 2010

The law in Tanzania is clear in that anyone who has a right of occupancy, what is commonly called a title deed, is required to develop it within a reasonable time or as per the directions given in the certificate of occupancy. We are not sure where this man was for over sixteen years. There is something seriously wrong here.

In Land Law, there is something called adverse possession, which simply means that if a person moves onto a piece of land, occupies it and develops it for twelve years or more with no interference whatsoever from the true owner of that plot, then that person who has occupied it for the twelve plus years acquires it by adverse possession. The person who acquires land under adverse possession has the same legal rights over the land to the person who was originally granted a right of occupancy over the land.

Furthermore, the law allows that the person with adverse possession over the land to apply and obtain a title deed on the said plot. Hence, if everything you have stated is true, and you have not withheld any information from us, then you are the rightful owner of the plot and the eviction is illegal.

As for the police interference, unless there is a Court order for your eviction, the police cannot evict you.

Mortgage v lease

We lent money to a company and created a mortgage on their building. Our relationship has been solid for the past three years. Earlier this year, the company has started defaulting and we issued them with a notice to proceed under the mortgage instrument. It seems like the borrower then informed the tenant, which is a very strong party in Tanzania, who obtained an injunctive relief from Court, claiming that they have prepaid rent for the next three years. We now cannot recover the money that is owed to us, nor can we sell the property, meanwhile the borrower continues to default. What should we do?

22nd November 2010

It is very difficult to guide you on this without reading all the documents. However, as a matter of principle, you should have had a clause in the loan documentation that disallows collection of advance rent for more than a period of a year. You might not have had that.

If the borrower has defaulted, and you do not wish to engage in a Court battle with the current occupier/tenant, we believe that subject to the injunction being lifted, you can proceed with the sale of the mortgaged premises, with the buyer purchasing it subject to the lease. Again, we would need to look at the lease – it is highly possible that there is some collusion here between the borrower and occupier, which may be hard to prove. The fact that there is a long term tenant will also affect the sale price, and these are factors you need to take into account prior to making any such moves. It is not unwise to contact your attorneys to find a practical solution that will take into account both the time and funds needed to get out of this.

Registration of debenture

We loaned money to an individual and created a third party mortgage. The debentures that have been duly signed have not been registered for the past six months due to issues with locating the file at the Business Registration and Licensing Authority (BRELA). Now that the file has been found, BRELA is refusing to register the debenture. What do you suggest we do?

22nd November 2010

The law is clear in that every security on a company's property created by the company is void against a liquidator, administrator, or creditor of the company if the particulars of the security (in this case a debenture) are not received by the Registrar for registration within forty two days after the date of its creation. A debenture falls into this category and hence should have been registered within the forty two days.

You have a couple of options. First you can re-date the debentures and get the borrower to sign them again with a current date and make sure this is properly documented. Most borrowers are reluctant to do this when they are in default. We hope that is not the case here.

Another option is to apply for an extension of time in Court to register a charge and invoke section 105 of the Companies Act 2002 (Cap. 212 R.E. 2002) which states, in so many words, that if a company fails to register a charge in time, then it may appeal to the Courts to extend the time for registration, provided that the failure to register in time was accidental or due to some other reasonable cause.

Your grounds are quite solid in that you failed to register the charge because of a misplacement of the company file, which unfortunately is not very uncommon here. Please be guided accordingly.

Reservation of company name

We are a foreign company wishing to register in Tanzania. Our company name is well known throughout Eastern Europe and Asia. I have heard some people in the local market talk about name stealing, whereby once we start the registration process, our name will be registered by someone else before we have fully complied, and then we would have to buy the name from these persons. How can we protect ourselves? We have informally searched for the name we intend to register and the name is available.

22nd November 2010

We have not heard of or come across such allegations, but will nonetheless proceed to answer the question. When you submit an application for a certain name, you may ask the registrar to reserve the name. The Companies Act is specific in relation to this, in that the Registrar may, on written application, reserve a name pending registration of a company or a change of name by a company. Any such reservation shall remain in force for a period of thirty days, or for special reasons the registrar may allow a longer period not exceeding sixty days, during which no other company shall be allowed to register that name.

You must note that no name can be reserved, and no company can be registered by a name which, in the opinion of the Registrar, is the same as or similar to a name appearing in the index of company names or is otherwise undesirable.

The law does protect you, and we suggest you appoint a good registration agent/law firm and proceed.

Agent principal relationship

I appointed an agent in Mbeya to deal in plastic products for our company. The relationship was very good in the first year of operations. But in the second year, the agent began delaying payment, not maintaining proper accounts, and lately has been claiming that his entire accounting system is such that he is unsure of the payables to us. How do we address this issue of him not being able to maintain proper accounts for the goods supplied by us? What should we do?

15th November 2010

It is the duty of an agent to keep accurate accounts of all of his transactions and to be prepared at all times to produce them to you, his principal. If he fails to keep proper accounts, then every presumption consistent with the facts will weigh in favour of the principal. Thus, if the agent has improperly mixed your property with his own, all that he cannot show to be his own will be presumed to belong to you. Furthermore, most normal agency agreements provide that all books and documents relating to the principal's business must, on demand, be produced to the principal.

In your case, you may proceed to terminate the agency agreement based on the termination clause. However, you should consider both the commercial and legal consequences of taking such action.

Detaining properties unlawfully

In August 2009, a friend of mine asked to use my Toyota vehicle to tour the Serengeti. My vehicle was to be returned in October, and to date the vehicle has not been returned. I have seen the vehicle being driven in Dar by other unknown people. What can I do to recover my Toyota? I am losing out on rental income.

8th November 2010

It is clear that your friend obtained your car with your consent for the two month period. After the said two months it seems your friend has wrongly detained your vehicle, for which you have a right of possession. You have demanded its return, but your friend has refused to return it. In law this is known as detenue and/or conversion and it is actionable under the Law of Tort. The remedy, upon proof in a Court of Law, will be the return/delivery of the vehicle or its value. In addition, damages may also be awarded. However, in order to succeed in the action for detenue, you must

prove that you demanded the return of the said Toyota and your friend refused. We advise you to consult your attorneys to write a formal demand notice which will serve as evidence during trial that you had formally demanded for the return of the vehicle.

TRA bullying us

Our company has heavily invested in Tanzania, and we expect returns in the long term. Over the past two years we have witnessed great bullying by the Tanzania Revenue Authority (TRA). The manager in our region openly tells me that they have targets to meet and hence they are stricter. For example, we get calls towards the end of the month to find out how much Value Added Tax (VAT) we shall be paying. It seems like the TRA are out to milk only the big corporations who are already paying a lot. There seems to be many untaxed people who the TRA is not auditing. My question now follows. We have just been sent an assessment to pay taxes that have no justification whatsoever. It is merely an assessment and there has been no audit. The tax manager tells me that we can talk about reducing the liability. In our opinion we have no liability. In the TRA's opinion we owe them over TZS 2B in taxes. The flip side is that TRA is yet to pay me back my VAT refund although I have been pushing for my refund for the past nine months. What should we do, as this is likely reciprocal action by the TRA? How can foreign companies survive in Tanzania with such abuse of power?

20th September 2010

The TRA is bound by the law and other rules and regulations. Much as the government wants to increase the amounts it collects through taxes, the TRA has to follow appropriate procedures. We are also shocked at how this assessment has been issued without an audit, unless of course your company did not cooperate with the TRA during the audit or after.

As per the Tax Revenue Appeals Act, any person who disputes an assessment made upon him may write a notice of objection to the Commissioner General. The notice of objection must state the grounds for the objection and be filed with the Commissioner General within thirty days from the notice of the assessment. Unfortunately, by the time we answer this question, the thirty days have expired and we hope that you have already done this.

The only catch to this objection to the assessment is that when you file it, the person filing it must pay the Board with a further appeal chance to the Tax Revenue Appeals Tribunal. And if you are still aggrieved, a final appeal can be made to the Court of Appeal where the buck ultimately stops. We recommend that you follow the above procedure.

When approaching the TRA staff, please be advised that as part of its quality customer care principles, courtesy and friendly handling of taxpayers is key. Should you have complaints about this, please write to the Commissioner General who should be able to address your concerns.

Court broker withholding sale proceeds

Two years ago I sued a person for breach of a commercial agreement. The judgment debtor's property was attached and sold. The Court broker who executed the decree gave me 1/3 of the sale proceeds and retained the rest. I feel that was improper – he merely said that this was the amount I was entitled to. Is this legal?

13th September 2010

We do not see any justification for such action, nor are aware of a law that allows such behaviour by the Court Broker. As a matter of

law, all fees, charges and allowances payable to the Court Broker and/or Executing Officers are supposed to be filed in Court. It is not for them to decide what to retain.

The Court Broker is supposed to file his Bill of Costs with the Court and within twenty one days the latter shall determine the amount payable after hearing the parties. The fees, charges and allowances charged include the cost of advertising, taking inventory, catalogues and all charges for safeguarding the property attached. The Court Broker may have contravened the law and you may have a cause of action against him.

In answering this, we assume that the sale proceeds did not fully meet the amount of the decree. If the amount realised from the sale is greater than the decreed amount, our answer is more involved. We suggest you contact your attorney for further guidance.

Termination by mutual consent

I have entered into a contract for the supply of raw materials for the manufacture of solar panels. The goods are to be exported to China, and the company has sent me a three year contract in Chinese. It is not terminable by me, but it may be terminated by the importer. I had the contract translated, and found that there is a clause of termination by mutual consent. Does that not defeat the purpose of having a contract in the first place? There is also a clause on renegotiation should the price of the material fluctuate plus or minus 10 %. Is that okay?

23rd August 2010

You have translated the contract into English, but are surely going to sign a contract written in Chinese. It would be wiser for you to request the importer to send you an English version of the contract. Translations have their challenges and there is no shortage of case law where one or two words in one language may not have an exact translation, leading to disputes that take years to settle.

The clause on termination by mutual consent does not defeat the purpose. Under the rules of contract law, the parties may not only freely conclude contracts but may also terminate them by mutual consent. This clause would simply say that should both parties want to terminate the contract, they can do so. However, we see it slightly conflicting with the non-terminability of the contract by you. For us to be extra sure we would have to read the entire contract.

We also wish to point out that the termination by mutual consent clause is infrequent, and does not have any add value to the drafting. You should, however, seek your attorney's opinion before concluding this deal.

Whether the renegotiation clause makes sense to your business is a commercial decision. We must point out that you must specify what will happen during the renegotiations, how long such negotiations will last, and what happens if they are unsuccessful. For example, you could have a clause that suspends the performance of the contract during renegotiations.

Effective vis a vis date of contract

I signed a contract in June 2009 and started performing my duties as a supplier under the contract. I completed my work in August 2009, only to be told that the commencement date of the contract was not June 2009. In the vast experience that I have, it comes to me as a great surprise how such a large company has misbehaved. Does such a provision in a contract make sense to you?

2nd August 2010

It is unfortunate that in this 'vast' experience of yours, you have not come across a contract that has an effective date (commencement date) which is different from the date of signing the contract. The date of signing does not automatically mean that you have to perform from that date. The effective date or commencement date is what applies as to when the performance of the contract should begin.

In your instance, you have completed the work before the completion date, and hence the delay in payment. It is very difficult to guide you on what to do without having read the entire contract. But one thing is certain – the company cannot deny that you have performed your duties, unless the service rendered is technical and one that has strict time frames. The company is stopped from reacting in this manner, if at the time you were performing the contract the company had noticed that the performance had begun, and it did not take any steps to inform you of the effective start date. This can get very complicated, depending on the wording of the contract.

Post-dated cheque cleared before date

I issued a post-dated cheque to a party who deposited it in their bank. Prior to the maturity date, my bank cleared the amount and debited my account. I then had to stop payment on the cheque, as the supplier to whom I had issued the cheque never delivered my goods on time. What should I do?

26th July 2010

There are two distinct issues here. The first is non-delivery of goods on time, which very likely amounts to a breach of contract. You can sue the supplier for that breach and recover your funds.

The more fundamental issue we see here is the act of your banker in clearing the cheque before the date on the cheque. A post-dated cheque is an instrument which bears a date later than the date of its issue. A drawee bank is not entitled to pay a post-dated cheque and debit its customer's account before the date of the instrument. The drawee bank also cannot treat the cheque as a bill presented for acceptance and hold a customer's funds to meet the amount on the cheque. You have a good case against the bank for making payment before the date of the cheque. Depending on other circumstances, you may also be able to recover damages against the bank.

Buying into a company

I am buying 15% of a company and am un-sure how the transaction works. The compa-ny secretary at times talks about share trans-fer, and then later about share allotment. My interest is the 15% shareholding in the company. Should I buy into the company? What are important agreements that I need to execute in such a transaction?

12th July 2010

We cannot decide on your behalf whether to buy the 15% shares or not. It is your decision and not ours and hence we cannot answer that part of the question.

The share transfer vis a vis share allotment seems to be either confusing you or the company secretary. A share transfer is where a shareholder would transfer his or her shares to you, for a consideration. That would dilute his or her shareholding and entitle you to become a shareholder. In such a transfer, you would pay the consideration to the shareholder who is transferring the shares to you. The share transfer is one of the ways you can own this company.

The second way of ownership is for the company itself to issue you shares at a certain value. The amount you pay for such allotment is paid to the company. In a share allotment, you would require a share allotment agreement to govern the relationship between you and

the company. Another important document for you in such a transaction is a shareholders' agreement that will govern the relationship between you and the existing shareholders. This type of agreement is often ignored by subscribers, yet it is a very important document for shareholders. It is unwise to negotiate a shareholders' agreement without reading and understanding the shareholders' agreement.

Forged signatures on cheque

Our Junior Accountant has been withdraw-ing money from a bank on our behalf for many years. Recently he used one of the cheque leafs, forged both of the direc-tors' signatures, and absconded with over USD 100,000. The forged signatures are very similar to the authentic signatures, but a closer look reveals that they are different. The bank is saying we have acted negligent-ly by trusting the employee, and they have paid the money in good faith. The bank also claims that he was an authorised agent of the company, and hence we cannot now go back and claim anything from the bank. What should we do?

19th July 2010

A paying bank acts as its customer's agent. As an agent, the paying bank is entitled to be indemnified for any given payment only if it has acted with its customer's authority. In your case the junior accountant was not authorised to sign cheques, but merely to draw funds. The bank was thus not acting on your instructions which has led to this loss.

Bankers do not budge easily! We are not surprised that they are denying liability. What the bank tells you, unless there is something you are concealing from us, will not hold as a defence in Court. We see no direct relationship between this trust element you have mentioned and the forged cheque, unless of course you have used the junior accountant to take advantage of the banks systems to steal the money.

We suggest you get a forensic expert to look at the signatures that you claim are forged. Once you are certain that the cheques are forged, send the bank a demand notice. Should that fail you can proceed to sue the bank for recovery of the said amount. From the facts above, we believe you have a good case against the bank. Our experience is that after obtaining a forensic report on the signatures that proves the signatures were forged, the bank normally gives in and settles.

Best price clause in a contract

I negotiate contracts on behalf of government agencies and other Tanzanian institutions though by training I am not a lawyer. I would like to know whether in a contract I can insert a clause whereby the supplier confirms that the price that has been quoted is the lowest price that they have ever quoted to anyone in Tanzania. In principle, I want to have recourse to an overpriced contract. How can I do this and is this common practice?

19th July 2010

As a negotiator you negotiate contracts. If all your suppliers agreed to such a clause, it would render you jobless! In a free market economy, many factors dictate the price of an item or service, the major ones being supply and demand. A price of a certain commodity may go up or down, depending on when you purchased it. Many other things determine the price as well. While you have thought of an interesting clause, it is unlikely that suppliers will agree to such a clause.

One clause that we have come across is the most favoured clause, which entitles the buyer to obtain a most favoured customer status. A clause such as this one would normally

read: 'The seller represents that the charges, costs, fees, other payments and discounts in this agreement are no less favourable to the buyer than the most favoured terms offered to or received by any other customer as of the time that this agreement is signed by the seller'. During this agreement when the seller signs any agreement for a similar product that contains charges, costs, fees, other payment and discount provisions that are more favourable to another customer, these provisions are to be immediately extended to the buyer.

Forceful change of name

The Registrar of Companies registered my company name twenty years ago. Surprisingly, the Registrar has now written to me saying that my company name is misleading. I do not understand how it took twenty years for the registrar to discover this. I have since found out that the name of my company is similar to the name of a bank in West Africa, which has moved the registrar to write to me. After doing some research on the internet, I found that the bank came into existence after my company was incorporated. Is this letter from the registrar fair?

5th July 2010

The Companies Act is clear in that if, in the Minister's opinion, the name by which a company is registered is misleading as to the nature of its activities and is likely to cause harm to the public, he may direct it to change its name.

You can challenge the direction by filing an application in Court. Such application ought to be within three weeks from the date of the direction you received. The direction must, if not duly made the subject of an application to the Court, be complied within a period of six weeks from the date of the direction or such longer period as the Registrar may think fit to allow.

It seems there is some real value in the name you have created, and it might be worth consulting your attorney.

Contractor, sub-contractor relation

I have been awarded a multi-billion Tanzanian shilling contract for construction of a project in Dodoma. I will have to sub-contract a large portion of the job, but do not have the cash flow to finance sub-contracting, and will be fully reliant on cash flow from the client to support the sub-contractor. What are the important things I should know?

28th June 2010

The contract between you and your sub-contractor will have to contain similar terms as the contract between you and your client. The completion time, scope of work, quality of material etc. must match.

One clause that you must include in your contract is the 'pay if paid clause'. This is a provision that makes the main contractor's payment to the sub-contractor for work performed contingent on whether the client pays the main contractor for the work done. In such a clause the sub-contractor assumes the risk of non-payment if the client fails to pay the main contractor. If your construction company is a small player, we are unsure whether the sub-contractors, especially if they much bigger in size than your company, will agree to such a condition. Alternatively, the sub-contractors may ask for a bank guarantee, which will be costly and difficult to obtain without any asset cover.

Personal guarantee in bank loan

I am a director in a family-run business but have no shareholding. My remuneration is limited to yearly director's fees. We have been borrowing heavily from some very large banks in Tanzania. Over the years, our turnover has been declining and we are losing market share, resulting in heavy liquidity problems for the company. In most of the bank documentation, I have been signing Personal Guarantees as part of the loan documentation. What is the effect of such guarantees in case the bank makes any moves? Ours is a limited liability company. Does that make a difference?

21st June 2010

Simply put, a personal guarantee is a guarantee that you, as the guarantor, will assume personal responsibility for repayment of the loan, should the company not honour its obligations.

Our experience in the market is that the personal guarantee agreements are very widely drafted to secure the bank. When you signed the personal guarantee, which is a one or two page 'innocent looking' document, you gave up your personal protection against liability, which is provided for by registering a limited liability company.

In principle, if the company defaults and the banks move in, should the banks not be able to realise what they lent to the company from the assets pledged by the company to the bank, the bank may then, subject to the Personal Guarantee agreement, come after your personal assets.

You will need to plan out how you will manage your personal affairs in case that happens. You need to see a good company law specialist.

Matching goods confiscated

I have been in the country for the past ten years and have always sympathised with the abject poverty here. Over the past few years, I have noted that the city authorities are disallowing petty traders from selling anything on the roadside. Tanzania is one of the poorest countries in the world, and it surprises me how the city authorities impose such conditions. Even the state of New York allows, to a certain degree, traders to sell their goods on roads. My question is twofold. First, is it legal for the city *askaris* to beat up a petty trader? Secondly, is it legal for them to confiscate and burn the poor fellow's goods?

21st June 2010

We must state that the city by-laws disallow this kind of trading and it is an arrestable offence. To answer your question, the city *askaris* are not allowed to beat the traders and can only use reasonable force to arrest them. As to whether these goods can just be confiscated, we answer this in the negative.

As per the law, the city *askaris* must take the goods to the City Court on Sokoine Drive to get an appropriate order for disposal of the goods, and then proceed with whatever they have been ordered to do. They must follow this procedure, they cannot simply confiscate and burn the items. Although you have raised some pertinent points, poverty is not grounds for breaking the law. The law applies equally to the rich and the poor.

ISP cheated on me

Twelve years ago I was in Tanzania and three of us who had been in the US studying together decided to start an internet service provider (ISP). At the time we had no money – I was the key technical person in charge of the project and spent a year doing all the ground work as part of my equity. The other two friends were in charge of raising the finance and looking for a suitable office. Too my dismay they failed, and the project collapsed. I then left the country for work abroad, where I am still based. It has come to my attention that the other two friends managed to get funding after I left and today the ISP is one of the largest in Tanzania. Do I have a claim over the company? Can I get an injunction?

14th June 2010

This is a very interesting question. In the question you have not mentioned if your company was registered with the other two friends or not. If it was, you were and would still be a shareholder. However, if that was the case, we presume you would not write to us!

There are a couple of scenarios we can come up with. One is that you had collectively registered a company that failed to get started. After you left, it is possible the other two friends of yours managed to find source funding, and proceeded in your absence to register a new company. In this instance, since you have not been compensated for your time preparing the technical papers, you have a cause of action against the company that is currently running.

The other scenario is where the same company that you registered proceeded to carry on the business and in your absence, issued new shares to prospective shareholders, and hence diluted your shares. That again can be looked at from a company law angle, and should have a remedy after your lawyers conduct a company search at the offices of the Registrar of Companies.

The third scenario is where the current ISP is independent of the ISP you were trying to set up. If so, we recommend that you consult your attorneys regarding the time that has elapsed since the occurrence of the aforementioned. There is a Law of Limitation Act that has a maximum time limit for certain suits.

Former partner using partnership trademark

In 1998, three friends and I established a partnership. We registered a trading name, which we also registered as a trademark. Our business has grown phenomenally over the years. Unfortunately, there was a misunderstanding amongst us, and in 2003 one of the partners left the partnership. In 2005, the partner who left established his own business, which is exactly in the same line of business that we used to do together. He is also using the same trademarked name as the one we registered under the partnership. We are losing clients, and our image is being tainted, as his product is inferior in quality to ours. How can we stop him from trading and using this registered name?

24th May 2010

As per the law, the trading name that you registered was for your partnership that the four of you owned together. When there is a change of the number or identity of the partners, the trading name and trademark will still stand and belong to the partnership, regardless of the identity of the partners involved. The partner who quits the partnership has no legal right to use the trademark of the partnership because it is not his personal asset, but rather the asset of the partnership. The act of him using the trademark amounts to infringement. Your partnership can institute a suit against him in Court seeking a permanent injunction against the former partner from using the trademark belonging to the current partnership.

From your question, it seems that the former partner also registered a company with a similar name (or exactly the same name) as the one you are running. This is surprising, as the Registrar of Business does not normally allow that. Again, this is challengeable, and we advise you to write to the Registrar of Companies seeking rectification.

However, your case is weak on the front of disallowing the former partner from engaging in a similar trade. The Courts are normally reluctant to entertain such arguments, as they are in restraint of trade and against public policy. You should consult your attorney for further guidance.

Signed a contract in French

I am a contractor based in Mwanza and signed a contract to do some work in Rwanda. The contract was drafted in French and I signed it without really understanding it. There have been some issues in the construction and I have not been paid, as the client is disputing some of the invoices. I recently received a notice from the client's lawyers that they are calling for me to pay damages as per the contract. I do not remember anything about damages in the contract. How can you help me?

31st May 2010

First, you should never sign anything you do not understand. Second, from your question, we can tell that you do not speak French, yet you signed a contract in French. This is baffling to us. Third, we do not see how you have anything to remember in the first place, since you signed something in a language you did not understand.

Is the contract valid in view of you not knowing the contents of what you were signing? This can only be answered after understanding the background of the entire deal. Are there any e-mails? Do you have the original tender documents? Did you write to the client? As a rule of thumb, you should never sign anything without understanding its contents. A second rule is that there is no such thing as a standard contract – always make sure you read everything in a contract. While it is highly unlikely that you can deny the existence of some item in the contract based purely on the fact that the contract is in a different language, there might be some hope somewhere after your attorneys look at the entire background of the deal.

Misleading name of company

A few years ago I received a letter from the Registrar of Companies, who had been informed by the Minister that my company's name is misleading to the public and

I should change it. I did not; as I believed it was not misleading. Recently I received a reminder informing me that action would be taken against me if I did not change my company's name. Is this legal? I thought Tanzania is a free market economy. If I change my company's name am I still liable for old taxes to the TRA?

12th April 2010

Tanzania indeed tries to adapt to free market economy principles, but even in such economies there are laws, rules and regulations to follow. A free market economy does not mean that the law does not apply or that one can do as they wish.

The Minister, as per the Companies Act, can order a change of name if the registered name is misleading. The procedure is that you either obey the order from the Minister and change the name of the company, or you make an application in Court to challenge the order. The option of keeping quiet can lead to a fine or default fine.

Also note that a change of name by a company does not affect any of the rights or obligations of the company, under its former. Thus, your TRA obligations remain the same. Otherwise everyone would change the names of their company in order to evade taxes!

Assignment clauses in contracts

I am entering into a contract with a log buyer from China. I am also in talks with a company that might be buying my assets and goodwill. What can I do to bind the log buyer to this company in the event this transaction goes through? I am more interested in selling my whole business and not parts of it. Is there an advantage for the buyer if he buys my goodwill and assets and not my business name?

12th April 2010

You need to be able to assign this contract to the company that is interested in buying you out. The assignment clause will transfer the contract to this new company. When you draft the contract, you must make sure that the assignment is automatic, as in when your business is sold, the contract is automatically assigned to this new company. Some assignment clauses require consent of the buyer, which can get very complicated.

To answer the second part of your question, the advantage to the buyer to transact in this manner is usually to protect the buyer from any tax liabilities that might be hovering over the sellers company.

No cooperation from co-owner

About twelve months ago I bought a residential place which is on the fifth floor of a certain building here in Dar es Salaam. This building has ten floors and there is a common gate. Recently we got a new co-owner, who is a very irritating and a difficult old man. He refuses to contribute for common expenses for cleanliness of the surroundings. Recently a balcony in his flat started leaking and everyone agreed to contribute funds for the repair except for this man. How does the law protect us from him? He says he is too old to do anything!

19th April 2010

There is no separate law for the old. The law is the law – it applies to all, including this old co-owner of yours.

According to the Unit of Titles Act of 2008, the rights and duties of all co-occupiers of premises who happen to share the premises like this co-occupier should contribute for collective expenses; also no co-occupier is allowed to interfere, even in his own unit, with the carrying out of work for conservation of the property approved by the rest of the occupiers including any urgent work.

This co-occupier is breaking the law and,

whilst morally we have to respect the old, legally you have your rights as well.

You can institute a suit against this co-owner and your chances of succeeding, as per the facts, are high. The co-owner may be held liable either to a fine not exceeding TZS 5M or a prison term not exceeding two years.

Not able to act as a director

I was appointed as a director in a company a year ago. Apparently, I was supposed to subscribe shares in the company as per the articles of the company. I was informed but had travelled and upon my return have been removed as a director from the company. Can the company do such a thing?

29th March 2010

Plainly put, the company has the right to do what it has done. The Companies Act is very clear in that it shall be the duty of every director who is by the articles of the company required to hold a specified share qualification, and who is not already qualified, to obtain his qualification within two months after his appointment, or such shorter time as may be fixed by the articles. It further states that the office of director of a company shall be vacated if the director does not within two months from the date of his appointment obtain his qualification and a person vacating office under this section shall be incapable of being re-appointed director of the company until he has obtained his qualification.

In short you will have to seek re appointment and in the interim please be informed that you are not a director and should not start acting like one.

Death of a party to a contingent contract

In July 2009, I entered into a contract for sale of a piece of land with my neighbour at Gongo la Mboto within Dar es Salaam. It was agreed that the contract would become effective upon approval and consent of the seller's brother residing in London who was expected to come to Dar at the end of 2009. Unfortunately, in January the seller died in a road accident and now the brother of the deceased, has decided not to approve the sale. What are my rights? Is the contract enforceable as we have already signed?

22nd March 2010

Any contract whose validity depends on the happening or no happening of an event collateral to such contracts in the future are called 'contingent contracts'. Your contract is a contingent contract as it is dependent on the happening of an event i.e. the approval of the seller's brother. In your case, unfortunately before the approval was obtained the seller died. In law, the death of one of the parties to a contingent contract has the effect of terminating the contract between the parties.

If you have paid the purchase price (consideration) of the land in question, depending on the terms of the contract, it is very likely that the money is recoverable. We advise you to follow up your money from the deceased estate or his/her successors.

Procedures to call a board meeting

I am a director in a company in Tanzania. Recently, I have realised that I have not been invited to a number of board meetings because I live upcountry. Does the law allow that? A few weeks ago I was given notice of a board meeting two days before the meeting. Is there no law that comes to my rescue?

15th March 2010

The fact that you live upcountry and may not be able to attend meetings does not mean that you should not be informed. The Companies Act provides that any board meeting should be convened after giving a minimum notice of twenty one days to the directors of such a meeting. The company is in breach of this law and any resolutions passed in such meetings can be challenged.

Market price fixing

I am a consultant in the telecom sector and have realised that two of the major mobile companies in the country regularly discuss their product and pricing strategy to the detriment of the phone users. Tanzania still has some of the highest mobile phone tariffs in the world. Is there no law that can stop them from doing this?

8th March 2010

The Fair Competition Act strictly disallows this. Section 9 of the Act is clear in that a person shall not make or give effect to an agreement if the object, effect or likely effect of the agreement is price fixing between competitors. The Act defines price fixing between competitors as to fix, restrict or control the prices, tariffs, surcharges or other charges for, or the terms or conditions upon which, a party to an agreement supplies or acquires, or offers to supply or acquire, goods or services, in competition with any other party to the agreement.

You can clearly note that the actions of the mobile operators are illegal. However, the challenge is proving that they are colluding and fixing prices. Mere same pricing in the market does not mean that they are colluding. You may, however, report this to the Fair Competition Commission who can also investigate.

Contract with option to buy

I entered into a contract to buy a restaurant, if and when the restaurant owner decided to sell it. It was agreed that he would give me the first chance to take over the entire business for a price to be agreed upon at the time. The owner has turned around and said

he is not willing to sell the business to me as he has another buyer. My lawyer wants me to take this to Court. What other options do I have?

22nd February 2010

This type of clause in a contract is sometimes referred to as 'first refusal clause or pre-emption clause', where one party undertakes to offer the beneficiary the opportunity in the future to conduct a particular transaction before concluding the transaction with a third party.

The best option is to appoint a mediator and see if he can get the two of you to sort this out amicably. In the absence of this, you will have to file a suit. You should also apply for an injunction preventing the owner from selling the business to anyone else pending determination of the suit. This is to prevent another battle with the new owner.

What we have noted, with concern, is whether the contract you entered into is really valid. A contract must have consideration which is defined as an act, forbearance or promise by one party to a contract that constitutes the price for which one buys the promise of the other. A contract without consideration is *nudum pactum* (naked agreement) governed by the maxim ex *nudopacto* non *orituractio* (a right of action does not arise out of a naked agreement). From your question, we are unsure if the agreement has any consideration i.e. did you pay a small deposit or the like to secure the pre-emption right? If not, then the contract is void and you will not be able to enforce it. After reading the contract in full, your legal team can guide you further.

Delivery of defective goods

I am a businessman in the tyre business in Mbeya. In mid December 2008, I ordered two hundred tyres from my supplier in Dar, who

FB

demanded the funds upfront. Having paid him, I was asked to collect the tyres from one of the bus terminals in Mbeya. Two weeks later, I discovered that forty of the tyres were defective. I have called up my supplier who showed me his invoice which clearly states that once goods are sold, they are non returnable or refundable. The supplier claims that I should have inspected the tyres before I bought them. It has been over two months and the issue is still pending. What should I do?

1st February 2010

The law of sale of goods generally imposes a duty on the buyer to inspect the merchantability of the goods he or she buys, especially if the buyer has an opportunity to do so. We have carefully considered the circumstances surrounding your case and find that the state of affairs of things did not, at the time of purchasing and receiving, give you time to inspect the goods. The principle of caveat emptor i.e. buyer beware, cannot apply against you. Even if the principle was applicable, yet your supplier, as the seller, would not be discharged from the duty to supply goods of merchantable quality. In supplying/selling defective tyres to you, your supplier committed a breach of an implied warranty.

His defence of 'once goods sold cannot be returned' cannot be generalized and extrapolated to situations where the quality of the goods is visibly inferior.

It seems like you have a good case against your supplier, unless of course there are additional details that you have not told us. Yours being a contractual transaction, means you can take action against the supplier up to six years from the date you were aware of this. If following up does not assist in getting your refund, you may sue the supplier and can consider not only recovering the purchase price of the tyres but also claim damages.

Bank loan default

I entered into a loan agreement where my company borrowed over TZS 2.5B from a bank in Tanzania. The same bank has been buying material from me and has not paid me about the same amount. The bank has taken me to Court and I have raised a counter claim on the equivalent amount. The case has just commenced at the Commercial Court. What are my chances of success? What else can I do to get out of this debt? What will happen if I lose the case?

25th January 2010

We are quite surprised that this particular bank has been buying 'material' from you. When we were answering this question, we were pondering over which bank in Tanzania buys material up to TZS 2.5B! It is also coincidental that the bank owes you the same amount. The whole saga smells of mischief, but we are duty bound to answer your question, as we do below.

You must appreciate that there are two independent transactions in your question. The first is your loan agreement where you have borrowed money and not repaid. On the other hand, you seem to have a supplies agreement whereby the bank has been buying certain material from you.

You are trying to protect your interest in the supplies agreement by not paying the loan agreement and have raised a counterclaim.

Most, if not all, loan agreements have a clear provision that the loan amounts are repayable without deduction, set off or counterclaim. We have not read your loan agreement but this standard provision is very likely going to be there. If that is the case, your counterclaim will fail. All you will manage to do is buy some time which will add up to the amounts you will end up paying. Boldly put, if the loan agreement is a standard loan agreement, you have very slim chances of succeeding.

Your second question on what else you can do to escape this debt is a question we choose not to answer. If you borrow money from a bank, you are duty bound to pay it back unless of course your company is going under and you have no choice (no means to pay it back).

If you lose the case, the bank will not only recover the funds from the mortgaged security, but may also pursue for recovery from you personally as you have very likely also signed a personal guarantee. The Commercial Court of Tanzania is also one of the most efficient Courts in the country and your dilly dallying may not last very long. You may end up deeper in the red.

Petrol spill in Kibaha

I had hired a truck to transport petrol from Dar to Kibaha. On the way, due to reckless driving, a few of the many simtanks in the truck leaked and I lost over 1000 litres of petrol. How do I recover this from the truck owner?

18th January 2010

The answer we are about to give you is not going to please you. Under the newly enacted Petroleum Act 2008, you are not allowed to transport a petroleum product in simtanks as you have done. You, your truck owner, the driver and any other director in your company, may be imprisoned and/or fined if you are found guilty of this offence. The Act mentions some very specific vehicles with specialised tanks that can carry such products.

Also be informed that the spill, as per the Act, is termed as a major spill. Where a government institution or local authority incurs costs or expenses as a result of the occurrence of such an incident, such costs shall be recoverable from those found responsible for the occurrence. In this case, it is very likely both you and the truck owner will have to pay for the clearing of the spill.

As for a claim on the truck owner, please be informed that since the action of carrying the petrol was illegal, there was no contract and when there is no contract, you cannot claim for any damages.

Legal item now illegal

I ordered a cargo of plastic material that was legal when I placed the order, but due to some recent regulations, the material is now illegal to import. The contract terms were such that I paid 50% on signing the contract, and the remainder when the goods have been delivered. In view of the new regulations, I cannot clear the goods at the port and am looking at re-exporting the goods or sending them back to the supplier. The supplier is putting pressure on me to remit the remaining payment threatening to call upon my bank guarantee for the difference. Do I have any recourse?

11th January 2010

Your contract has been 'frustrated'. The doctrine of discharge from liability by frustration has been explained in various ways – sometimes by speaking of the disappearance of a foundation which the parties assumed to be at the basis of their contract, sometimes as decided from a rule arising from impossibility of performance, and sometimes as flowing from the inference of an implied term. Whichever way you put it, the legal consequence is the same. This definition is as per a very famous English case, Joseph Steam Line v Imperial Smelting Corporation.

It is held that where the doctrine of frustration applies, there is no breach of contract. What happens is that the contract is held on its true construction not to apply at all from the time when the frustrating circumstances supervene.

Put simply, frustration is the unforeseen termination of a contract as a result of an event that either renders its performance impossible or illegal or prevents its main purpose from being achieved.

Unless there is a specific provision in the contract for the frustrating event, a frustrated contract is automatically discharged.

In your case, assuming what you are telling us is the truth, your contract has very likely been frustrated and you need not pay the balance. Also as per the terms of the payment in the contract, you would only be liable to pay if the goods were delivered. You have not defined delivery to us but we assume it means delivery in your warehouse. That has also not happened.

As for the bank guarantee, your legal team needs to look at the wording of the guarantee to guide you further. The doctrine of frustration may or may not apply there.

Price adjustment clauses

I have entered into a contract for the supply of a unique material at a certain price. However, when I sent the invoice to the buyer, he reduced the amount claiming that the market prices had reduced. He referred me to a price adjustment clause at the end of the contract which reads that my price shall be 12.5% higher than the market price at the time of delivery or USD 1,000, whichever is lower. My entire calculation was based on USD 1,000 and that is the rate I invoiced. Contracts are made for certainty. Isn't this an illegal clause? I have been duped and need your help.

4th January 2010

From the facts mentioned, you have not been duped. It seems like in the excitement of signing this contract you have not read the contents of it. It does not matter that the clause is at the end of the contract.

Price adjustment clauses are very common in contracts especially when it comes to items whose prices are dictated by international demand and supply and whose market price is readily available from international markets.

You should avail your lawyers with all other facts and maybe they might come across something that will give you some recourse. If the issue above is read in isolation, we do not see how you can get what you want.

Illegal transfer of funds

One of my competitors is known to transfer funds into overseas bank accounts, from illegal proceeds here and in the Congo. Are such transfers allowed? Are there no restrictions on such illegal funds? What happens if a limited liability company is involved in such behaviour? What is the liability on the directors?

11th January 2010

This falls under the Anti Money Laundering Act which came into effect from January 2007. It defines money laundering as engagement of a person or persons, directly or indirectly in conversion, transfer, concealment, disguising, use or acquisition, of money or property known to be of illicit origin and in which such engagement intends to avoid the legal consequence of such action.

Section 12 of the Act reads that a person who engages directly or indirectly, in a transaction that involves property that is proceeds of a predicate offence while he knows or ought to know or ought to have known that the property is the proceeds of a predicate offence commits offence of money laundering.

The Act has very widely defined predicate offence which covers what you have mentioned in your question.

The Act further reads that any person involved in money laundering shall be fined a minimum of TZS 100M to a maximum of TZS 500M or to imprisonment to a maximum of ten years. The financial penalties are even stiffer if the person is a corporate where the fine is a minimum of TZS 500M to a maximum of TZS 1B

The Act makes it very clear that if the offence is committed by a corporate, a director, manager, controller, partner or anyone concerned in the management of its affairs, these individuals are personally liable.

Suppliers claim on insurance policy

I am a supplier of steel based in Dubai sourcing material out of Eastern Europe and India. In a CIF contract, I insured goods for a Tanzanian company at 105% of the value. The insurance was initially in my name and upon being paid, I transferred the rights under the insurance to the name of the buyer. The goods were a total loss and the buyer managed to claim the entire amount I had insured. I wish to institute a claim on the buyer for the portion that I had over insured i.e. the 5%. Should I institute a suit in Tanzania or Dubai?

28th December 2009

Although you have not asked us to do so, before we discuss the point of where you should file a suit, we wish to discuss the merits of this case.

The issue of excess insurance, as against the insurer, has long been settled in that a buyer receives full benefit of the insurance, even if the market has fallen since the contract date. The seller, having transferred outright his interest under the insurance policy, will be in no position to demand that the buyer turn over a sum representing the market decline. Suppose now that the seller insures the goods for an amount in excess of that required under the CIF contract. In the case of Strass v Spillers and Bakers Ltd, the seller insured the goods at a value higher than that required under the CIF contract. It was held by the Court that the seller did not have to account to the buyer for the additional amounts received under the claim. It was observed by the Court that practice allowed speculating sellers to cover themselves against market rises. Furthermore, it was understood in the insurance community that this practice was ancillary to the trade in grain and that the policy was binding and effective. However, it has been held in other cases that if the seller takes out insurance in excess of the contract value and assigns the insurance to the buyer on the documentary exchange, the buyer is under no obligation to the seller to account for the extra moneys received from the insurer.

Your case falls very close to the latter – you have not mentioned who paid for the additional premium. If it was the buyer, you will definitely not have a cause of action. However, if the additional premium was paid by yourself, you need to get yourself a lawyer to study the facts in detail. We, however, see little chances of success as the policy has also been transferred to the buyer.

As for where to file the suit, your lawyer can guide you after going through the case in detail.

Inequality of bargaining power

I own a small time agency that produces music in Tanzania. I do work for many corporates and was recently assigned a job by a very large brewer. The brewer has a standard contract template for its suppliers which I duly signed. I have completed my assignment and because of a very small technical point in the contract, my payment has been stopped. Every time I inquire, they tell me that I am in breach of contract. However, the music I produced is being used by the brewer and liked by everyone who hears it. My lawyers tell me that I am totally bound by the contract and that it is very difficult to recover the outstanding amount. I feel that this big player is acting very unfairly with me. What should I do?

14th December 2009

In short, from the long question that you had written (that we had to reduce to accommodate the space we have for this column), you are being bullied by the brewer. You have mentioned that this was a standard drawn contract that you 'just' signed but the fact remains that on the face of it and as per your lawyer, you did sign and hence agreed to the terms and conditions of the contract.

Within the classical Law of Contract, the relative bargaining strength of the parties is not a question for judicial inquiry. The Court is appealed to when a foul is alleged, and the Court has no substantive function beyond that since it is not the Court's business to ensure that the bargain is fair, or to see that one party does not take undue advantage of another or impost unreasonable terms by virtue of its superior bargaining position.

The modern view of Contract Law, however, is rather different. Although a doctrine of inequality of bargaining strength is not recognised as such, the relative bargaining power of the parties is often relevant consideration, particularly where the issue concerns the validity of exemption clauses in standard form contracts.

You can try looking at the problem from the angle as suggested by the modern view of contract, bearing in mind the contract you signed. In future do not blindly sign on contracts.

Security over sold goods

I am a Ugandan company starting operations in Tanzania. I have noted that many a times when goods are delivered, the buyer does not pay for the goods on time. Is there a way I can protect myself by being able to at least take the goods back in case I am not paid?

16th November 2009

Apart from the normal precautions that you should take of making sure there is a proper contract in place, you can insert a' retention of title' clause.

Under the retention of title clause, a seller of goods seeks to retain ownership of the goods, even after they have been delivered to the buyer, until he has received full payment.

From a sellers point of view, it is particularly important to retain ownership of goods where the buyer becomes bankrupt or goes into liquidation before paying them. The drafting of retention of title clause must be approached with caution as the goods are likely to be in the possession of the buyer who may have stored them somewhere unknown to you, or the buyer may have mixed the goods with other similar goods that he owns.

Some other important points to note when drafting such a clause include setting out clearly what the buyer can and cannot do with the goods and whether the goods can be sold by the buyer until final payment.

Holding company letter of comfort

My company deals in the mining industry. We are in the final stages of buying a machine from a manufacturer whose holding company is based in the far east. The supplier is not known to us and we have asked for a performance guarantee from the holding company. The holding company has sent us a one page letter of comfort – can we go ahead with the transaction.

23rd November 2009

A document is not a guarantee unless intended to be legally binding. A letter of comfort – for example, a letter confirming that it is the issuer's policy to ensure that its subsidiaries are at all times able to meet their liabilities – may be so framed as to indicate an assumption of liability but is usually designed to provide no more than moral reassurance. This is particularly the case where the party issuing the letter has refused to give a guarantee. There is a presumption that an undertaking given in a commercial context is intended to be legally binding but this is rebuttable by evidence showing that this was not the intention of the parties, and it is that intention which is the task of the Court to ascertain.

It is difficult to guide you without reading the drafting of the letter of comfort, but it is very likely that this is not a guarantee and if your pre condition to enter into this transaction is a guarantee, you should not proceed.

Time is of essence in contracts

I am entering into a contract to service software and computers for a bank in Dar. The contract that has been sent to me is very strictly drafted and mentions on several occasion that 'time is of the essence' to the agreement. Is there something that the bank is trying to trap me into by mentioning this over and over again? What do you advise I do?

16th November 2009

The first advice is for you to make sure you read the contract thoroughly. This is not a normal client – this is a bank you are dealing with and software and hardware in banks are what makes the banks run these days. There are also clear Bank of Tanzania regulations that govern the type of contracts that banks can enter into.

A breach of 'time is of essence' will usually entitle the other party to terminate the contract. Whether all, or any particular terms

of the agreement are to be subject to the stipulation that time is of essence will depend on the bargaining position of each party. Frequently, as seems to be the case in this contract, a general clause is inserted providing that time to be of the essence in relation to all the terms of the agreement; in such a case you should scrutinise these terms carefully to ensure that punctual performance is in each case feasible.

You should not get excited and simply sign the contract. You must be upfront in what you can and cannot do, within the time frame provided. You may also want to check if the consequences of failing to meet the set time spelt out in each case and if all times and dates to perform are set out.

The bank is not trapping you – the bank is upfront in what it expects of you. If you want meet their expectations, as long as they are realistic, you can go ahead and sign the contract. If you cannot, you should not sign this contract – you will land into problems in the future.

Rights of a partnership

In October 2007, I entered into an oral partnership with a friend to start up a business of buying and selling various produce. It was agreed that I be a silent partner and my friend was supposed to keep all books of accounts of this business. Ever since we have started my friend does not want to show me the books of accounts. He does not dispute the partnership either and always procrastinates in giving me any records. There is something fishy going on. What should I do?

9th November 2009

As we have said many times before, oral contracts are recognised by the law but hard to prove. They also bring in a lot of ambiguity. It is always advisable that contracts should be written down and signed by both parties. Your case is a typical case of entrusting someone with funds because they are your friend, relative or partner.

Unfortunately, the law recognises everyone separately from one another and hence for any transaction you do, you must make sure that everything is documented and all doubts are addressed at the onset and not when the parties cannot see eye to eye.

You are lucky that your friend does not dispute the existence of the partnership, although you have failed to tell us how he has acknowledged this. If it is orally, then you will have the case of proving that it does exist, if he denies it at a later stage.

Your interest for now is to get to know how the business is running. As a partner, you have the right to your company's financial statements. Assuming you have tried all other ways to convince your partner to produce the documents, we advise you to institute a suit in a competent Court of Law for an order to compel your partner to produce the documents for your inspection and determination of their correctness.

Private contract enforceability

Two of us entered into a private contract for a certain transaction. We had it written down with all the terms and conditions. The other party has defaulted in its promise and I have paid an advance based on the contract. I went to a lawyer who tells me that it will be hard to enforce it. Should I appoint a debt collector?

23rd November 2009

From your question, there seems to be some information you are hiding. We are unsure what you exactly mean by a private contract? It sounds more like an illegal contract.

An illegal contract is a contract whose formation, object, or performance is so iniquitous, against the law of the land, or contrary to public policy, that no Court will entertain or enforce it. Technically, it is a 'no contract.' In situations where two wrong doers enter into an illegal contract and one of them takes advantage of the other, the law normally will not intercede to rectify the situation.

If your contract is illegal you will not be able to enforce it. Examples of illegal contracts include supply of prohibited drugs, procuring and engaging in prostitution, illegal remittances of funds overseas and the like. A contract can also be held illegal if it is contrary to public policy. A debt collector cannot enforce an illegal contract.

Contractor's mistake, developer sued

I am the developer of a very large piece of land in Dar. Recently the crane that was being used to work on my site caused some damage to the neighbouring plot. I have now been taken to Court as a developer. How can I be taken to task for the wrong of the contractor? I am also under the Tanzania Investment Centre (TIC) certificate of incentives and was informed that I am fully protected. How can a large scale investor be frustrated like this?

30th November 2009

You have raised some very interesting points here. Before we answer your questions on whether you are liable for the acts of your contractor, we wish to answer your other questions and remarks.

To begin with, just because you have a TIC certificate of incentives does not mean that you cannot be sued. With or without a TIC certificate, you still have to follow the rule of law in Tanzania, as you would anywhere else in the world. This certificate protects your investment not your actions.

We are unsure about the frustration; you have been sued in Court and must defend yourself. It is part of the business world out there. Very bluntly put, the TIC certificate reduces° many bottlenecks but will not, and cannot, offer protection to you from incidents such as the one you mentioned. What you can perhaps do is inform TIC about this for record purposes in case there is someone who is maliciously trying to take away your focus from the project.

Are you liable for the actions of your contractor? There is a very famous English case – Rylands v Fletcher in which it was held that the liability for such cases is strict and it is no defence that the event happened without your wilful act, default or neglect or even that you had no knowledge of its existence. Interpreting this rule, you could be held liable but surely you also have a contract with the contractor where he indemnifies you for such mishaps. The contractor should also have a contractor's all risks insurance policy that should cover the damage done by the crane. If you do not have these in place, you may end up paying for the damages done.

Confidential information protection

My firm is negotiating with a company from Kenya on an acquisition. I am releasing some information to them that they can take advantage of, at a later stage. How can I be 100% protected against this party, who might end up competing against me, in case the transaction does not go through?

9th November 2009

This is a very pertinent question. We would suggest that you get the receiving party to sign a Non Disclosure Agreement (NDA) that will offer some good protection.

A confidentiality or NDA is crucial for any other party who needs to protect confidential information. As the importance of the confidential information increases, so does the relative complexity of the agreement.

In your NDA, it is important to have a definition of confidential information, which is one of the most important parts of such an agreement. Ideally, the contract should set forth as specifically as possible the scope of information covered by the agreement unless of course, if the confidential information would end up being disclosed in the NDA itself. Whilst the agreement will offer very good protection, it is very hard to quantify it to 100%.

Fraud in bank

An amount that my company was meant to pay the Tanzania Revenue Authority (TRA) was debited from my account but not remitted to the TRA. TRA is now after me and the bank is claiming that I should have checked my bank statement. It is quite obvious that the fraud was done at the bank. The bank is not admitting any liability. What should I do?

2nd November 2009

Generally, a customer owes his bank a duty to take reasonable and ordinary precautions against forgery. One decision in the Courts has said (and we quote) 'Primarily, the relationship between a banker and customer is that of debtor and creditor. And the drawing and payment of the customer's cheques as against the money of the customer's in the banker's hands the relationship is that of principal and agent.'

The bank also owes fiduciary duties to you as its client and it has been held in many cases that *prima facie* every agent for reward is also bound to exercise reasonable care and skill in carrying out the instructions of his principal.

It seems that the exact amount meant for the TRA was debited from your account and remitted to a third party. There has to be some collusion between the third party and the bank officials. If that can be proved, you have a very good case against the bank. The mere fact that you did not discover the mistake from the bank statement will not limit the liability of the bank. If the bank does not cooperate to credit your account or remit the funds to the TRA, you should consider taking the bank to Court. From the facts, unless there are details that you are withholding from us, you have a very good case.

Warehouse insured twice

My brother insured our warehouse and innocently, so did I. Recently, there was a fire and the warehouse was totally gutted down by fire. We claimed against one of the companies, which somehow found out that we have two insurance policies. The insurance company is trying to extract 50% of the claim amount from the other insurer. We are stuck in between. Is this fair?

26th October 2009

Insurers and also we, as lawyers, view this very suspiciously. You have a double insurance and the word 'innocent' is very important for you to succeed. For if the two insurance companies find out that there is 'material non disclosure of facts', your claim will not be payable. You sound very hopeful that the amount will be paid just 'waiting' for the other companies 'equal contribution' to the claim amount – we are unsure where such optimism emanates from. Insurance companies will also look at the previous years to see if you have been double insuring all these years or is it this year, when you have a total loss. We know that insurance companies around the world are hated but you must appreciate that there is a lot of insurance fraud in Tanzania. Just as any other business entity, insurance companies also have to protect their interests.

Most policies normally include a rateable proportion clause. The principal effect of this is to prevent the insured, who has double insurance, from claiming the full loss under the policy. The clause makes the insurer liable only for their rateable proportion and requires the insured (not the insurer) to pursue the other parts of the claim from the other insurers. In your case, your insurance company is, very kindly, trying to recover money from the second insurer and then pay out your claim. You will appreciate that such clauses are typically justified as a way of preventing fraud.

Is this fair? The answer is in the affirmative. If it was genuinely an innocent mistake, you should get paid, unless of course there are facts that have not been brought to our attention.

Too many conditions in assignment clause

I have signed a long term contract with a company a few years ago. The contract is for the supply of certain raw material. I wish to assign the contract to another company as I intend to wind up operations in Tanzania. The other party informs me that there is a procedure for me to follow and that the assignment cannot be done automatically. They pointed out to the assignment clause in the contract. Shouldn't an assignment clause automatically allow assignment?

12th October 2009

The contract you have signed on restricts rather than prohibits assignment. Such clauses are sometimes referred to as restrictive assignment clauses. They have the advantage of being more rigid than a normal assignment clause, but more flexible than disallowing assignment.

You have not mentioned what the procedure is for assignment. Often such clauses provide for the formal requirements of any consent to be given and mostly make the compliance with such requirements a condition precedent of the assignment of the contract. Such clauses also provide various criteria on which a refusal to consent to the assignment may be based.

You have asked whether the assignment clause should be automatic. It all depends on the wording of the clause in question. Your clause is a restrictive one and it seems like you will have to fulfil the requirements before the assignment. Otherwise you will be in breach of contract.

One additional point you may wish to consider is to see if there is any formal requirement under the contract for you to inform the other party of change of shareholders or directors. If not, you can sell the whole company to the person you intend to assign the contract to, unless of course there are reasons (tax reasons) which are barring you from doing that.

Compensation for burnt cosmetics

I own a shop selling cosmetics in the city centre. Last week a person who identified himself as an inspector from the Tanzania Food and Drug Authority seized some cosmetics in the shop and burnt them claiming they were dangerous for human use and the government had banned their sale. Can I claim for compensation since I was trading with a valid licence to sell cosmetics?

5th October 2009

The Tanzania Food, Drugs and Cosmetics Act of 2003 clearly prohibits any sale of cosmetics; unless such cosmetic product conforms to requirements prescribed by the Tanzania Food and Drugs Authority (TFDA). The Minister for health may also, through the Government gazette, declare any cosmetic product prohibited to be used or offered for sale.

If the cosmetics that you were selling were advertised as being banned for sale, then the inspector's action were within the law. The interest of the TFDA is to protect citizens from

using dangerous drugs and cosmetics.

If you have any reason to believe that the cosmetics were not part of the banned list, then you may appeal to the Minister against the action even though there cannot be personal liability on the inspector, if he was performing or executing any function under the Food, Drugs and Cosmetics Act, in good faith.

As far as compensation is concerned, if the goods burnt were actually not banned, you have a good case and can pursue to claim for the goods and other damages.

We must mention that just because you have a licence does not mean that you can sell banned cosmetic products.

Memorandum of Understanding

I came to Dar es Salaam to negotiate a certain deal in the mining sector. After many weeks of negotiations, a detailed Memorandum of Understanding (MOU) was signed with the local party, and I met all the conditions as per the MOU and paid the amounts agreed. The other party has now refused to perform based on the MOU claiming that it does not bind them. Please advise.

28th September 2009

Defining an MOU depends in the context it is used in. However, usually an MOU designates any kind of pre contractual document by which one or both parties intend to organise negotiations and execution of the contract. It seems the stage you reached at was beyond this and you might have actually signed a contract, which will very likely work for you.

Whilst we lack all the details and a copy of the MOU, it seems like your MOU was perhaps drafted as if it was a contract and just because it reads MOU, does not mean that it cannot be interpreted as a contract. We suggest you present your MOU to your lawyer to interpret its contents.

Family debt in contract

I have been trading in the timber business with my father until recently when I decided to start my own company. After being conned by a supplier, I went into some serious debt which my father undertook to pay. This was all done through signing of letters. My father has not paid the debt yet and the due date has already elapsed. The businessman has threatened to institute a civil suit against me. Do I have any liability? Please guide me.

28th September 2009

In the Law of Contract, there is a doctrine of novation which recognises that one party to a contract can release the other and substitute a third person who then undertakes to perform the released person's obligations. From the facts you have given us, it is clear that your debt has been officially 'taken over' by your father under the doctrine of novation. By virtue of the letter your father signed, a new contract was created between your creditor and your father

As per section 62 of the Law of Contract Act, if parties to a contract agree to substitute a new contract for it to rescind or the parties alter it, the original contract need not be performed. Therefore, even if there was originally no privity of contract between your creditor and your father, by the doctrine of novation a new contract between them was created when your father signed on that letter.

It is your father who is bound to pay the debt. If that businessman decides to institute a suit for the debt recovery, then it should be against your father. You cannot be made party to that suit and it will be a misjoinder of parties if he decides to sue you. Strictly speaking, your father should be the one worrying and not you.

Threat of demolition and injunction

The Kinondoni authorities had given me a permit to develop an office in a certain area on Toure Drive, Dar es Salaam. We are now on the third floor and have been served with a notice to demolish within thirty days. Our lawyer advises us to go to Court and file a case and get an injunction. I have never been involved in a case and do not want to fight in Court. What should I do? What is an injunction and what are the conditions of this injunction? Will the Judge be willing to grant such an order against the same authorities who appoint him?

21st September 2009

Your lawyer is right. You should file an application in Court for an injunction. We have noted you have never been to Court – however, you are going to Court to fight for your rights, assuming that you have a valid permit unless you do not mind demolishing.

You have two options, the Court option being the first one. Second option is trying to sort this out amicably with the Kinondoni authorities but make sure that you get their blessing in writing.

An injunction is a judicial remedy whereby a person is directed to restrain from doing or to do a particular act or thing, and in your case the injunction would be directed to the Kinondoni authorities, its servants and agents. It is a preventative relief to preserve status *quo* in respect of the subject matter of the suit.

The main principles governing exercise of discretion for the granting of the type of temporary injunction you should be looking for are that you must satisfy the Court that there is a *prima facie* case, meaning that there is a serious question to be tried in the suit and on the facts there is probability of you being entitled to relief; that there is irreparable injury likely to be suffered and that the Court's interference is necessary to protect you from this injury which is irreparable and that on a balance of convenience the inconvenience likely to be caused by withholding the application for injunction is greater than by granting it. Simply put that you have more to lose than the Kinondoni Municipal Council.

Your last question is whether the Judges will be fair in granting an injunction against the very system that appoints them. It must be pointed out Judges are appointed directly by the President without interference from anyone least of all the municipal councils. And just like in many other counties, the Judges in Tanzania uphold the rule of law. It does not matter who is fighting against whom. We believe the judicial system will be able to protect you, provided you have not been party to any mischief.

If you go through each one of the main principles above, you will notice that you have very good chances of getting an injunction. Just a cause of concern – due to the backlog of questions, we have only managed to answer your question three months after you sent it. We do hope you took your lawyers advice, filed a suit and got an injunction!

Breach of tender procedures

I applied in a tender for the supply of large vehicles to a government department. Due to time constraints, I was verbally told that I should go ahead and import the vehicles. Having placed the importation order and after several follow ups for the contract, I was informed that everyone who tendered, including myself, had been rejected. I am in shock. Please advise.

7th September 2009

Procurement in Tanzania falls under the Public Procurement Act. Under the Act, the tender body does have the right to reject the entire tender. This is only justified if there is lack of competitive tendering, tenders are not substantially responsive to the tender document, the economic or technical data of the project have been altered or the tendered amounts are higher than the budgeted amounts. If the rejection of the tenders is due to lack of competition, then the tender body may re advertise the tender widely again.

In your case, we are unsure why the tender has been rejected. It may be due to one of the above and hence legal. There is not much you can do at this stage.

As for the importation of the vehicles, you have not mentioned as to who gave you the go ahead to import. It is quite shocking to learn that you placed an order for vehicles without having a written contract. In any case, if this is how you have been operating with the same department for years, you might have a very slim chance of claiming that there was indeed a contract. However, your chances of success for specific performance or damages are very slim. You need to see your attorney for further guidance.

Aircraft searched before departure

I am a Kenyan small time charter flight operator. Recently, I was flying from Mombasa to Pemba when I had to make an emergency landing in Dar. I was carrying two Yemeni nationals and a Somali, all working for the same company. Upon landing, I was greeted by a bunch of policemen who claimed that they suspected I was involved in terrorist activity, and hence needed to search the aircraft and passengers. We were in Dar for over four hours and I lost a lucrative return flight because of this. Was the search legal? How come we do not have such behaviour in our country? Can I claim for loss of business?

14th September 2009

It does not matter whether you are a small time operator or a tycoon. Our law treats everyone equally. Under the Prevention of Terrorism Act, a policeman is allowed to stop, board and search any aircraft, vessel or vehicle if he has reason to suspect that there is in it evidence of a commission or likelihood of commission of an offence and hence the search was legal. As for not having 'such behaviour' back home, we are not sure what you mean. Tanzania is a sovereign nation that has its laws that must be followed. It does not matter whether you are our neighbour – when you are in Tanzanian air space or on the ground, Tanzania law applies. And since in our opinion the search was legal, it is very unlikely that you will be able to claim for any damages.

Claim back a gift

I have been in touch with my childhood friend for many years. During the course of our friendship we have exchanged various gifts. Some time ago, my friend, now living in Dubai, shipped a car in my name as a present. I incurred expenses in clearing the car and now that I am driving the car, my friend wants the car back. What should I do? Can he just claim back the car like this?

17th August 2009

A gift is a voluntary transfer of property from one person or entity to another made without charge or consideration, with the full intention that the property shall not return to the donor and with the full intention on the part of the receiver to retain the property entirely as his own without restoring it to the giver. For a gift to be valid, however, there must be a giving on the party of the donor and a taking on the party of a donee, an intention to give and an intention to take, a delivery of the property to the donee and a gift must be complete. Short of any of these, a gift can be revoked at any time before delivery.

In your case, there was a clear intention to give the car to you and you had the intention to accept it. Since you have cleared it, registered it in your name and are in possession of it, unless you want to give it back, legally the car now belongs to you. If there is nothing you are hiding from us, you can continue to enjoy your car.

Time of the essence in contract

I am a fish importer in Europe currently negotiating a contract with a Mwanza based fish processing plant. How do I approach the issue of timely delivery which is fundamental to the working of the contract?

24th August 2009

This must be stipulated clearly in the contract. Since you are in the perishable foods business, it is absolutely essential that you include a 'time is of the essence' clause. Unless this clause is included in your contract, a 'reasonable' time for performance will be implied if a problem arises as to any timing issue. In this way, you have made the precise timing of performance critical, and if this timing is not met, you can claim a breach of the contract. This clause should be tailored to reflect the specific timing issues within your contract.

A sample clause that we can suggest: 'Time is of the essence with respect to all provisions of this agreement that specify a time for performance; provided, however, that the foregoing shall not be construed to limit or deprive a party of the benefits of any grace or use period allowed in this agreement'.

Another aspect that you must consider is the payment terms – consult your lawyer for further guidance.

Definition of incoterm in contract

I have entered into a contract with a foreign supplier. Surprisingly the contract is just a few pages although the goods are worth millions of dollars. The contract refers to Incoterms. What is this and am I protected?

10th August 2009

You should have asked this question before you signed the contract! The old jibe that the larger the transaction the longer the contract should be, does not hold any water. Just because you are buying goods worth millions of dollars does not mean that the contract should be long. A good contract covers the parties in all scenarios. Just because your contract is short does not mean that it is not properly drafted – you need to look at the contents of the contract to determine whether you are protected or not.

Coming to your question, Incoterms are a universally recognised set of definitions of international trade terms, such as Free on Board (FOB), Cost and Freight (CFR) and Cost Insurance and Freight (CIF), developed by the International Chamber of Commerce (ICC) in Paris, France. It defines the trade contract responsibilities and liabilities between buyer and seller. It is invaluable and a cost-saving tool. The exporter and the importer need not undergo a lengthy negotiation about the conditions of each transaction. Once they have agreed on a commercial term like FOB, they can sell and buy at FOB without discussing who will be responsible for the freight, cargo insurance, and other costs and risks. The Incoterms in current use are the 2000 edition.

The Incoterms are quire comprehensive and offer clear unambiguous obligations on both the parties. Whether these were discussed is unclear but normally Incoterms offer good protection to both buyer and seller. In your case, you will need to read the contract to be sure whether you are adequately protected.

Notice to demolish from NHC

I am a 'co-owner' of a building with National Housing Corporation (NHC) and have been served with a three month notice for demolition. I am not a tenant of NHC and hold a title deed although the two other flats in the building are owned by NHC. I do not pay rent to NHC and am shocked at the notice which has surprised me. Should I not be compensated? What are my rights? How can NHC just sell the plot without my authority? What should I do?

17th August 2009

This is an issue that many are facing. Demolition notices on properties that are 'co-owned' with NHC are, in our opinion, challengeable based on the fact that you were neither involved nor considered for a joint venture. Your position is different from that of a tenant and hence you have a good case.

Historically, buildings that were acquired by the government during nationalisation were placed with the current NHC. At the time landlords also became tenants but at a later stage, the government decided, under administrative powers, to return those flats in which the owner himself/herself was residing. A long lease was negotiated and what you call a 'title deed' was issued.

You have not been involved in the process only to be served with a demolition notice. Your question is pertinent – how do you get compensated or rather how can you salvage the situation.

We would suggest a two tier strategy. Our opinion is that you have a good case against NHC and possibly the joint partner developer, and thus recommend that you meet NHC to look into the possibility of sorting this issue amicably.

In the event you are not satisfied with the discussion or the compensation NHC offers, if any, you can file a suit at the High Court lands division. It is also advisable to get an interim order against demolition.

Must my contract be in writing?

Why do people advise me to have contracts

in writing when the law recognises oral con-tracts? I have been in business for over sixty years and believe that the word rules the world. Contracts bring mistrust. What is your opinion?

10th August 2009

We are unsure where you got the term 'word rules the world' from but it is surely interesting to learn this.

A proper contract reduced to writing reduces any ambiguity in any of the terms or conditions. It is also important for continuity that contracts are written clearly. If God forbid one of the parties to the oral contract dies, how would the heirs take over? We have always advised our clients that the time for oral contracts is gone – gone are those days where you could just rely on someone's word. Contracts do not bring mistrust but ensure that relationships are maintained.

We totally disagree with you, unless of course, you run a very small business where the amount in question is so negligible that the cost of even the paper on which to print the contract would be more expensive than the amounts involved in the contract. Otherwise you must reduce your agreement onto paper – it could even be handwritten and in plain non legal English, but it must be written down. You have definitely been very lucky for the past sixty years.

Demolition for non-payment

I entered into a contract with a company which promised to pay me within thirty days of me supplying a very sensitive service. To make the contract payment terms very strict, we agreed that if the company does not pay me within the stipulated time, I would be entitled to demolish one of their buildings. I have not been paid and have also been served with an order from the Lands Court that I cannot demolish the building. What should I do?

3rd August 2009

This is a very weird contract. Why would you want to demolish the debtors building if you are not paid? How would that offer you relief unless the land would be surrendered to you after demolition, which is not the case. This sounds like a Shakespearean play and we wonder if this is a real contract. In any case, we shall answer this as if it does exist.

From the facts above, it is clear that the company you supplied to has not paid. The primary objective is for you to recover such funds under our civil procedures based on the contract you entered into.

As far as the demolition is concerned, this is against public policy and also implies injury to the property of the debtor and is illegal. Even if the company signed such a contract allowing you to do such an act, the Courts will come to the rescue of the company. The Court has rightfully issued the injunctive order. We would suggest that you focus your energy on the recovery of the funds outstanding rather than the demolition of the property.

Change of use of right of occupancy

I have a piece of land near Kibaha with a certificate of occupancy of thirty three years beginning 2002. The plot was meant for a school and says so in the title. However, I now wish to construct a petrol station instead. Do I need any approvals?

17th August 2009

As per the Land Act, you will have to apply to the Commissioner for Lands for a change of use to undertake this new development. Your application should also state why you intend to change the use of land.

Upon application, the commissioner shall consult with and take account of the views of the authority in charge of that township, the local authority and any other authority whose consent to that change of use is necessary.

Upon approval of such authorities you shall be required to take your certificate of occupancy for endorsement for the change of use. You must not start any development until approval is granted as such development shall be illegal and may result in demolition of the development or revocation of the certificate of occupancy. You must also be informed that the change of use in your case may be disallowed based on public policy if the plot was and is meant to be specifically for the construction of a school.

No changes clause in contract

I entered into a contract with a company in Dubai in which they stated that any changes to the contract should be in writing. Is this a fair clause? I am used to doing my work on the mobile phone and even for a small change in quantity, they want me to do so in writing. It is wasting my time. What should I do?

27th July 2009

The supplier is trying to protect both you and his company. This clause you are referring to is called a NOM clause (No Oral Modification clause) and it is in common use in international contracts. The clause requires that any changes, even if they are very minor, be done in writing. It is a very fair and important clause which unfortunately does not seem to work for you.

A way to go around this is for you to request the company to amend the contract with another clause that allows you to request for a variation by way of electronic mail or sms, although the admissibility of a sms message in Court is debatable. We understand that you might be on the move and not available to write to the company all the time. Both e-mail and sms are available to you on your phone

and may be used. You must appreciate that it becomes very hard for either party to prove their case when verbal instructions are given.

Director's conflict of interest

I am a director of a mining company where I have realised that one of my fellow directors is also a director of another company to whom we have been giving supplies contracts. This has only recently come to my attention. These contracts are all properly tendered and I am not trying to say that my fellow director is a crook. What does the law say?

20th July 2009

In the mining industry, there is no law that disallows a director of one company to be a director of another company. It would not be in the interest of the public to have such a law.

However, the issue of disclosure is clearly stipulated in section 209 of the Companies Act where it is stated that it shall be the duty of a director of a company where he or any connected person is in any way, directly or indirectly, interested in a contract or proposed contract with the company to declare the nature of that interest at a meeting with the director of the company.

Hence, your fellow director should have declared the interest he has in the supplies company. This applies even if he became an interested party after the contract was made.

In your question you seem to have conveniently ruled out fraud or misuse of powers. If any of these apply, it may cost your fellow director his directorship.

In any case, with the facts presented to us and as per the Companies Act, your fellow director is liable to a fine for not declaring his directorship in the other company.

Shipping contract gone sour

I hired a large ship to carry goods to and

from East Africa. In the contract, it has been stipulated that in the event that there is a dispute we shall first refer the matter to arbitration in the UK under the laws of the UK before commencing proceedings at the Commercial Court in Tanzania. We are having problems with the contract and the other party has referred the matter to some very expensive arbitrators in the UK. Can I move this to the commercial Court?

20th July 2009

Arbitration differs from litigation in Court in that the procedure is not available as of right in the event of any dispute, but is dependent on prior agreement between the parties, as is in your case. It also possesses many attractions to the prospective litigant as it is sometimes cheaper than going to Court, is faster and less formal. Arbitrators selected by the parties are usually experts in the field who do not regard themselves as so strictly bound by the precedent of the judiciary.

In this case, it is very unlikely that you shall be able to move this matter to the Commercial Court without going for arbitration in the UK. The law that will apply during Arbitration will be that of the UK Arbitration Act 1996. Next time you should pay extra attention to the arbitration clause you sign. We advise you to appoint an attorney in the UK.

Compensation for counterfeit coins

I am a manager in a bank here in Dar. In the course of receiving and issuing of coins, we received coins from customers which are counterfeit. I have had to take them to the Bank of Tanzania for impounding and destruction. Shouldn't the Central Bank compensate our bank?

13th July 2009

Counterfeiting is to make an exact copy of something in order to trick people into thinking that it is the real thing. It should

be remembered that issuing coins which are counterfeit is a criminal offence and punishable under the law.

Our Penal Code is quite clear on this that any officer of the Government or the manager of a bank who receives, during the performance of his duties, any coin which he or she has reasonable ground of believing to be counterfeit shall impound such coin and transmit it to an officer of the Bank of Tanzania who shall cut, deface, or destroy it with or without compensation, as he thinks fit. The decision of an officer of the Bank of Tanzania whether compensation should be granted or withheld shall be final, and no person shall be entitled to claim, and no proceedings or action shall be brought, against the Bank of Tanzania or the Government in respect of any loss or damage suffered by reason of such impounding and cutting, defacing or destruction.

Hence, the Bank of Tanzania has discretionary powers when it comes to compensating your bank. Going by the market practice, it is unlikely that compensation shall be given but the Bank of Tanzania has the final say.

Money wrongly transferred to my account

My bank mistakenly credited my account with a large sum of money. I did not know about this and ended up spending the money. Now the bank is after me. How can I claim a right over the money?

27th July 2009

Banks can make mistakes as they are operated by humans. This is not the first time we are hearing of such a mistake. We also find it very hard to believe when you say that you did not know about the amount credited and yet ended up spending the money.

Your bank has a right to 'come after you'

for a full refund of the amounts mistakenly transferred into your account. You have no right over the money that was transferred unless you can prove that the funds were meant for you. Because you have spent the money and need time to repay, you may need to contact your bank manager, who upon making a proper assessment may or may not grant you time to repay the funds.

Winding up of company

There is a company based in Dar that is not paying a long outstanding debt of a company I own. I have been told that I can wind up this company if they fail to pay me. What does this mean?

13th July 2009

Winding up or liquidation is a procedure by which a company can be dissolved. It may be instigated by members or creditors of the company or by the order of the Court. It involves the appointment of a liquidator to assume control of the company from its directors. The liquidator collects the assets, pays debts, and distributes any surplus to company members according to their rights.

The threat of being wound up is a serious one, prompting most companies to react. Usually, if the debt is due and not disputed, the best course of action for a company, which is the subject of a winding up petition, is simply to pay.

Section 279 of The Companies Act allows you to petition for winding up of the company if the company is unable to pay its debt, and has failed to do so, twenty one days after you have demanded for such payment. On hearing a winding up petition the Court may dismiss it, or adjourn the hearing, or make any interim order, or any other that the Court thinks fit.

Annual returns for companies

Why do I have to send annual returns to the registrar of companies? Is it necessary for me to do that? It is adding to the bureaucracy in Tanzania.

20th July 2009

The filing of returns is to ensure that your company file is updated at the registrar of companies. This is a requirement by law and is mandatory. The annual returns should be made on the anniversary of the company's incorporation anniversary, or the anniversary of the previous returns.

The Companies Act is very clear on the need for such returns. If a company fails to deliver an annual return within twenty eight days, the company or officers of the company in default shall be liable to a fine.

We disagree with you on your last comment about adding to the bureaucracy – most countries have a system of annual returns.

Holding company guarantee not valid

I signed a contract with a mining company in Tanzania and during negotiations we agreed that in the event of any defaults on their part, their holding company would cover any such liability. The clause heading in the contract reads 'Holding Company Guarantee' but when you read the clause, it surprisingly excludes the holding company from guaranteeing the performance of the subsidiary. The heading of the clause and the clause itself therefore contradict each other. What should I do?

29th June 2009

It is very difficult for us to give you an answer in the affirmative or negative without reading the entire contract but from the looks of it, it seems unlikely that you can enforce the clause the way you would like to. You will be bound by the contract as it stands.

However, you might still want to check if there is an entire agreement clause. Such a clause is drafted so as to make the contract

FB

the final document upon which to rely on, irrespective of what you agreed upon prior to signing. You should also check if there is a clause that says 'headings are used for convenience of reading or convenience of reference only, and shall not affect the construction or interpretation of any of the terms of the contract'. If these two clauses appear, you might not be able to call upon the holding company for performance. You should also consult your attorneys for further guidance.

Seizing goods when not paid

I have been selling goods to a customer and wish to know how I can protect myself when he does not pay and I want my goods back. What should I do?

22nd June 2009

If you specifically want your goods back, you can incorporate in your contract of sale a clause called 'retention of title' (reservation of title). The retention of title clause will say you continue to own the goods you supplied until you are paid, and you can enter the customer's premises, with or without notice, to take them over when payment is not made or overdue. Depending on the goods you are selling, you may need a more sophisticated retention clause, if for example, your customer has sold your goods to some other party or processed your goods to produce another product.

You should also make sure that it is worth recovering your goods. Make sure you can also tell which goods are yours. If you cannot tell your goods from other similar goods at the customer's premises, you might not be able to take them back. Your trading terms should require the customer to store your goods separately until you are paid. In practice, customers rarely comply, so mark your goods in some way – with your name or logo, or batch or serial numbers – so you can identify

them even if they are mixed with other goods.

Disposition part of right of occupancy

I have sold a portion of a registered land and want to make sub-divisions so that the buyer has a separate title. What are the laws applicable and the procedures to be followed for the process of sub-division?

29nd June 2009

All matters concerning disposition of registered land are regulated by the Land Act No.4 of 1999. Under that law an occupier of land under a right of occupancy who wishes to dispose his/her land may apply to the commissioner of lands for approval for disposition of the whole or a part of that land, whatever the case may be.

In practice, application for approval of sale of land to the commissioner of lands is done simultaneously with filing relevant forms. These include filing a form for notification of disposition of the right of occupancy and a form for transfer of right of occupancy, and attached to these the sale agreement dully signed by both the seller and buyer. The sale agreement should provide in full the description in terms of measurements and price of the portion of the right of occupancy being sold.

Once the sale is approved, the registrar of titles will enter names of both seller and the buyer in the registry and the ownership of the plot will now be determined by the shares each has in the plot.

For the purposes of subdividing the plot, the law requires you to then apply to the director of the municipality concerned for approval. The letter of application attached with your subtitle, must state reasons for the subdivision. The application is likely to be successful if, for example, both plots are already developed with houses built thereon and that such houses were built with the requisite building permits.

The permit to subdivide the plot may, however, be rejected if the size of the plots, after being subdivided, are too small compared to the neighbouring plots in the area.

Penalty clauses in contract

I entered into a contract with a construction company in Tanzania and had a liquidated damages clause for any delays in completing the job. When there was a delay, and I claimed for my liquidated damages, the other party decided to take the matter to Court and challenge the clause saying it was a penalty clause. What is the difference? Am I not entitled to my liquidated damages?

15th June 2009

A contract can include a 'liquidated damages' clause setting out what compensation will be payable if one party fails to fulfil their contractual obligations. But if it amounts to a 'penalty clause', it is unenforceable.

Liquidated damages clauses are often used in construction projects – agreeing the level of compensation if the project overruns.

Negotiating compensation in advance and including it in the contract has several advantages which include both customer and supplier benefit from increased certainty, damages which might otherwise be difficult to quantify, such as lost profits are specified, the likelihood of litigation in case of breach of contract is reduced and the need to fulfil the contract is reinforced, reducing the risk of breach of contract.

Normally, terms freely agreed between two contracting businesses are enforceable. However, a liquidated damages clause will not be enforceable if it is a penalty. A liquidated damages clause that was a reasonable estimate of the probable loss is enforceable.

A clause which attempts to intimidate the supplier into fulfilling the contract, rather than to compensate the customer for a breach, is a penalty. Also an unreasonable estimate is likely to be considered a penalty and whether the clause is referred to as liquidated damages or a penalty is irrelevant.

So how can one tell whether a clause is a liquidated damages clause or a penalty clause? Characteristics of a liquidated damages clause are: Reasonable estimate of the probable loss (regardless of what the actual loss turns out to be), does not have to be a genuine pre-estimate but should be justifiable, reasonable at the time of entering into the contract rather than when the breach occurs and negotiated terms are more likely to be considered reasonable than a liquidated damages clause that is unilaterally imposed. This is to protect the interest of smaller suppliers when dealing with giants.

Characteristics of a penalty clause are: compensation that is clearly greater than the greatest possible loss that could be suffered as a result of the breach, in the case of failure to pay a specified sum a larger amount than that sum and as much compensation for a minor breach of contract as for a major breach that causes significant damage.

Such liquidated damages clauses must always be carefully drafted and particular care should be taken where a liquidated damages clause is to be the only remedy for a breach of contract. If the clause is unenforceable, there may be no other way to claim compensation. One should also keep evidence of the negotiations to agree any liquidated damages clauses, and of the basis on which the amounts of compensation were agreed.

In your case, the contractor is trying to 'get away' with the damages by claiming that it is a penalty clause which would be unenforceable. You need to consider the clause in light of what we have said above. Your attorney should also be able to guide you.

Ship hijacked by pirates

A ship that was carrying cargo destined for Tanzania was declared to have been hijacked. The ship owners have declared something called 'General Average' and want us to sign some papers. What is general average and what should we do?

8th June 2009

The law of general average is a legal principle of Maritime Law according to which all parties in a sea venture, proportionally share any losses resulting from a voluntary sacrifice of part of the ship or cargo to save the whole in an emergency. In the exigencies of hazards faced at sea, crew members often have precious little time in which to determine precisely whose cargo they are jettisoning (throwing off board). Thus, to avoid quarrelling that could waste valuable time, there arose the equitable practice whereby all the merchants whose cargo was on board would be called on to contribute a portion, based upon a share or percentage, to the merchant or merchants whose goods had been tossed overboard to avert imminent peril. While General Average traces its origins in ancient maritime law, it still remains as part of the law.

For General Average to be declared, the Courts have accepted these three elements to be present. First, a common danger in which the vessel, cargo and crew all participate; a danger imminent and apparently 'inevitable,' except by voluntarily incurring the loss of a portion of the whole to save the remainder.

Second, there must be a voluntary jettison, jactus, or casting away, of some portion of the joint concern for the purpose of avoiding this imminent peril or, in other words, a transfer of the peril from the whole to a particular portion of the whole.

'Lastly, this attempt to avoid the imminent common peril must be successful'.

From what you have said about the pirates, it seems that the declaration of General Average is a fair declaration. However, we cannot advise you on whether you should sign all or any of such papers until we know the contents of what you are signing. We advise you to contact your Attorneys to interpret the contents of the letters sent to you.

Agency relationship

I am a supplier to a large retailer and wholesaler in Mwanza. I have recently heard him telling customers that he is our agent. How can I protect myself from him committing on my behalf?

1st June 2009

We are glad you have spotted this. Very few people do. First and foremost, do you have a contract with him to supply him with the goods? If not, we advise you to consult your attorneys and make sure that a contract is drafted in which you make it very clear that the buyer in Mwanza is not your agent.

In law, agency is the relationship that arises whenever one person (the agent) has authority, express or implied, to act on behalf of another (the principal) and consents so to act. Hence, the agent is in a position to place the principal in a contractual or other relationship with a third party. In most cases, parties wish to deny the existence of an agent/principal relationship because of the liability that can arise.

In the contract that you draft, request your attorney to include, and based on your business model improve upon, the following clause: this agreement shall not constitute or imply any partnership, joint venture, agency, fiduciary relationship or other relationship between the parties other than the contractual relationship expressly provided for in this agreement. Neither party shall have, nor represent that it has, any authority to make any commitments on the other party's behalf.

Tips for contract signing

I am going to be entering into a contract very soon. What are the important things I should consider before signing?

18th May 2009

First and foremost, make sure you read and understand each and every word of the contract. There is nothing like a standard contract so make sure to ask questions if there is something that you do not understand. Also make sure that the amount agreed upon is clearly stated including the terms of payment i.e. when such amounts become payable.

We have noticed that many contracts do not clearly describe the goods or services being sold – insist that such descriptions are properly recorded in the contract. Check if the amount in the contract includes taxes. Other things that you should check include: whether or not the party is able to enter into this contract, is the contract legal, are you entitled to sign this contract on behalf of your company, what are the remedies for a breach of contract, what is the performance time of the contract, to perform the contract are there any approvals from any authorities required. You should also make sure that all that has been agreed upon has been recorded in the contract – it is pointless signing a contract and then claiming that it did not capture what was agreed upon. Remember that a good contract is not ambiguous and is clear to understand. There may be other guidance that your attorney can give you prior to signing.

Agreement dates confusion

I signed an agreement on a certain date and assumed that my obligations started on the day I signed, only to realise that I should have started providing my services a month later. Why is there such a dates confusion? Shouldn't the agreement start on the day it is signed?

25th May 2009

It seems like you are confusing the commencement date of an agreement and the date of signing. These two dates need not be the same. This is a common confusion amongst many people. For example, you can sign an agreement today and agree that you will start performing under the terms and conditions of the agreement two weeks later.

The commencement date of the agreement is normally specified in the agreement. If it is not, you can normally assume that the agreement comes into effect on the date of signing. You have not specified if the agreement you signed has a commencement date. If it does then the agreement comes into effect from that particular date. You will need to check the document you signed.

It is critical that you read agreements carefully, understand what the terms and conditions are before you sign. If you do not understand any part of the agreement, you should always seek legal advice. It becomes very difficult to challenge terms and conditions of agreements after you have signed. We have noted many cases where parties do not read agreements after being told by the other party that it is a standard agreement! There is no universal definition of a standard agreement so be careful.

No licence, no insurance

I was stopped by a traffic policeman for a certain offence. Can one get imprisoned for a road traffic offence? If so how and charged with what? How serious an offence is driving without a licence and without insurance? Can I complain?

18th May 2009

Yes, you can get imprisoned for a road

traffic offence. Our Road Traffic Act imposes different penalties for various offences ranging from a fine to imprisonment or both. However, it is trite law that in any offence, if the relevant law provides for different options of penalties starting with sentence of a fine like many of the offences under our law, the convicting Court should impose a sentence of a fine unless there are compelling circumstances to justify the imposition of any other optional sentences. The Court may for instance, opt to impose on the accused imprisonment instead of a fine, depending on the evidence of previous conviction and the accused's general character, for example, if it is established that the accused is a habitual offender of the same traffic offence. This is so irrespective of the offence.

Under the law, all traffic offences are serious offences. However, in practice there are two categories of offences – major and minor offences. Major offences include those offences which are directly and potentially dangerous to persons. These include offences like causing bodily injury or death through carelessness or dangerous driving and driving without a driving licence or insurance. These offences are triable by the Court of Law and their penalty is either fine or imprisonment or both, depending on the circumstances of each particular case.

Minor offences include offences like driving a motor vehicle on the road with defective tyres, failure of the owners to give identity of a driver or driving a bicycle in a prohibited manner. Offenders to these offences are punished instantly by having to pay prescribed fines to the nearest police station from the place where the offence is committed or directly to the charging traffic officer, and getting an official receipt.

Your question does not specify what offence you were stopped for and whether you were fined or not. However, from the questions you are asking, it seems like you neither had a driving licence or insurance. Please take note that both these offences are punishable by imprisonment as they are serious major offences.

As for complaining, we are unsure what you want to complain about. It is pointless complaining about the traffic police officers when you are on the wrong side of the law. Reports in recent newspaper articles estimate that road accidents are going to be one of the leading causes of death in Sub Saharan Africa by 2012.

Child injured in friend's house

A 7-year-old child from our Msasani peninsula neighbourhood came to play with my daughter at our house, which we have rented from a company. Whilst playing the neighbour's child sustained some injuries when our outside roof collapsed. The child's mother is acting like a gold digger and intends to sue us for damages and costs of treatment for injuries sustained. Am I liable to compensate her?

11th May 2009

It is very uncommon for roofs to just collapse. From the facts, your house seems to be a dangerous place to live in. The Occupier's Liability Act imposes upon you a duty of care to control the premises you are occupying and the safety of all those people occupying and entering the said premises. It is not a defence to say that you are a mere tenant and not the owner of the house.

The law imposes a common duty of care to the occupier of the premises as it does to the owner. The law expects every occupier, be it a tenant or owner, to take reasonable steps to prevent the development of such dangerous situations in their premises.

If the child's mother can prove that you or the owner of the premises did not take reasonable precaution, you will be liable. Exceptions lie when the person injured, knew of the risk, accepted it and then got injured. However, such an exception cannot apply to a 7-year-old child.

As for the mother being a gold digger, it is very difficult for us to comment. Everyone wants to protect their child; claiming her right as per the law does not necessarily make her a gold digger.

Entire agreement clause in a contract

I signed an agreement which had a clause that all the terms of the agreement were contained within the agreement. However, the person who marketed me the machine had promised more than what was documented in the agreement. The agreement is for the supply of machinery worth billions. How do I approach this? I have insurance – can I claim on the policy?

27th April 2009

You should always carefully read any documents including agreements before you sign them. The clause that forms part of your agreement is sometimes referred to as the entire and final agreement clause. The aim of such a clause is to state that all the terms of a contract are contained within the written agreement between the parties to the contract. In consequence, a clause like this attempts to exclude other documents or statements from forming part of the contract. These might include statements made by a party's representatives which may have induced the other party to enter into a contract and/or documents such as sales literature or any other exchanges of correspondence between the parties.

Before signing the contract, you should have insisted on the inclusion of the promises that the marketing person had mentioned. You have not told us what these promises

were but from the facts given, it looks like you have a very tough case to fight. And the fact that the machinery is worth billions does not offer you any more or less protection.

As for the insurance, the contract of insurance is one in which one party (the insurer) agrees for a payment (the premium) to take monetary provision for the other (the insured) upon the occurrence of some event or against some risk. For such contracts to be enforceable, there must be some element of uncertainty about the events insured, which we do not really see in your case. You have not mentioned what type of insurance you have, but it is very unlikely that insurance will offer you any protection. We recommend that you engage an attorney who can read the entire contract in light of what you are saying and see if there is anything else in the other clauses that can offer you protection.

Bank reference turned sour

A well known bank in Tanzania gave a reference for a certain customer of the bank. The reference was general in nature. I transacted with the customer and have now lost TZS 285M, in advance payment. Can I sue the bank?

13th April 2009

You are trying to sue the bank for what we call negligent misrepresentation which involves statements made honestly but without reasonable grounds for the belief.

Normally banks give reference letters that are general and very vague. They also have disclaimers on such letters. This is to limit or avoid liability that could potentially arise, in circumstances such as yours. Banks are normally not credit reference agencies and the same applies in Tanzania.

If the bank was acting honestly when it gave you the reference letter, it is very unlikely that your suit will succeed. In any such transactions in the future, we suggest you should get an advance payment bond or a bank guarantee for sums you pay in advance. You might still want to consult your lawyers to interpret the letter the bank gave you to see if an action for a suit arises.

Contract with non standard definition

I am a Tanzanian businessman having entered into a contract with a British company for the supply of certain software. After signing the contract, I was surprised at how they have defined a certain term. It is a common word in the industry but their definition in the contract is not what the ordinary definition is. I would like to interpret the contract based on the ordinary definition and they are refusing, saying it is well defined in the contract I signed. What should I do?

6th April 2009

To begin with, before signing any documents, you should read every word contained in such documents. It is unfortunate that you have entered into a contract and have then decided to challenge a definition that is already in the contract document. In your question you have not mentioned what 'that' word is and what the contract defines it as. We will, however, answer your question generally.

The clearest way in which a contracting party can give a special meaning to a word, is to include a definition of that word in the contract, as is the case in your contract. Generally speaking, the Court will apply definitions given by the parties, no matter how different the definition may be to the ordinary meaning of that word. Even if a word is not specifically defined, the Court might decide that the parties have used the word in a special sense, and not in accordance with the ordinary dictionary meaning. However, in coming to such a conclusion, the Court will only look at evidence found in the contract

itself i.e. the particular context in which the word was used.

In your case, it is very unlikely that a Court will accept the ordinary meaning of the word, since the same word is clearly defined in the contract that you have signed.

Shop robbed, no compensation

My shop was robbed and the guards were found guilty by the Court. I got nothing of the stolen goods back. Can I recover from the security company?

30th March 2009

The fact that the guards were found guilty does not mean that the Court would order for compensation against the security company for the goods that were stolen. This is because as far as the criminal Court is concerned, its duty is only to determine the criminality of the accused persons.

However, it is likely that you have a contract with the security company. The fact that the guards have been found guilty of an offence arising from the robbery of your shop is sufficient evidence that the security company has breached the said agreement. You have a good cause of action against the security company for the value of the goods stolen from your shop and general damages, for breach of contract. Depending on the amounts involved, you can consider suing your security company.

Contract not on legal paper

I was recently asked to sign each page of a contract. Does the law force me to do so? I also noted that the draftsman used white paper instead of the normal coloured legal paper. Does that invalidate my contract?

2nd March 2009

A contract is a deliberate engagement between two competent persons to do or abstain from doing an act upon legal consideration. A contract may be oral or in writing and parties to a written contract are bound by the letters (words) of the contract itself so that in case a dispute arises, as to the terms and conditions of the contract, reference will be to the agreement and not to any other extraneous matters.

You have been asked to sign each page of the contract. There is no law that compels you to do so. It is just a precaution by the draftsman to avoid any forgery in the future. Many a times, dishonest parties to a contract substitute pages, to favour their needs, resulting in legal wrangles. The signing of each page reduces the chance of pages being illegally substituted in the future and is standard practice.

As to the use of white paper, this is more of a professional issue. It is also easier to notice any forgery or mischief on legal paper than normal white paper and hence the usage.

Sign contract or go to jail

My son was working for a very large foreign company in Tanzania. One of his subordinates was involved in stealing of company property and my son was questioned by the police. The police continued to harass my son. I approached the employer who threatened me that he would make sure my son was imprisoned unless I signed a contract agreeing to pay. I come from a poor family and after also being threatened with violence, I did not read the contract and signed it, just so that I could leave the employer's premises. I do not have the money to pay and the employer now wants to take me to Court. What do you suggest?

16th February 2009

A contract is a legally binding agreement and constitutes an offer and acceptance by each of the parties. A number of other requirements must also be satisfied for an agreement to be legally binding. There must be lawful consideration (unless contract is by deed), the parties must have an intention of creating legally binding relations, the parties must have the capacity to contract, the agreement must comply with any legal requirements and must be entered into mutually and freely by the parties. The contract must be legalie one cannot enter into an agreement to sell and deliver for example cocaine, otherwise the contract is null and void.

From the brief facts you have given us, it seems that you were put under duress to sign the contract. Duress is defined as pressure, especially actual or threatened physical force, put on a person, to act in a particular way. Duress may consist of violence or threats of violence to the claimant or members of his family. The threats need not be the only cause of entering a contract. It is sufficient that the threats are a factor influencing one to enter into the contract.

Contracts entered under duress are voidable and can be set aside, at the option of the victim. You have a good case to challenge the validity of this contract and we advise you to contact your attorney.

Why should I arbitrate?

I made a contract with a party which has defaulted on payment. The matter has been referred to arbitration. Why should I arbitrate? Please advise.

19th January 2009

It is very likely that your contract has an arbitration clause that refers the matter to arbitration. Arbitration is the determination of a dispute by one or more independent third parties (the arbitrators) rather than by Court. These arbitrators are appointed by the parties in accordance with the terms of the agreement. The arbitrator the rules of natural justice. Depending on the arbitration clause and the 'fairness' of the decision, the award made by an arbitrator can be challenged in Court. You have not mentioned if the contract you entered into has an arbitration clause. If it does you will have to go for arbitration for it is the law, that parties to a contract with an arbitration clause cannot submit themselves directly to the Court. If there is no arbitration clause, you need not arbitrate and can file a suit.

Suit time barred

In 2001, I entered into a contract with a company in Dar to supply certain material, to be delivered by the end of the same year. However, the Company did not honour the contract. What can I do to recover my money?

12th January 2009

Every cause of action has a limitation of time to sue. Suing under a contract is six years from the time the cause of action arose. In this case you are therefore time barred. However, this is not the end of your right to institute a recovery suit. You still have a chance to make an application to the Minister of Justice and Constitutional Affairs to sue out of time by stating the reasons for the delay and explaining what you are claiming against the other party. The Minister after consultation with the Attorney-General may make an order for extension of time. This is provided under section 44 (1) of the Law of Limitation Act (Cap 89 R.E 2002). Some of the reasons that are acceptable to be allowed to sue out of time are sickness, documents having been misplaced, having been imprisoned and not being able to institute a suit having travelled overseas. In your case, you are not specific enough as to what caused the delay in filing the suit. If your reasons are accepted, you will be granted with leave to sue out of time and

can proceed to file a case in Court for breach of contract.

Breach of contract

I made an agreement with a company for the supply of certain goods and whilst they have been partially delivered, the quality is not what was agreed. They have also failed to deliver the rest of the goods and have been avoiding me. What can I now do?

5th January 2009

The supplier has not, as per the terms and conditions of the contract, delivered what was contractually agreed upon. Finally, a restitutionary remedy is most appropriate where a party has performed their side of the contract but has not received the agreed counter performance. You must note that the primary remedy for breach of contract is normally placed on damages. This is reinforced by the fact that although a victim of a breach may seek specific performance or an injunction, such orders are equitable in nature and therefore discretionary. In your case, the details are a little sketchy. We are unsure what percentage of the consideration (bargained price) you have paid, whether the contract was specific enough as to the quality and that there is no ambiguity and what the reasons are for the further delay. We suggest you consult your lawyers immediately.

Importing first time

I wish to import goods by sea freight from a supplier in the Far East. They are giving me two types of contracts – FOB and CIF. What do these mean? How do I make sure that the goods will be delivered to me in Tanzania after I make the payment? The supplier is asking for 100% advance.

12th January 2009

The terms referred to in your question are the common types of contracts for the international sale of goods. FOB stands for 'Free on Board'. Here the seller undertakes not just to get the goods to the ship, but to see them loaded on to the ship. The sellers obligations extend to all charges incurred before shipment, including loading charges, but exclude freight and insurance. You as the buyer will be responsible to pay the freight and the insurance. In the absence of a contrary intention, the buyer has the right and the responsibility of selecting both the port and the date of, and generally making the arrangements for, the shipment of the goods. Once the goods have been delivered over the ships rail, the seller has delivered them to the buyer and the risk has passed to the buyer. If you decide to go for a FOB contract, we would strongly advise you to insure the goods with a local insurance company. CIF stands for Cost, Insurance and Freight. In a CIF contract, the seller agrees not only to supply the goods but also to make a contract of carriage (pay for freight) under which the goods will be delivered to the port of destination, and a contract of insurance, to cover the risk while the goods are in transit. The seller performs his contract by delivering the relevant documents to the buyer, an invoice specifying the goods and their price, a bill of lading as evidence of the contract of carriage, an insurance policy and any other documents, as specified in the contract.

Coming to the second part of your question, we would strongly advise you not to pay 100% advance, or any advance. Customary practice is for you to open a Letter of Credit (LC) with your bank. This is a document whereby your bank will undertake to pay money to your supplier via your supplier's nominated bank on presentation of documents specified in the letter. For example, if your contract is CIF, then your bank will only pay the suppliers bank upon receiving bill of lading and the insurance policy with an invoice.

Matters of Court Procedure & Ethics, Dealing with Lawyers

Lawyers may not agree but the bottomline is that the Court of conscience is a higher Court than the Courts of justice.

Guilty until proven innocent! Guilty or not guilty everyone is entitled to a fair and just trial. This chapter answers questions on Court matters, illegal arrests, summons, Court proceedings, giving evidence, filing a defence, appealing, calling a witness and Court related procedures. It also responds to questions on the various Courts and managing your legal fees, not a lawyer's favourite topic!

The best way is to stay out of trouble and out of Court.

Award for costs too low

I am a Tanzanian businessman and resident of Sumbawanga. In 2009, I successfully defended a suit that my customer had instituted against me in the Resident Magistrate's Court at Kisutu on allegations of breach of contract. I was extremely disappointed with the minimal costs awarded to me by the Court in comparison to the amount I spent defending the suit, which included transport, taxis, food, entertainment and accommodation costs for my witnesses. I feel that the Court has not been fair to me. What should I do?

25th April 2011

Taxation is the legal term given to the process of the Court assessing the costs that the successful litigant incurs in prosecuting the suit. The taxing master, normally the registrar, deputy registrar, or resident Magistrate in charge in case of the lower Courts, is the officer of the Court responsible for taxation. The process starts with the successful litigant presenting a list of costs in Court, commonly known as the 'bill of costs'. This refers to the amounts he or she has spent in prosecuting the suit and should be submitted within sixty days from the date of judgment. Only necessary costs are considered by the Court.

Costs incurred entertaining your lawyer or witnesses are not accepted. The bill of costs must normally be supported by receipts and vouchers for all disbursements, together with any documents, drafts or copies, and must be reasonable. What is reasonable depends on the judicial discretion of the taxing master, who considers the facts, complexity, public importance, and other circumstances of the case and decides on what figure the 'bill of costs' should be taxed at. If the taxing master erred in these principles, the aggrieved party can refer the matter to a High Court Judge,. The decision of the taxing master on the

quantum is final. With regard to your question we are not in a position to fault the taxing master, for we lack sufficient facts. We do not have details of the 'bill of costs' you presented in Court, nor do we have a copy of the taxing master's ruling. However, should you think that the taxing master erred in his assessment of the costs, we advise you to refer the matter to the Judge.

Reference to the Judge is made by way of 'Chamber Application', supported by an affidavit made within twenty one days after the certified copy of the taxing master's decision has been issued. In case the deadline has passed, you can apply for an extension of time upon showing good cause for such delay.

Defending myself in Court

I have been charged with the offence of theft and wish to defend myself. Is that allowed? What do you suggest I do? Any books I can read?

28th February 2011

In law, there are principles of Natural Law which are basic and sacred principles that must be observed. One of them is 'the right to be heard'. This means that whoever is charged with any kind of offence has the right to defend himself or herself. The procedure is as follows: during your arrest you must be informed of your right to an attorney, your right to remain silent, and be promptly taken to a police station. Once you are arraigned in Court, the charge will be read to you and you will have to plead either guilty or not guilty.

Theft is a bailable offence and bail shall be open only if you satisfy the bail conditions. It is likely you will plead not guilty. After such a plea, a preliminary hearing is conducted where the prosecution will produce a list of witnesses and you will be required to provide your list. Trial then begins, whereby the Prosecution brings its witnesses and you can cross examine them. You need to counter the testimony of the witnesses to disprove the allegations against you.

This all might sound sensational as we write it, but please be reminded that Court rules can get quite technical and we advise that you engage an advocate to represent you.

Several high profile personalities, including former Liberian President Charles Taylor and former Yugoslavian President Slobodan Milosevic, defended themselves in trials. For more tips, we recommend you read a book by a well known retired Judge, B. D. Chipeta, titled 'A Handbook for Public Prosecutors.'

Driving offence and jail

I was involved in a road accident and am now threatened with imprisonment. The offence is that of causing harm by driving dangerously. I always thought that traffic offences are resolved by paying a fine. What should I do?

4th April 2011

Dangerous driving is one of the most serious offences under the Road Traffic Act. In order to prove this offence, the following ingredients must be present: (1) the accused was driving the car, (2) the driving was dangerous or reckless which resulted in injury or death. Most traffic offences are resolved by payment of a fine. However, in view of the seriousness of this offence, and in the interest of public policy, it is true that on conviction you may be imprisoned. You may not be able to deny that you were driving the car, but whether or not you were driving dangerously is subjective and depends on the facts of each case. You should get your attorney to guide you further.

Substitution of charge during trial

Two years ago my uncle was charged with unlawful wounding. He pleaded not guilty and the prosecutors brought three witnesses. Surprisingly, when the third prosecution witness appeared, the prosecution side substituted a charge to that of causing grievously bodily harm, and after the defence hearing he was convicted and sentenced to three years in jail. Was it fair to substitute a charge?

11th April 2011

Substitution of a charge is governed by section 234 of the Criminal Procedure Act, which says that the prosecution side can amend and/or substitute a charge at any stage of the trial for a number of reasons such as defectiveness of the charge in its substance or form. However, after the substitution, the accused has a right to enter a new plea, this time to the amended charge. The Court shall also inform him his right to recall witnesses to give evidence afresh or to be further cross-examined. All these procedures should be indicated in the Court records.

Any omission of these procedures is treated as a serious error capable in law of vitiating the decision arrived at the end of trial. Since your facts are silent as to whether or not all these procedures were complied with, we advise you to consult your Attorneys with Court records for further advice. Whether or not it is fair to substitute a charge is subjective. In the eyes of the accused it might look unfair; in the eyes of the prosecution it might be fair. However, the law clearly states that the prosecution can substitute a charge.

Claim after limitation period

In 1999, I entered into a contract with a friend to pay TZS 50M that arose out of a transaction. However, due to my financial constraints, I could not pay as promised. A few months ago I received a fourteen day demand notice from my friend's lawyer claiming the amount and other associated costs. I have replied to the demand notice and acknowledged the debt, but the creditor is anxious to go to Court immediately after the said fourteen days without further notice. Please advise.

11th April 2011

There is no doubt that your relationship with your friend is regulated by your written contract of 1999. However, under the law, the time limit for proceedings under the written contract is six years. In your case, there are two distinct dates – the date of your contract in 1999 and the date of your acknowledgement of the 1999 debt, which you said is a few months ago. By virtue of the Law of Limitation Act, no acknowledgement shall be operative, if it is made after the expiration of the period of limitation.

Under the Law of Limitation, your friend cannot make a claim against you if it has been more than six years since your default. Under special circumstances, the Minister in charge of justice may extend the period an additional three years, which would take period of limitation to 2008. After 2008, your friend would not be able to claim against you, even if you had acknowledged the debt afresh. While you might have a moral obligation to pay, legally you have a good defence in case you decide not to. However, we that you recommend see your attorney for further insight and guidance.

Electronic evidence in Court

At the bank where I work, there is a loan that was made in which all of the documents were exchanged only by e-mail, which is very strange. The borrower is a good friend of the credit manager and an informal overdraft facility was allowed, contrary to procedures. The overdraft is unsecured, save for a guarantee by the individual who has now refused to pay back the funds. Our legal team says we have no case, as the Court will not accept electronic evidence and that it would be hard to prove the debt. Is this true?

4th April 2011

On the face of it your legal team is correct. However, logic defies what your legal team is saying when it is quite clear, as you have pointed out, that a loan was granted, and the funds were disbursed to the borrower. From your question, it seems to us that you can prove an overdraft that was utilised, and that the borrower had exchanged e-mails with your credit manager. Why then should the Court not support your case? The cardinal rule is that the Claimant must prove what he or she alleges.

The Evidence Act here is very old and does not provide for electronic evidence, as it was adopted from the Common Law system in England. The Best Evidence Rule states that only original documents in written form are admissible in Court. You have no originals – what should you do? Well, the High Court Commercial Division, in a landmark case, allowed the admittance of electronic evidence. The main issue before the Court was whether electronic evidence from computer printouts is admissible under the provision of the Evidence Act. The Judge held that Courts have to take due cognizance of the technological revolution that has engulfed the world. In concluding, the Judge added that the law can ill afford to shut its eyes to what is happening around the world in the banking fraternity. While electronic evidence was allowed in the above case, there are tens of dozens of instances where the Courts have not allowed electronic evidence. Whilst this is being looked at a little more leniently by the Courts, the facts of each case will decide the applicability of the admissibility of electronic evidence. In your particular context, that being a bank, is a somewhat of a throwback to the past in that record keeping in banks is to a large extent old fashioned.

Your bank has no option but to file a suit and invoke the above when the defence raises an objection to the evidence you produce. The learning point for you and other bankers is twofold: first you need to have checks and balances even for senior managers to ensure that they stick to your lending guidelines (it must be pointed out that some banks in Tanzania still do not have proper guidelines) and secondly, everything that a banker does must be formally documented and signed. E-mails are convenient, but can turn out to be costly.

Contempt of Court

I was summoned as a witness in a case in which it was quite apparent that the Judge was siding with the plaintiff's lawyer when I was being questioned. I was very uncomfortable, and it reached a stage where I could not handle it anymore and was a little aggressive in Court. The Judge held me in contempt of Court and has set a date to sentence me. Is this normal?

14th March 2011

Contempt of Court is defined as disobedience of a Court order or process, such as a breach of injunction. For example, if an injunction is served on a defendant with a penal notice attached, breach of the injunction can result in the defendant being imprisoned. Other contempt of Court examples are when one deliberately interferes with the outcome of legal proceedings, uses threatening language or creates a disturbance in Court and unreasonably attacks the integrity of the justice system. We have also heard stories of people being sentenced to jail because their phone rings in Court! The general notion is that Judges should use this discretion very sparingly. In your case we are unsure as to

how aggressive your behaviour was in Court. You must be warned that contempt of Court can lead to a custodial sentence of up to six months. We suggest you contact your lawyer for further guidance.

Plea of guilty

I was arrested for an offence in which the public prosecutor and magistrate informally told me to plead guilty and that would be the end of the matter as I would be fined. It seemed like a reasonable quick fix arrangement and I did exactly as I was instructed. To my utmost surprise I was passed a sentence of one month in jail. Can the magistrate and prosecutor misguide me like that?

14th March 2011

We begin by saying that neither the prosecutor nor Magistrate is allowed to guide you in such matters. They do not act for you, and hence this guidance was inappropriate and perhaps even illegal. Unfortunately you have not told us what the offence was, but many offences have the option of a fine and/ or custodial sentence, and the general rule is that a fine should be imposed first. By the time we have answered this question (because of the backlog we have), you should be out of jail. We do sympathise with you, but wish to reiterate the importance of proper legal representation when in Court.

Traffic police asking for a ride

I was stopped by a traffic police and asked to give him a ride. I am a foreigner and do not really know how things work here and hence declined. The officer then called the traffic officer at the next junction, who again stopped me. I was subsequently taken to the traffic police and questioned. Is it mandatory for a driver to give a ride to a traffic police?

28th February 2011

We are not aware of any law that compels you to give a lift to a traffic police officer. Being taken to the police station for not giving a ride amounts to misuse of power of the officer and you can report this to the head of traffic police in Dar es Salaam. Make sure your complaint is in writing and you get an acknowledgement of the letter. You do not want the letter to 'get lost.' You should then follow up and seek a written response. We hope you know the ID number of both police officers.

Child caused fire

We live 55km from Mbeya in southern Tanzania, where the climate is very cold. Our 9-year-old child was in the forest. In order to warm himself, he lit a fire. Unfortunately and unknowingly, he lit a fire on hardened and dry grass, and the fire spiralled out of control and burnt down a small hut belonging to a family. At the time of the fire, there was no one present in the hut. The matter was reported to the police and my child was taken to Court. The final outcome of the judgment was that I was to compensate the hut owner with a certain amount. Is this fair? I do not have the means to pay such compensation. What should I do?

14th February 2011

The Penal Code provides that a person under the age of 7-years-old is not responsible for any act or omission, and that a person under the age of 12 years is not criminally responsible unless, at the time of the act, he had the capacity to know that he should not have committed the act. The burden is on the prosecution to prove that your child should have known not to light the fire.

When a child is convicted of an offence, and the Court is of the opinion that the case would be best disposed by payment of a fine, in the interest of the child, the law allows the parent to pay the fine. However, a parent

against whom such an order is made must be given the opportunity to be heard. It seems like you were not availed such a chance and can appeal this order.

Appeal to begin after prison sentence

In 2007, my brother who was employed by a certain public parastatal was charged with stealing monies from his employer. He was tried, convicted and sentenced to jail for a term of three years. Despite being found guilty and having been sentenced, the Republic appealed to the High Court to challenge the decision of the District Court, alleging that the sentence of three years in jail was too lenient. This came to all of us as a shock. In May 2009, my brother completed his prison sentence and was released from jail. He has now been served with a Court summons calling him to attend the appeal against him. Is the Republic's appeal allowed by law? What are the chances of success in the appeal? Is the appeal fair, especially considering the fact that he has already served his punishment and been released from jail? What will happen in the event the appeal against him succeeds? Please advise, as all of us are confused.

24th January 2011

The matter is indeed confusing. It seems to be quite clear that the Republic was aggrieved with the sentence of three years imposed upon your brother. The Republic wants to see the sentence enhanced, which is allowed. The same would have been the case had your brother thought the sentence is excessive – he could have appealed. Considering that your brother was charged with stealing property from the public parastatal, which is a specified authority, under the Minimum Sentencing Act the correct sentence for this particular offence should have been five years imprisonment and not three years. This is not what you want to hear but it is the plain truth.

Since the Trial Court imposed a lesser sentence, which is inconsistent with the provisions of the Minimum Sentencing Act, the High Court will likely have no other means of preventing the due process of the law from being carried out, and will likely impose the correct sentence, even if this leads to undesirable consequences for your brother.

Whether your brother has completely served his custodial sentence is immaterial, as the time already served will be taken into account in computing the correct duration of stay in jail. Unless there are other facts that you have not disclosed to us, it is likely that the appeal will succeed and your brother will have to serve a further two years in jail.

Protection of witnesses against prosecution

In November 2009, my wife appeared in District Court where she testified on behalf of the accused in a case involving my neighbour, who was charged with the offence of assaulting the wife of a rich businessman, also our neighbour. During cross examination, the public prosecutor confused my wife with tricky questions and ended up accusing her of being a liar and abettor to the offence. My wife has now fled from our home, fearing that she will be arrested because she testified. Is there any possibility that she will be charged? Please advise.

4th January 2011

We are not aware of what questions were put to your wife and how she answered those questions. With the limited facts you have given us, we do not believe that there is anything your wife needs to worry about. The general principle of law is that a witness in Court cannot later be arrested or prosecuted on the grounds of any personally incriminating evidence given, nor can that evidence be used as proof against the witness

in any subsequent proceedings. The law gives immunity to witnesses from being prosecuted on the basis of evidence they give in Court, unless they purposely give false evidence, which is not the case here. Unless there are other reasons why your wife left you, we are sure she can return without being arrested.

Calling witnesses during appeal

In 2000, three of us were charged in the District Court with two counts: stealing by public servant and being in possession of offensive weapons. After a hearing at the Trial Court, I was found with no case to answer. This was not the case with my co-accused. The director of public prosecutions appealed to the High Court, and the Judge recalled three witnesses and called one new witness to hear evidence against me. The High Court then proceeded to reverse the acquittal order, held that I indeed did have a case to answer, and ordered that I join my co-accused for defence at the Trial Court. Was the Judge right and fair to hear new evidence? Please advise me.

24th January 2011

Under the Criminal Procedure Act, the law clearly allows the High Court to summon any person or recall any of the witnesses if their evidence appears to be essential to the just decision of the case. The High Court is also empowered, when dealing with appeals from the subordinate Courts, to take additional evidence (if necessary) itself or direct that such evidence be taken at the subordinate Court. However, the High Court must record its reasons for taking additional evidence and it should not misuse this and turn it into a retrial, filling gaps in the prosecution's case or changing the nature of the case against an accused person. The evidence added by the High Court shall be taken as if it were evidence taken at the trial before the subordinate

Court. As we have no Court records to view, which would have helped us guide you as to whether additional evidence was necessary for such a decision, we advise you to consult your attorneys for further advice.

3% Fees at commercial Court

We are a company registered in South Africa that supplies goods to a company based in Tanzania. Our relation with the purchaser has gone sour and we intend to take them to Court. Our appointed attorneys have quoted us Court fees of 3% on a claim of about TZS 4B and legal fees of an equal amount. Are these fees not exorbitant? What is the average time to completion of case at the Commercial Court?

3rd January 2011

The Commercial Court is the preferred Court for the business community in Tanzania. The fee at the Commercial Court is 3% of the first TZS 200M, and 1% on amounts above the TZS 200M. Hence, for the TZS 4B claim, the Court fee will be TZS 6M plus TZS 38M totalling TZS 44M. The figure you have been quoted of TZS 120M is definitely in error. We do not wish to comment on the legal fees you have been quoted, as this is a commercial decision.

Presently, the Commercial Court takes an average of about fourteen to sixteen months to complete cases. However, it depends on the complexity of the matter and whether it involves any applications. The Commercial Court is very serious about the pace with which matters get disposed and is weary of delaying tactics by attorneys.

We also wish to warn you that since you are not a Tanzanian registered entity, it is likely that the defendant, your debtor, will apply for security for costs. You should prepare funds for such an application to avoid delays.

Power of attorney donor dead

A close relative of mine gave a power of attorney to his lawyer to act on his behalf for the sale of a property in Shinyanga. Unfortunately, the relative died, and the lawyer seems to be misusing his power of attorney. How does such a power work? Can the power only be given to an attorney? When power of attorney is given, does it also mean that the proceeds of sale go to the person holding the power of attorney?

3rd January 2011

Power of attorney is the authority given by one person to another to act on his or her behalf. The power dies when the donor, in this instance, your relative, dies. After the death the Will of the donor comes into effect, and the lawyer has no right and cannot act on this power of attorney.

As for the proceeds of the sale of property, it is important for you to read the power of attorney. The power of attorney would allow the lawyer to act for the donor (giver of the power of attorney), but does not necessarily mean that the lawyer retains the amounts raised under the transaction. In the transaction you mentioned, if the transaction was done after the death of your relative, then the power of attorney had expired and the person who had been given the power acted without any power, and any contract he has entered into is void.

Although the phrase 'power of attorney' somehow denotes that an attorney is involved, the power does not have to necessarily be given to an attorney.

Technicalities in Court

I made an application at the High Court in Iringa for certain reliefs based on merit. It was a strong application to block a bank from selling my property for non-payment of a loan. To my utmost disgust the application was not even heard, and the application was cancelled on a mere technicality. Instead of citing a certain section 68 of a law, my attorney quoted another section which the Judge said was not the right section to cite. Because a mere numerical error, we were thrown out of Court. What kind of justice is this? Why would a Court just throw us out on these minor matters without addressing the major issue at hand?

20th December 2010

It is now well settled that non-citation or wrong citation of an enabling provision of the law renders the application incompetent to be heard. This seems to be the case in your application for injunctive relief against the bank. Some counsels have argued that such matters are not the heart of the matter, as you also claim. But the Court of Appeal of Tanzania has made it very clear in a number of cases that citing of the correct provision of the law is a fundamental matter. And if it the wrong section is cited, then the legal foundation is bound to collapse.

The constitution of Tanzania in Article 107 supports your view that mere technicalities should not prevent the Court from looking at the substantive issue, which in your case was not addressed at all. However, in response to this, the Court of Appeal has said that it is these same rules and procedures that are used to facilitate the administration of justice; and they are not mere technicalities.

We suggest you contact your attorney and consider refilling the application for injunctive relief in Court.

Twenty one days to file defence

I was presented with a summons to appear in Court. However, I did not file my written statement of defence within twenty one days, which is what the Court clerk told me I should have done. What should I do? I must also add that I have been very unfairly sued, as I should be the one suing. How do I do initiate my suit whilst I am already the defendant?

20th December 2010

There is a difference between a summons to appear and a summons to file your written statement of defence. It seems you were served upon a summons to appear. The law says that when a summons to appear is issued and if you are required by the Court, you shall at or before the first hearing or within such time as the Court may permit, present a defence of your case. We are unsure as to what the summons said, but if it only was for your appearance, and if no other order as to filing of a defence has been made, then you may not be time barred.

If the summons was for filing a written statement of defence, then the law is very clear in that you shall file your defence within twenty one days of being served with the summons. You count the twenty ones days from the next day of having received the summons, and if the twenty first day falls on a weekend, the following Monday is deemed to be within the twenty one days. If the twenty first day is on a public holiday, then the next working day is deemed to be the twenty first day.

You need to understand what kind of summons you received and get an attorney to advise you. If you are time barred, you will be required to make an application in Court to file your defence late, and cite the reasons for the delay. As for having a claim against the same person who has sued you, this is possible within this same law suit by way of a counterclaim. It is imperative that you move rapidly on this issue without wasting any more time.

Surety ordered to pay expenses

Two years ago, my uncle was accused of stealing a car and the case was brought before the Mtwara District Court. My uncle denied the charges against him and bail was granted. I became his surety and signed a bond of TZS 500,000. In one hearing, my uncle could not appear, as he had travelled to Mwanza to attend to his sick mother. I appeared and informed the magistrate who ordered me to pay TZS 150,000 as expenses for the witness from Dar es Salaam and TZS 40,000 for the witness from Masasi. So as to avoid being sent to jail, I paid up. Was this a fair order?

6th December 2010

Assuming what you are saying is the truth and your uncle is not engaging in delaying techniques, and that his mother was really ill on the hearing day, we see no justification for the said orders issued by the trial Magistrate.

The absence of the accused had been caused by circumstances beyond his control, which you could not have done anything about. Hence, it is not justified for you as surety to pay expenses incurred by the prosecution witness, regardless of where they travelled from. You are at liberty to appeal to the High Court to set aside the said orders. Your legal advisor can guide you further.

Warrant of arrest for tax matter

Over the past four years we have had an issue Tax Revenue Appeals Board related to Value Added Tax of a colossal amount. The case had been dragging on until a few weeks ago when the Tax Revenue Appeals Board issued a warrant of arrest for me as chairman of the board of directors of the appellant company. This was not only shocking to me, but also very damaging to my reputation. Can the Appeals Board order my arrest, and if so, what can I do to avoid it? Just for your information, I am an investor with investments in twenty African countries including Tanzania. Can there be no preferential treatment for such investors?

29th November 2010

Being an investor in twenty African countries does not absolve you of a tax liability. Even companies with a worldwide presence pay taxes in Tanzania. That is no ground to win an appeal, and it is very unlikely that any preferential treatment can be given to you or your company.

We wish to point out that having a case run for four years is quite unusual, as cases at the Tax Revenue Appeals Board are usually fast-tracked. We hope you are not confusing the Tax Revenue Appeals Board and the Tax Revenue Appeals Tribunal, which is the appellate body to the board.

From our reading of your question, this warrant of arrest was probably issued because you did not appear as a witness at the Appeals Board. Rule 13 of the Tax Revenue Appeals Boards rules provides that a person who has been served with a summons to appear before the board and fails to comply with such summons without reasonable excuse commits an offence under the Act. It further adds that when a person who has been served with a summons to appear before the board as a witness and fails to comply with such summons, the board may issue a warrant of arrest in order to ensure the attendance of that person before the board at the date, time and place specified in the warrant. Your attorneys should address this issue immediately before an arrest is made – you may have to give reasons as to why you failed to appear before the board. Please be informed that the Government, as any government would, takes the duties of this Appeals Board very seriously, as it is this very body that addresses the critical aspect of government revenues through tax collection.

Deaf person as witness

I am a law student and have been attending cases in Arusha. Recently there was a case whereby the prosecution brought a witness who was deaf and dumb. Without a flicker of doubt the Judge disallowed the evidence. In fact the deaf man was the key witness, as he was at the scene of the crime. Do you think the Judge was right? Is this not discriminatory?

15th November 2010

The law is clear in that a person who is unable to speak may give evidence in any other manner in which he or she can make it intelligible, such as by writing or sign language, if they can be written or made in Court. A person who is a deaf-mute is not incompetent as a witness if he or she can be made to understand the nature of the oath, and if intelligence can be conveyed to and received from him or her by means of sign language. He may be examined through the medium of a sworn interpreter who understands the sign language. In our opinion, if an interpreter was available, we do not see why the Judge should disallow the evidence.

Court to draft my agreement

I hear of so many problems where people are fighting in Court trying over the interpreta-tion of contracts. Why do we have to go to Court when there is a problem? Can we not get a Court to draft a contract that will then not need to go to Court? Is this drafting not a money making machine for you lawyers?

1st November 2010

Your ideas are good in theory, but make no practical sense. A Court is manned by a human called a Judge, who is also trained in law. It is not manned by God. The Judge's pen is not God's pen; there is no magic that the Court can do that law firms cannot. One cannot go to Court to get agreements drafted because Courts are there to interpret the law. What would happen if a Court drafted your agreement and there was a dispute? Who

would adjudicate the matter? Just because an agreement is drafted in Court does not mean that there will be no dispute. World over there is an outcry that Courts are slow in their proceedings, so you can imagine the efficiencies of Courts if it was mandatory for all agreements to be drafted by Judges.

Drafting a contract involves a great deal of skill; lawyers try to cover most eventualities, yet inevitably there are events that lawyers might not anticipate, at the time of drafting.

Your comment on drafting being a money making machine for lawyers is unfounded and uncalled for in the circumstances. Most problems arise because people wait too long before consulting their attorneys . The English proverb – 'a stitch in time saves nine' – sums this all up.

Attending police station during pendency of case

In July 2010, I was arrested by the police on allegation that I was involved in breaking and entering. I was charged in a District Court and was posted bail. During the pendency of the case, I was summoned again to the police station for further interrogation. Is this procedurally correct? How can I stop this?

1st November 2010

Unless you were called to attend the police station for a different incident, which does not seem to be the case, then it is likely that the act of summoning you to the police, while the case is pending in Court, was unlawful. The police move is suspicious because once an accused person is taken to Court, he is subject only to the jurisdiction of the Court; the reserve powers of police to summon or arrest persons under the law are meant to deal with criminals before cases are taken to Court. In a situation like yours, police can only, deal with accused person with leave of the Court, which is rarely granted. That being the case, we advise you to report the incident to the Court for necessary orders. Alternatively, you can directly complain to the Director of Public Prosecutions for his intervention.

Proceedings in camera

I am a 21-year-old girl studying at a Dar es Salaam secondary school. Our neighbour's daughter, who is also my friend and class-mate, was raped one night when she had gone out to a kiosk to buy water. Fortunate-ly, the suspect was arrested and charged in the District Court. We attended Court every time the case was called. However, when the witnesses started to testify, we were ordered by the Court to leave the courtroom. Is this fair? We wanted to observe the Court's pro-ceedings from the beginning to the end to make sure that justice was done. Is it not our right to observe Court proceedings? Do you think that the magistrate planned to side with the accused, and hence wanted to con-duct the proceedings in a secretive manner?

1st November 2010

As a general law, everyone has the right to be present in Court, provided there is sufficient accommodation and there is no disturbance of the proceedings. It is usual, however, where cases involving indecent details are called on, to direct females and boys to leave the Court, but if an adult woman should insist on being present at the hearing of the case, there is probably no power to prevent her from being present. It is expressly provided under our laws, the Sexual Offences Special Provision Act and the Criminal Procedure Act, that in rape cases, or when a witness who is under 16-years-old is call in any proceedings relating to an offence pertaining to decency or morality, the Court may order the exclusion of all persons not being members/officers of the Court or parties or their counsel. However,

this does not preclude witnesses to be called to testify. Kindly be informed that the course taken by the Court is normal in cases like this one and therefore nothing to worry about, unless you have concrete evidence to the contrary. Moreover, if you are on the list of witnesses, you may be called to testify.

Prohibition to arbitrate outside Tanzania

One of the local parties I am entering into a contract with informs me that according to local law, all arbitration must be conduct-ed in Tanzania. This does not surprise me because of the country's socialist back-ground, but is there some flexibility?

25th October 2010

We are surprised to hear this. We are not aware of any law that prohibits you to choose a venue for arbitration outside the country. The other party may be trying to save on costs, as Arbitration outside the country is very expensive. If the party is misguiding you about arbitration, you may want to read the entire contract and see what else you have missed!

Failure to inquire marital status

In December 2008, I was sued in the Pri-mary Court for compensation for adultery, although I produced strong evidence that I did not know that the woman with whom I was alleged to commit adultery was the complainant's lawful wife. In fact, before I started the relationship, the lady had told me she was not married, which I believed to be true. I question whether the Trial Mag-istrate was fair to decide the way he did, as demonstrated by his conduct during the case. During the trial, he did not record my evidence, and at times interrupted my tes-timony. Is there any way I can challenge the findings of the Trial Court, considering that fter delivering the judgment I was ordered o pay TZS 150,000 to the claimant, which I lid immediately?

1th October 2010

Your letter implies that you feel your rial was not conducted properly. Without joing through the records of the Court, ve are unable to comment on whether rour accusations against the Magistrate are tenable. However, it has always been jifficult to impeach the records of the Court, especially when a complainant had the right and opportunity to ask the trial Magistrate or Judge to read evidence over to him/her and did not to exercise his/her rights. It appears that you did not opt to exercise this right.

As to the strength of your evidence, again we cannot comment because we do not know what evidence you presented, nor the strength of the complainant's testimony. This being a civil matter, evidence as a matter of law is weighed on a balance of probabilities. It seems that your opponent's evidence outweighed yours. We advise you to proceed with the appeal process. Guidance of a lawyer is recommended.

Usurpation of prosecutor's powers by a magistrate

My brother was charged and later convicted of breaking into a shop and stealing. It started when he was found to be in possession of stolen goods, and called to be a state witness. During his testimony against the accused, the Magistrate ordered that my brother be added to the charge sheet, along with the accused because the magistrate strongly believed that my brother had played a role in the offence. Is this fair? Does a magistrate have such powers?

4th October 2010

If all your facts are correct, your brother was wrongly added to the charge sheet

and hence wrongly convicted. The Criminal Procedure Act only empowers Courts of Law to amend a charge sheet where it is defective in either substance or form. The law does not give power to the Court to usurp the prosecutor's powers and order that a person be included in the charge sheet. In your case the Court misdirected itself. You have all the right to appeal – hopefully you are within the statutory period to appeal to the High Court of Tanzania.

Execution for vacant possession

In 2005, I won a case against a man whom I had sued in the High Court of Tanzania for adverse possession of my piece of land. The man died a few years later. The background is that the deceased had built a house on the land which he rented to another family. Last year, well after I had won the case, I filed an application for execution for vacant possession of my land, but my application failed because the occupants of the said house objected, alleging to be the owners, having bought the suit land from the deceased. The Judge entertained their objection, despite there being a judgment against the deceased. Is the Judge's decision not wrong? How can a judge make a mistake?

27th September 2010

The facts you have given us do not give detailed particulars of the objection put forward by your opponents (objectors), to enable us understand why the Judge made that decision. However, from a legal point of view, we can say that as far as you and the objectors are concerned, there is no basis of treating your application for vacant possession as being in execution of the decree you obtained against the deceased. Your victory against the deceased was a Judgment good only against the deceased and any one claiming under him. Strictly speaking, these objectors are not claiming under the deceased. They allege to be lawful owners of the suit land. The Court cannot, on the basis of that Judgment alone, order for vacant possession against the objectors. From the facts, our opinion is that the Judge was right in entertaining the objectors' objection. Unfortunate for you, but you will now have to file a suit for trespass against the objectors.

You have also asked, 'how can a judge make a mistake?' A judge is not an angel or a superhuman. He or she is a normal human just like you and us. There is no shortage of case law where judges have made mistakes – some of these mistakes have embarrassed some of the most senior Judges, not only in Tanzania, but around the world. This is the reason that there is an appeal mechanism, to ensure that justice does prevail.

Value of evidence by complainant's relatives

In 2007, my elder brother was accused of assault with intent to cause grievously bodily harm, and the incident was reported to the police station by the complainant's mother. The matter was brought before Mbeya District Court, where the case was heard, and he was convicted and sentenced to a prison sentence. In course of the hearing, the prosecution side brought five witnesses to prove their case. However, four of the prosecution witnesses, upon whom conviction was based, were the complainant's relatives. I sincerely state that my brother did not commit the alleged offence, and the Court should not have found him guilty, but had it not acted on the complainant's relatives' evidence, which in fact was unreal. What value does the evidence of the relative have in law? Can the Court convict solely on the testimony of relatives, and what are the chances of success on appeal? My brother filed his appeal to the High Court, but since 2008 his appeal has not been heard. The Court's clerks have failed to give any firm answer as to the date of the appeal. Is it not possible that the complainant's relatives are playing foul against my brother? Please advise me on the appropriate steps to take.

13ᵗʰ September 2010

From the facts, your main issue is whether a complainant's relatives can legally testify on his behalf. The law of evidence is very clear that every person is competent to testify unless the Court considers them to be incapable of understanding the questions put to him/her or cannot give rational answers to those questions by reasons of tender age (14-years-old or under), disease (whether of body or mind), or any other reason. There is no rule of practice or law which requires the evidence of relatives to be automatically discredited. In the absence of the exceptions given above, the evidence of a relative is as good as of any other person, and the Court can solely rely on it for proper conviction. However, if the said witnesses appear to be biased or have questionable credibility, the Court will receive such evidence with caution and will warn itself before relying on it during conviction. In such instance the Court will require some other evidence for corroboration. The defence counsel also plays a significant role in assisting the Court in reaching a just conclusion.

With regard to chances of success in your brother's appeal, this will depend entirely on the evidence in the Court records. The Appellate Court will examine the evidence and determine if the case was proved to the standards required by law, which in this circumstance is proof beyond reasonable doubt. It is the prosecution's side which is duty bound to prove their case beyond reasonable doubt, and should the defence be able to raise even the slightest doubt in the mind of the Magistrate or Judge, as the case might be, the Magistrate or Judge shall acquit the accused.

FB

Since the appeal is before the High Court, you are advised to contact the District Registrar of the respective High Court, who will inform you as to why your brother's appeal has not yet proceeded. There could be various reasons for the said delay.

New evidence in Court of Appeal

I have been in litigation in the High Court for the past eight years. The case has now been concluded and I have lodged an appeal. There is one particular key piece of evidence that was not produced at the High Court that I have requested my attorney to present. However, he has declined, saying the Court of Appeal disallows additional evidence. Is this true?

30th August 2010

The Civil Procedure Code Cap 33 (RE 2002) reads as follows: 'The parties to an appeal shall not be entitled to produce additional evidence, whether oral or documentary, in the Court. But if the Court from whose decree the appeal is preferred has refused to admit evidence which ought to have been admitted; or the Court requires any document to be produced or any witness to be examined to enable it to pronounce judgment, or for any other substantial cause, the Court may allow such evidence or document to be produced, or witness to be examined.'

It is not entirely true that you are disallowed to produce additional evidence. Unfortunately, we are unable to fully guide you as we are unsure what this evidence is and why you did not produce it at the trial Court. Your attorney should make an appropriate decision.

Courts misbehaving

I am a banker with twenty five years of experience and have worked in Tanzania for the past year and a half. In my Tanzanian experience I have noted that Tanzanian Courts are lenient towards borrowers who have defaulted. The Court does not seem to take cognizance of the fact that the borrower has taken money from the bank. Lawyers in Tanzania plead on behalf of the borrowers as if the defaulter has not taken any funds from the bank. How does one prosecute a case in Tanzania effectively? What other remedies does a banker have?

30th August 2010

There is no shortage of defaulters in this market – your observation is correct. However, we must draw your attention to the fact that in the eleven years of the existence of the High Court Commercial Division, banks have been highly successful in recovery cases. It is the Court of choice for bankers, and the Court has delivered some great results.

However, bankers are also at times to be blamed. For example, in third party mortgages, many banks in the past years have been exposed because they have forgotten to take spousal consent, allowing the property, mostly matrimonial property, to be mortgaged without such a consent. Banks have also failed to conduct due diligence and many disburse funds prior to perfection of securities. We do not believe that the Courts are to be blamed in isolation. Bankers tend to pin the blame on Courts, perhaps to impress their board of directors.

Turning to your question on other remedies that are available; please be informed that the law is very strict for borrowers. The law allows the bank to sell the mortgaged property after giving a sixty day notice, and without going to Court. You must appreciate that no law can substitute for banks conducting their due diligence before disbursement. The market here is challenging but has great potential. We hope your bank is not one that has engaged itself in loan disbursements prior to perfection of securities – the banks often defend themselves by claiming that the customer exerted a lot of pressure and hence the disbursement!

Judge made fun of my lawyer

I filed a suit at the High Court in Mwanza and lost the case. My lawyer told me during the Judgment the Judge made fun of him, clearly showing the Judge's bias. He has made jokes at my lawyer's expense, which is clear from the judgment. What can I do?

23rd August 2010

Among other things, a judgment contains facts from both parties' cases, a summary of witnesses' testimony, reasons for the decision, and the decision itself. We have not read the judgment, but merely because a Judge used some humour, which judges do use at times, does not mean that he was biased.

Different Judges have different writing styles – some are sober and straight; others write in a sarcastic and humorous manner. We have read judgments of Judges in the western world who have actually written judgments in the form of poetry. As long as the Judge has addressed the issue at hand, we do not see any valid reason for your lawyer to complain. He may be complaining about the Judge merely because he lost the case.

Instead of focusing on trivial points, look for important mistakes of fact or law in the Judgment and file an appeal.

Matters that can go to Commercial Court

My issue stems from a transaction I entered into, as an individual, to supply spare parts to a firm in the agriculture sector. I have not been paid on grounds that I supplied substandard parts, an allegation that I believe has no basis at all. I wish to file a case at the High Court Commercial division in Dar es Salaam, but have been informed by lawyers that I will not be able to file a suit at this Court because my matter is not a commercial dispute, as I am an individual. While I do acknowledge that I have not been trading as a company, I do not understand the rationale behind being disallowed. Do I have any remedy?

23rd August 2010

The High Court Commercial Division is a Court that has proved to be highly efficient and we understand why you want to file your case there.

Under the law, a commercial case is defined as one which involves a matter of commercial significance, including but not limited to the formation of business or commercial organisation, the governance of a business or commercial organisation, the contractual relationship between a business or commercial organisation with other bodies or persons outside it, the liability of a commercial or business organisation or its official arising out of its commercial or business activities, the liabilities of a commercial or business person arising out of its commercial or business activities, the restructuring or payment of commercial debt by or to a business or commercial organisation or person, the winding up or bankruptcy of a commercial or business organisation or persons, the enforcement of awards of a regional Court or tribunal of competent jurisdiction made in accordance with a treaty or mutual assistance arrangement to which Tanzania is signatory and which forms part of the laws of Tanzania, the enforcement of arbitration award, admiralty proceedings and arbitration proceedings.

The definition of a commercial matter is quite wide, and we fail to see why your matter, according to your lawyers, cannot be classified in any one of these categories above. Unless the value of the claim is below the pecuniary jurisdiction of the High Court, Commercial division, we do not see why you should not be able to file your case there. You may want to seek a second opinion.

Abuse of police powers

For the past four months, I have been arrested more than five times by an officer at a particular police post in my area on flimsy and vexatious allegations by my neighbour, who is unmarried and a rich business woman. There have never been any charges against me, and instead I end up spending the night at the police station. I have since found out that the woman is having very close relations with one of the officers at the station. How can I stop these arrests? Can I get a Court order to stop the police from arresting me?

9th August 2010

You have not informed us what the source of conflict is between you and this woman. There surely has to be something in her allegations that is causing all this friction. It might be a good idea to this find out.

You mentioned getting a Court order. You can lodge a complaint with the director of Public Prosecution's office, who will resolve your problem.

The matter does not end here. If the higher authorities conclude that the police officer has been arresting you for no good reason, or because of his relationship with the woman, you will have civil recourse against the police officer for abuse of office powers. Such tortuous acts, if proved in Court, are actionable, and there are damages that can be recovered by a victim thereof. In other jurisdictions the misuse of power by the police officer is called misfeasance in a public office.

Debt and civil prisoner

I failed to pay a debt because the money I

borrowed was used on another project. The Court ordered me to re-pay the amount, plus interest, and damages of TZS 100M. The lender is now threatening to imprison me for failure to settle the order of the Court. Can I be taken to jail simply for not paying the amount? This failure to pay is surely not equivalent to a criminal offence? Can the lender bully me like this?

9th August 2010

You must first realise that you did take the money, and did not use it for the purpose for which you borrowed it. If the lender is a bank, you must understand that it is the bank's depositors' money that has been lent to you. Unless there are details you have not provided us, we do not see any bullying here by the lender.

When it comes to civil imprisonment, the law is clear in that every Court decree for payment of money may be executed by the detention as a civil prisoner of the judgment debtor or by the attachment and sale of his property, or both.

Prior to being taken as a civil prisoner, the decree holder must deposit subsistence allowance into Court for the upkeep of the prisoner whilst he or she serves the sentence. Such a civil imprisonment sentence is for a maximum of six months and still does not relieve you of the debt you owe.

I do not know who to sue

I own a piece of un-surveyed land in Dar es Salaam. I have recently found 'fundis' constructing a wall on my land under instructions of the man who they simply refer to as their boss. My efforts to identify the alleged boss and his whereabouts have been futile. What should I do in the situation whereby the *fundis* are speeding up construction and I have no clue who to take to task?

2nd August 2010

Not being sure of who to sue should not mean you allow the *fundis* to continue building the wall. The *fundi* himself might be the trespasser! In such a situation, the law allows you to sue jointly all involved in the construction of this wall. You may sue the company constructing, the *fundis* in the company and any other person or company you reasonably believe is involved in this illegal activity. During the pendency of the suit, you should seek for temporary injunctive orders to restrain further construction of the wall.

Suing a magistrate for wrongful conviction

I was prosecuted for armed robbery before the district Court in the Morogoro Region and convicted to serve a thirty year sentence. Throughout the case I continually plead with the magistrate that I did not commit the said offence, but nonetheless she went on to sentence me. I appealed to the High Court, was successful, and was acquitted of the charges against me. I was wrongfully in prison for seven years, and I now want to sue the trial Magistrate for ruining my life and falsely imprisoning me. Can I sue the magistrate?

19th July 2010

In performing their duties, our Courts (Magistrates and Judges) are duty bound to conduct cases faithfully, without fear or any other interference. In the event of proved judicial misbehaviour or misconduct on the part of the presiding Magistrate or Judge, any affected party to the case can apply to the Court and require him/her to withdraw from conduct of the case. Magistrates and Judges hear and decide cases based on the evidence before them, and our laws clearly provide that no Magistrate or Judge will be liable for any wrong done, if the said act was done in the exercise of his/her official duties.

In your case, you have not mentioned any overt act of misconduct committed by the Trial Magistrate. The Trial Magistrate may have misled herself in examining and/or evaluating evidence adduced before her, but that alone cannot justify liability on her unless it is established that she acted malafide or unfaithfully, which does not seem to be the case here.

Right to be heard

My case at the High Court was heard in my absence. I neither received the summons, nor was I aware of the judgment against me. How do I get justice from our system if I am not informed? How could the Court Broker have managed to locate where I live to execute the judgment, whereas the Court Clerk who delivers the summons did not manage to locate me?

12th July 2010

Courts are guided by the principal of natural justice which states that no one should be condemned unheard. There are several judgments of the High Court and the Court of Appeal of Tanzania which elaborate on the right to be heard. The Courts have held that decisions reached without allowing the one party to be heard are a nullity and capable of being nullified. What you should immediately do is file an application to set aside the ex parte decision reached by the Court, stating the grounds for your non-appearance. You should also contact your attorney for further guidance.

Law firm fees

I am a citizen from Eastern Europe and have invested in Tanzania under the Tanzania Investment Centre (TIC) Certificate of Incentives. In 2008, I fought a major suit against a company here in Dar and used a Dar based law firm. The fee note that I have been sent s for 3% of the amount we litigated. Is that not absurd? Can the TIC assist in this, as I am a foreign investor? Investment agencies in other countries take complete care of their investors, including investor immunity. Please advise.

th July 2010

First and foremost, the TIC cannot assist in negotiating your legal fees for you. TIC looks for and facilitates investment for investors. It does not, and is not supposed to, micro-manage your project. We are not sure which countries' investment agencies negotiate legal fees for investors!

And as far as Tanzania is concerned, no one is above the law, and hence there is no investor immunity as such. While there may be some incentives for investors, these are all within certain limits, and no blanket immunities are issued.

Regarding the legal fees, the Advocates Remuneration and Taxation of Costs Rules covers the 3% that you are concerned about. The rules and the schedules to the rules are clear in that an attorney should charge 3% of the claim amount as a fixed fee. We are not sure of all the facts of the case, but we do not see anything wrong or peculiar in the percentage quoted to you.

Right of silence

I have read many times about one's right to remain silent when arrested. Can this be used against me in a Court of Law if I am prosecuted? Why does the law want me to remain silent when I am not guilty?

14th June 2010

We must mention at the outset that the law does not want you to remain silent. It is you who makes the decision to remain silent or not.

The Right to Silence is the right of someone charged with an offence, or being tried on a criminal charge, not to make any statement or give any evidence. It is often cited as a prime example of the fairness of the criminal justice system; it is meant to protect the innocent. However, many a times the Right to Silence has been criticised as unduly hampering the conviction of the guilty.

Normally the Right to Silence cannot be used against you in a Court. When arrested, because of the confusion that the arrest may cause, you not only have a right to remain silent, but have a right to a friend, relative or attorney. This, however, also depends on what you have been arrested for and the seriousness of the offence.

Civil imprisonment for judgment debtor

I lost a case at the High Court and been ordered to pay TZS 118M plus interest. I am not denying the amount, but have no means to pay this. What are the consequences of non-payment? My lawyer frightens me that if I fail to pay this amount, I shall be imprisoned. Can one be imprisoned for a civil case? If so, for how long?

21st June 2010

You are what is called a judgment-debtor, that is, a person whom a judgment has been obtained ordering him to pay a sum of money and it remains unsatisfied. The law is clear in that a judgment-debtor may be arrested in the course of the execution of a decree at any hour and on any day, and shall, as soon as practicable, be brought before the Court, and the Court may order his detention. The law further provides that where a judgment-debtor is arrested in execution of a decree for the payment of money and brought before the Court, the Court shall inform him that he may apply to be declared an insolvent, and that he will be discharged if he has not committed any act of bad faith regarding the subject matter of the application, and if he complies with the provisions of the law of insolvency for the time being in force. Should you not file an application for insolvency, the period you are likely to be imprisoned for is six months. During such imprisonment, the judgment creditor is supposed to pay the judgment debtor a subsistence allowance. The answer to your question on whether one can be committed to civil imprisonment is therefore in the affirmative.

Suing a prisoner

I have instituted a recovery suit against a friend of mine who is now serving a three year prison sentence for a criminal offence. The Magistrate is unwilling to serve the summons on the defendant, claiming that he is already in prison. Is there a law that does not allow me to sue this prisoner? How do I proceed? My lawyer says we should file an application to proceed with the case ex parte.

21st June 2010

The Magistrate is wrong in not proceeding with the case. There is no law that bars one from suing someone in prison. In fact, the prison authorities would allow the prisoner to go to Court to defend his suit, if he is summoned to do so. We do not see why the Magistrate is preventing you from proceeding with the case. If this continues you may pray for the Magistrate to withdraw from the case and the case to be reassigned.

We are not comfortable with the strategy suggested by your lawyer. What he is proposing, an ex parte hearing, is a hearing conducted without the other party being present. It is against the principles of natural justice to proceed with an ex parte hearing when the defendant has not been served or is already in default. In the unlikely event that you get such an order, it may be challenged at a later stage and delay your recovery.

Warrant of arrest for non appearance

A warrant of arrest has been issued against me for non-appearance when my criminal case was called. The arresting police officer insisted on arresting me, despite the good explanation that I gave that I was actually at the Court premises and I did not hear my case being called. What should I do? Can the Court just convict me like this?

7th June 2010

In a case of this nature, a warrant of arrest is not the end of the case. The order for arrest will always require the person being arrested to demonstrate why he should not be punished for his non-appearance when his case was called. If the Court is satisfied with the explanations given, then the order for arrest will be vacated. In your case, we cannot see any problem if what you have said is true and you can clearly explain, to the satisfaction of the Court, that you arrived on time and did not hear your case being called.

Regarding the arresting police officer's refusal to accept your explanation, our opinion is that the police officer was right, for an order of arrest is a lawful order of the Court, and cannot be amended by the police. The police officer's duty and obligation is no more than to arrest and place the person arrested before the Court for further orders or directives. Should you still worry, we advise you to seek legal assistance.

As for what you call the conviction, please note that this is not a conviction on the main charges you face. The case will still have to proceed before a final judgment is delivered.

Charged with traffic offence

I was charged with a traffic offence of driving on the road side, despite this being common practice in Dar es Salaam. The traffic officers insisted that I am liable for the offence. Is this just? Why only me? I was asked to pay the fine at that instance, but refused as I was not getting a receipt for the payment.

7th June 2010

From the facts you have given us it is not in dispute that you committed an offence you are charged with. Although the fact that it is a tendency for most drivers in Dar es Salaam to drive on the road sides, this alone does not justify your action. It can merely apply to mitigate seriousness of the offence and may lead to your acquittal depending on how you put up your defence. Under the Penal Code of Tanzanian Law, a person who commits an act under an honest and reasonable, but mistaken, belief as to the existence of any state of things, may not be criminally responsible for the act, to any greater extent than the real state of things had they been as he believed them to be. In your situation, survival of conviction will depend on the prosecution's evidence and the way you will put up your defence.

As for the payment of the fine on the roadside, it is likely that it was a demand for a bribe. When paying a fine, a receipt is what you should demand for. Bribes usually come with no receipts.

Policeman slapped me

I was driving peacefully one day when a traffic police officer on a motorbike pulled me over. He asked me for my driving license and registration card, which I duly complied with. He then checked my insurance sticker, extinguisher, lights and triangle and could not find any fault in my car. Then, without even looking at my tyres, he said that my tyres were worn out and that I would have to pay a fine for driving a vehicle unfit for the road. I decided to check the tyres myself, as I was driving a brand new Toyota Land cruiser, and was unsure if his allegations were true. The tyres were brand new, and I informed the officer accordingly. He was not amused and he started giving me a lecture on how arrogant we the *mzungu* community are in Tanzania. He then took my license and pulled my insurance sticker to which I protested as I had no clue why he was taking such action. I was sure this was unfair and we started arguing, and a few minutes into the argument he slapped and pushed me. I have been in the country for less than six months. Is it legal for a traffic police to act like this? Can he call me a *mzungu*?

31st May 2010

Unless the policeman was acting in self defence (assuming you tried to attack him), he cannot slap anyone, including a traffic offender. From the facts, we do not see any signs of aggression from your end, so the slapping amounts to an assault and is a criminal offence. You can file a complaint against this policeman at any police station, and he may be charged for acting beyond his powers. We recall that a few years ago there was a similar occurrence, and it had resulted in the dismissal of the police officer. We suggest that you also lodge an official complaint with the head of traffic police at Dar es Salaam, who shall investigate the matter.

As for calling you a *mzungu* (white person), the word *mzungu* is not derogatory in its ordinary meaning so we do not see anything offensive about the word. Other commonly used words in Kiswahili include *mhindi* (Asian) and *mwarabu* (Arab). From the facts above, we do not believe that you have a cause of action against the police officer for calling you a *mzungu*.

Also note that a police officer cannot just take your insurance sticker and driving license. When he does so, he is acting ultra vires (beyond his powers).

Release of convicted offenders on probation

I am a business woman owning several chicken farms. Near one of the farms there are street children who have been stealing chickens. I reported the matter to the police and two of the culprits were arrested and also admitted the offence. They were sentenced to imprisonment, but the magistrate released them on probation for a period of six months. I wanted them to be imprisoned. Is it correct for the magistrate to let them go on probation? I want to teach the children a lesson. What should I do?

24th May 2010

We start answering your question with sympathy for both sides – whilst you have lost some chicken, you must be mindful that these are young children, maybe orphans, with no shelter or food. These are also children who have no education and have lost all hope in life. You might want to reconsider your aggressive approach and behave in a more humanitarian fashion.

Coming back to the law, according to the Probation of Offenders Act, if the Court is of the view that considering the age, the nature of the offence and mental condition of the offender, it is better to release the offender under probation, the Court is empowered to release the offender for a period not more than three years, and the offender will be under constant supervision by the police. If the offender commits the same offence within the three years, then the offender will be re-arrested and he/she will finish the rest of his/her sentence in prison. This is also to reduce the congestion in prisons.

Much as you would like the offenders to go to prison, Magistrate has done nothing wrong and it is unlikely that you can influence the Magistrate's decision.

Admission of loss

My younger brother was working in a company as a store keeper. The company deals with wholesale and retail power equipment.

Whilst stocktaking, there was a loss that was observed. My brother admitted the loss and was taken to the police, where he is currently being investigated. What should we do?

8th March 2010

The entire case depends on the investigation of the police. In Criminal Law, admission of loss does not necessarily mean it is an admission of theft. In order to commit the offence of theft, there must be a dishonest taking or appropriation of another's property. In this case, it will depend on the evidence adduced by the prosecution. It is very difficult for us to predict his guilt or innocence without knowing the contents of the investigation. It is also possible that the loss could have occurred because of bookkeeping errors or pilferage by others, not necessarily your brother. This questioned has been answered on the basis that your brother admitted the loss. Should he have admitted to the theft, our opinion will change in its entirety.

Acquittal of the co accused

A relative of mine and two others were arrested for an offence and sent to Court, where we bailed him out. The case has been proceeding in Court and when the prosecution completed their case, the magistrate surprisingly released the other two but not my relative. It shocks me that the case is over and my friend is still in prison.

3rd May 2010

Criminal cases are different from civil cases. Normally, when the investigation is complete, the prosecution side has to proceed with a preliminary hearing to determine facts which are in dispute and facts which are not in dispute. After this, the prosecution will bring witnesses to build their case. When all the witnesses are called by the prosecution, and before the accused persons are called upon to open their defence, the Court must deliver a ruling as to whether the accused have a case to answer or not. The Court has to pass this ruling based on, among other things, the evidence adduced by the witnesses on the accused's participation in the offence.

The law is very clear in that if it is clear to the Court that a case against the accused person is not sufficient to require him to make a defence either in relation to the offence which he is charged with, or in relation to any other offence of which he is liable to be convicted, the Court shall acquit the accused person.

It is likely this is what happened in the case you are referring to. From the face of it, it seems like the two co-accused have no case to answer, whereas the Magistrate believes your friend has a case to answer. This is not the end of the case – your friend will now open his defence. But having a case to answer does not mean that your friend is guilty. The case is yet not over for this friend of yours.

Prosecutor agrees bail, magistrate refuses

My young brother was brought before the Resident Magistrate's Court where certain charges were read out. The prosecutor did not object to bail but the magistrate blindly refused. Is she not going to convict the accused at the end of the day? What should I do?

26th April 2012

First of all, be informed that the granting or refusal of bail by the trial Court does not necessarily mean that the accused will be convicted or acquitted. Denial or grant of bail in criminal proceedings has no connection with the outcome of the case. Whether the accused will be acquitted or convicted in a criminal case depends on the proof adduced by the prosecution and the defence.

In any criminal case, whether bail should be granted or not is the judicial discretion of the Court itself, which depends on the nature and circumstances of each case. If the prosecution does not challenge bail, bail is not automatically granted. You have not mentioned what your brother has been charged with; in any case, the Magistrate has powers to deny bail on various grounds. Should you think that the Court's order was improper then you can appeal against the order to the High Court. Your attorneys can guide you further based on the charges against the accused.

Threats to commit an offence

My house was set on fire while I was travelling. The police have not taken the person who had previously threatened to set my house on fire and who is obviously responsible for this act to Court. What should I do to make sure this man is prosecuted? I am informed that the brother of the man who burnt my house has already spoken to the Police and hence the delay in taking him to Court.

12th April 2010

First of all, we wish to inform you that the police do not take every case reported to them, to Court, except those cases which are supported by evidence. Also the allegations that your offender's brother has been dealing with the police officers to avoid the offender from being taken to Court are mere allegations which unless proven cannot hold any merit.

Coming back to your issue – as indicated before, threats alone cannot be conclusive evidence that a person who uttered threats in the past has committed the offence. It might be likely that he committed the offence but that is not conclusive. There must be something tangible other than the occurrence of the threatened act to indicate that the offender did carry out his threat. In your case for example, you have not told us whether there are any witnesses who can prove that the alleged man set fire to your house The reason the purported offender may not have been taken to Court is that the evidence against him maybe weak. Unfortunately, we do not have enough information on the evidence that you have presented to the police to guide you further. In any case you may lodge a complaint letter to the principal state attorney in charge at your zone for his intervention.

Failure to reply to counterclaim

The Court has passed a default judgment against me on pretext that I have not responded to counter claims raised by the Defendant in his defence against me. This is despite the fact that my case is not yet determined. How can I suffer when I am the claimant? Can I successfully appeal against this ex parte decision?

15th March 2010

Claims raised by the defendant in his defence against the plaintiff are in legal language called a 'counter claim'. A counter claim bears the same characteristics and requirements as a plaint (a statement of claim by the plaintiff). A counter claim is a statement of claim which states claims by the defendant against the plaintiff in the latter's case. Such claims by the Defendant need not be the same as those of the plaintiff or arise from the same transaction. Since a counter claim is a cross suit, the law requires a person (plaintiff) against whom a counter claim is brought to respond to it within the prescribed time set by law, which is usually twenty one days. Failure to file a defence to the counter claim, empowers the Court to pass any adverse orders against the defaulter which includes but not limited to default judgment depending on the interdependency of the

claims of both the plaintiff and the defendant.

Whether you can successfully appeal against the default judgment passed against you will also depend on the facts and legal issues pertaining to the counter claim itself. However, as a matter of procedure you will need to make an application in Court to set aside the default judgment. Chances of succeeding in this application will depend on the reasons that you present on why you failed to reply to the counterclaim.

Confiscation of passport

I travel to China every few weeks to purchase female clothing. In mid-September I was arrested for under declaring goods on arrival and of forging invoices which is common in Tanzania. I do not see anything wrong in this as changing invoice value is common here. After being arrested I was taken to the police station where I spent the weekend. The following week I was charged at the Kisutu Court, and was bailed out. As a condition to bail, the magistrate demanded that I deposit my passport with her. However, due to the nature of my business I need to travel a lot. What should I do? Can the Court not release the passport back to me so that I can temporarily travel? I am losing business due to this. Please help.

5th April 2010

Any person accused of committing a crime is presumed innocent until proven guilty in a Court of Law with competent jurisdiction. Such a person charged with a crime has a right to bail unless the person is charged with offences which are unbailable such as murder, treason and armed robbery.

Bail is to set at liberty a person arrested or imprisoned, on security being taken for their appearance on a certain day and a place. In granting bail to accused persons, apart from the bond executed with or without sureties is sufficient security for his appearance, the Court may also impose mandatory conditions which are for the accused person to surrender his or her passport or any other travel document and restrict movement of the accused to a certain area. In addition to these requirements the Court may require the accused person to report at a police station or other authority within the area of his residence, abstain from visiting particular locality or premises or associate with certain specified persons and any other conditions which the Court may deem proper and just to impose. The condition to surrender passport and other travel documents is to ensure that the accused will attend Court on a fixed date. We suggest that on the hearing date, your attorney makes an application for the release of the passport, by giving reasons that will convince the Magistrate that you will show up during the course of the subsequent hearings.

We also wish to add that forging invoices is indeed a criminal offence and your defence of it being common practice or rather market practice holds no legal basis. The mess that you are in now is as a result of your own doings; without sounding like preachers, you should refrain from this kind of behaviour.

Denial of bail on grounds of safety

My brother has been arraigned for a criminal offence at the Resident Magistrate's Court of Mara region at Musoma. The prosecutor has successfully moved the trial Court date so as to avoid granting bail to the accused on the ground that the accused's safety will be in jeopardy if granted bail. Is this a good ground for denying bail?

22h March 2010

Bail is the accused's right. However, Courts have been vested with discretionary powers to refuse or grant bail to the accused depending on the nature of the offence with which the

accused is charged. Under section 148(5)(d) of the Criminal Procedure Act the Court is empowered to keep the accused person in custody for his own protection or safety when or if the situation renders so necessary. Before the Court can exercise such powers, it is the duty of the prosecution to satisfy the Court with definite reasons supported by proved and admitted facts showing reasonable cause for the belief that the accused's safety will be in jeopardy if released on bail. Vague fears or suspicion by the police that accused safety will be in danger can not suffice. The test under the law is not whether it would be better for the accused to be kept in custody for his own safety but rather whether it is necessary that the accused should be kept in custody for his own good. The prosecution must therefore give concrete evidence to show clearly that the accused safety is in danger and such information must be verified as to its authenticity.

In your case you have not told us the offence your brother is facing nor have you availed to us the information or reasons the prosecutor advanced to Court for the prayer to enable us give our views. However, should you think that the decision of the Court was not based on proved facts, you can refer this matter to the High Court.

Dismissal of a suit despite advocate's letter for adjournment

I have been in litigation over a claim for two years now. Recently the trial magistrate dismissed my suit despite both the advocates' having jointly filed a letter to the Court for adjournment. Is this fair? Can I successfully challenge the dismissal order?

29th March 2010

We cannot guide you in depth since we do not have the facts as to why the advocates were seeking an adjournment and why the

Judge refused to grant the same.

Whatever the facts may be, we wish to point out the law to you. The Civil Procedure Code, Cap 33 (R.E 2002) has given discretional powers to the Courts to regulate their own proceedings, including powers to adjourn or not to adjourn cases. Although a consent letter by advocates might be a factor which may be taken into consideration in an application for adjournment, such consent cannot automatically result in adjournment. A High Court Judge once said 'in a case that business of the Courts is not subject to the vagaries of the business activities of advocates engaged by the litigants'.

You may decide to appeal and the success of your appeal will depend on the circumstances of your case and more particularly on the reasons stated in the joint adjournment letter. You may also wish to note that Courts are now becoming increasingly strict in granting adjournments as cases are getting delayed, to the detriment of the party seeking justice.

Service of summons through newspapers

Recently, I learnt from a local newspaper that a suit has been instituted against me at the Kisutu Court and that I should appear to defend it. Unfortunately, I was busy with official matters and thus could not appear. Astonishingly, I have been served with Court papers showing that an ex-parte judgment has been passed against me despite all the correspondences with the Magistrate in charge where I have clearly stated that I shall advise the Court when I could appear before it. Despite my openness with the Court, this has happened. Is this fair?

22nd March 2010

Being summoned to Court is not an appointment at a hairdresser that can 'just'

be rescheduled. A Court dispenses justice and it cannot necessarily agree to follow your schedule, especially when you have unreasonably told the Court that you will get back to it without a firm commitment.

From the facts given above, it is clear that you were properly served with the summons and hence you cannot claim that you were unaware of the proceedings in Court. Where proceedings are instituted and summons served on the defendant, the procedure is for the Defendant or his/her advocate to file a Written Statement of Defence in accordance with the law (Civil Procedure Code, CAP 33 (R.E. 2002)) You are to blame for the situation you are in now. You can only rescue the situation by making an application to Court to set aside the ex-parte judgment if you can show good cause why you did not appear in Court when summoned. The application to set aside the ex-parte judgment has to be made within thirty days from when the said ex-parte judgment was communicated to you otherwise you will have to apply for extension of time. We suggest you seek legal advice.

Arbitration at the ICC

I entered into a contract with a foreign supplier where the arbitration clause reads 'ICC rules Paris'. I signed the contract and we are at loggerheads now. How do I refer this issue to the ICC and how does the process work? What are the charges and can a Tanzanian refer the matter to ICC? Can I not arbitrate in Tanzania?

29nd March 2010

The ICC, International Court of Arbitration was created in 1923. This Court is composed of members from ninety different countries. It does not itself settle disputes but supervises the arbitration process from its inception to the rendering of an enforceable award. All ICC awards are scrutinised by the ICC

International Court of Arbitration.

ICC does not require, or give official endorsement to any standard form of Request for Arbitration under its rules. This is to preserve the necessary flexibility and adaptability of ICC arbitration, which is international in scope. Article 4(3) of the rules states, however, that: 'The Request to ICC shall, inter alia, contain the following information: the name in full, description and address of each of the parties; a description of the nature and circumstances of the dispute giving rise to the claims; a statement of the relief sought, including, to the extent possible, an indication of any amount(s) claimed; the relevant agreements and, in particular, the arbitration agreement; all relevant particulars concerning the number of arbitrators and their choice in accordance with the provisions of ICC articles, and any nomination of an arbitrator required thereby; and any comments as to the place of arbitration, the applicable rules of law and the language of the arbitration.'

According to the ICC, parties should be aware that: the place of arbitration is fixed by the Court unless agreed upon by the parties; the applicable rules of law are those which the Arbitral Tribunal determines to be appropriate, unless otherwise agreed by the parties; and that the language(s) of arbitration is (are) determined by the Arbitral Tribunal in the absence of an agreement by the parties.

The parties' position and views on these issues may be included in the Request and the Answer, which may constitute an agreement on one or more of the issues. Failing agreement, the parties' comments will be considered by the Court or the Arbitral Tribunal in making their decision(s) on such issues.

You may want to note that each Request for Arbitration must be accompanied by a non-refundable advance payment of USD 2,500. Our experience is that ICC arbitration is effective but also very expensive. It all depends on what amounts are being contested to make it economical to pursue.

As for whether you can arbitrate in Tanzania or not, our answer is in the negative. You had the chance to read the contract, to which you agreed to this ICC clause. It is very unlikely that your request for arbitration in Tanzania will be granted unless the other party consents to this request.

Court moving sua moto

Can a Court, on its own, summon a witness although both parties have not asked for such a witness to be examined? In a case that I filed, I was shocked to see that the Judge sent a summons to some person we had mentioned during the course of the trial, whom neither the defence nor plaintiff's lawyers required. Is this procedurally correct?

8th March 2010

Generally it is the duty of the parties to a claim to prove a claim. The Court usually summons witnesses if asked by the parties to do so and a failure to call a witness cannot be blamed on the Court. However, should the Court think it is in the interest of justice to summon appearance of a certain witness, to prove or disprove a certain fact, it has all the powers to do so sua moto, provided the parties are given a chance for the witness to be cross examined. There is nothing procedurally wrong with what was done in your case.

Appeal on guilty plea

What does the law say about a person who pleads guilty in Court and then appeals, claiming that he did not admit the offence on the ground that he did not understand the charge? There have been two instances of such cases in Mbeya that I have seen.

15th March 2010

A person who pleads guilty has the right to change his plea before the judgment is entered. As a general principle, once judgment is entered under the assumption that the charge has been read, explained and understood by the accused, he cannot appeal against the conviction. We do not have all the facts pertaining to the case and how the plea of guilty was entered. Courts in Tanzania have held that when a conviction is likely to proceed on a plea of guilty, it is most desirable that every constituent of the charge be explained to the accused and that he should be required to admit or deny every element of it, unequivocally. For instance, if one is asked whether he is guilty or not, and he responds by saying 'it is true', that does not, in the eyes of the law, necessarily mean that he meant a plea of guilty. We suggest you get on board an attorney to assist you decide on the chances of succeeding in your appeal.

Circumstantial evidence leading to acquittal

I own a bar that works till late at night. Last year, my accountant, who was the only person left in the bar, calculating sales and tallying cash, reported a cash loss of TZS 2M. It could not have been anyone else but him who took the funds. There was no lock or safe broken into. Both the keys to the safe room and the accounts room were with the accountant. I reported this to the police who charged the accountant with stealing. The accountant has now been acquitted. Is this fair? My insurance is also reluctant to cover for this loss? What should I do?

1st March 2010

In Criminal Law, the standard of proof is beyond a reasonable doubt. Hence, if the defence attorneys can raise even a little bit of doubt in the mind of the Magistrate, that there exists a chance, be it a very slim chance, that the accused is not the one who committed the offence, the Magistrate will pronounce an acquittal.

In your case, it seems that the prosecution was relying on circumstantial evidence, that is indirect evidence, which did not convince the Court to point out, irresistibly, to the guilt of the accused, and hence the acquittal.

As for your burglary insurance, it is standard insurance practice that there should be a theft for the insurance to come into play. In the standard burglary insurance cover, theft by employee is not covered. Theft by employee is normally covered in fidelity insurance. In this instance, proving theft will be a challenge as there is no break in. Both the safe and the doors were found to be intact indicating that it is likely an inside job or an error in the calculation. We suggest you contact your broker for more advice on the exact scope of cover you have.

Assessors in a trial

I am a law student and attended a criminal session at the High Court in Dodoma. During the trial, I noticed that the Judge was not availing an opportunity to the assessors to ask questions to the witnesses. Does this not jeopardize the dispensation of justice?

22nd February 2010

The assessors' duty in a trial is to aid the trial Judge in accordance with the Criminal Procedure Act and to do this they may put their questions. The assessors cannot be stopped from putting their questions although the Judge has discretion to prevent the asking of questions which are biased or improper to the subject matter.

Denying the assessors the opportunity to direct questions to witnesses means that the assessors were excluded from fully participating in the trial and effectively disabled from aiding the Judge. This is improper and on appeal this could be held as a mistrial.

Irrelevant questions to witness

I was summoned as a witness in a certain case. It really bothered me because the defence counsel kept on asking me irrelevant questions. The magistrate was also not very useful as she insisted I answer some of the questions adding more questions herself. How can we make sure justice is done?

15th February 2010

The defence counsel are known to ask witnesses difficult questions to challenge the credibility of any witness. That is what a defence counsel is trained to do. Without knowing what questions were asked, we cannot tell if they were relevant or not.

Also, there is nothing wrong in the Magistrate asking you questions unless he or she was forcing you to answer in a manner that you did not want to.

Change of plea before sentence

A 17-year-old boy, with a questionable state of mind, was charged of raping my 15-year-old daughter. When arraigned he volunteered a confession and the juvenile Court accepted his plea of guilty. He was remanded awaiting a medical report. On the adjourned hearing he sought to change his plea and the trial magistrate agreed. The magistrate then rectified her records and ordered that the case proceed by calling upon the prosecution side to produce witnesses. Was this procedurally correct? How can one change a guilty plea to not guilty?

8th February 2010

In criminal proceedings, arraignment is said to be complete when the accused has pleaded. It can be a plea of guilty or not guilty. Plea of guilty is a confession by the accused of the offence he or she is charged with. Once a plea of guilty is entered, the trial Court proceeds to enter conviction. It should be noted that this is not the end of the trial for the trial of a criminal case ends upon a Court imposing the sentence. However, the law does not, unless the sentence is passed, bar an accused who has pleaded guilty to withdraw his plea of guilty and substitute it with that of not guilty. When this happens, the trial Court has to accept the withdrawal of the accused's plea of guilty, short of it will render the whole trial a nullity. While we sympathise with you for the inhuman action done to your daughter, we decline to say that the procedure adopted by the trial Court was improper. After all, changing plea does not rescue the accused; the law will take its course.

Single witness conviction

In March 2009, I was charged with the offence of obtaining a large amount of money by false pretence. I was tried and convicted based on the testimony of only one witness and was sent to three years imprisonment. How could I be convicted based on the evidence of a single witness?

1st February 2010

From our experience as advocates and trained lawyers, we are sorry to inform you that there is no way one can successfully fault a decision of the Court solely on the ground that the Court had acted on the evidence of a single witness unless one can show that the prosecution evidence, as a whole, was insufficient to warrant a conviction against the offence or that in convicting the accused, the Court had acted on the wrong principle of law.

Like in many other jurisdictions, our law of evidence is clear in that what matters is not the number of witnesses but the weight of evidence.

Unless the evidence of the sole witness in a case is weak, or if such evidence which desirably requires corroboration, which does not seem to be the case here, there is no way the appellate Court can disturb the findings of the trial Court.

Should you believe your situation to be different from the one referred to here, we advise you, subject to limitation of time, to appeal against the decision of the trial Court.

Preliminary objection on lease

My lawyer has raised a preliminary objection on a lease claiming that the lease never existed and that I, as the tenant, never signed on the lease. He tells me that this will dispose of the suit? Is this correct? Do you think I should go ahead?

25th January 2010

You have raised some very interesting points. First, after you have admitted in the question that you are a tenant and you also further assert that there is no lease. You cannot say that there is no lease at all because there has to be a landlord for there to be a tenant. We are unsure of your motives!

In our opinion, the preliminary objection will not succeed purely because such an objection normally raises a point of law which is argued on the assumption that all the facts pleaded by the other side are correct. It cannot be raised if any fact has to be ascertained. In your case, your lawyer's opinion is that a lease does not exist. The other party seems to be relying on it. Since there is a need for the Court to look into the existence of the lease, the preliminary objection cannot be upheld and stands to fail.

Effect of plea of guilty on sentence

In January 2009, my friend and I were charged with armed robbery at the Ilala District Court in Dar es Salaam. When called upon to plead, I pleaded guilty to the offence and was accordingly convicted and

sentenced to jail for a term of thirty years. The trial then proceeded against my friend and at the end of the trial he was also found guilty, convicted and sentenced to jail for a term of thirty years. Was the sentence of thirty years imprisonment against me fair? Was I not entitled to a more lenient sentence due to pleading guilty to the offence? Can I successfully appeal against such a sentence?

18th January 2010

It is a well established principle that the offender's remorse expressed inter-alia in a plea of guilty is a mitigating factor which may reduce the sentence below the level appropriate to the offence; the offender's insistence on being tried does not justify a sentence above that level. However, allowance in mitigating for remorse is at the discretion of the Court and does not automatically follow a plea of guilty. In some cases Courts are entitled to consider the extent of the offender's remorse and make greater allowances. In a case of an example where the offender does not dispute the prosecution case which is supported by overwhelming evidence or in a manslaughter case where the offender deeply regrets the killing as a result of say drunkenness.

In your case, things are slightly different. Armed robbery is a scheduled offence i.e. offences whose sentences are fixed by the law. Courts have no discretion to give any allowances in sentencing for scheduled offences. Since you pleaded guilty, we have no advice to offer except to tell you to serve your custodial sentence.

On whether you can appeal or not, the law i.e. Criminal Procedure Act bars appeals against convictions upon which a plea of guilty is entered unless it was an equivocal plea of guilty and the sentence imposed was excessive. Unless you are telling us that you did not clearly understand what you pleaded, we are sorry to inform you that the sentence imposed against you was proper in the eyes of the law. Armed robbery is a serious offence and the law takes it very seriously.

Time limit to sue

I am a businessman who used to own a tourist safari company in Tanzania. For the past ten years I have lived in Sweden. My uncle who is a fellow shareholder was taking care of the business until it collapsed because of a reduction in the number of tourists. I have now moved back to Tanzania only to find that the company went under because there was a massive fraud in the company. I now want to recover the money from my uncle who was involved in this. My lawyers inform me that since this is based on a contract, I cannot sue since the time limitation to sue has elapsed. What law is this? Please advise on how I can recover the money.

18ᵗʰ January 2010

It is the Law of Limitation Act (CAP 89 R.E. 2002) which prescribes periods within which proceedings to enforce a right must be taken or the action becomes time barred. It is true that the Limitation Act has set a limitation period of six years for suits founded on contract save only where it is specifically provided otherwise.

However, in your case there is a fraud issue and hence the limitation to sue on contract does not start to run until the time you discovered the fraud. You are hence within the time in which to sue based on your contract.

Also note that in criminal matters, such as fraud, there is no time limitation as far as the criminal justice system is concerned. We do not see any obstacles in you suing for recovery.

Arbitration cheaper than Court

I am negotiating a contract and the other party wants to insert an arbitration clause that in case of a dispute, we submit fully to arbitration because it is cheaper. I am wor-ried as we have not even signed the contract and the other party is sceptical about it. Do you think I should go ahead?

11ᵗʰ January 2010

The principle alternative to a Court of Law is to submit to arbitration. Arbitration gives the parties the opportunity to choose a neutral forum and a neutral tribunal and it also leads to a decision which is enforceable against the losing party not only in the place where it is made but also internationally under the provisions of such treaties as the New York convention. While arbitration is also generally faster than going to Court, in our opinion arbitration is certainly not cheaper than going to Court. There are various fees that need to be paid – the arbitrators fees, rental of the arbitration hall, travel expenses for the lawyers handling the case and the lawyer's fees. These all add up to make arbitration even more expensive than going to Court. The major advantage is the speed with which a result is achieved. Other disadvantages of arbitration include the limited powers of arbitrators, conflicting awards and the general inability to bring multi-party disputes before it. The creativity that lawyers have in Courts is quite widely diminished when you go for arbitration.

A party that proposes an arbitration clause in a contract need not be viewed suspiciously, unless of course there are other factors that worry you. It is better you negotiate a contract properly in the beginning rather than start looking for excuses later.

We do not wish to comment on whether you should proceed with the contract or not; that is a commercial decision.

Kenyan judgment in Tanzanian Court

I have lost a case at the High Court in Kenya. The judgment Creditor, has registered the Kenyan Judgment at the Commercial Court in Tanzania, which has in turn issued a summons where I have to show cause why my assets should not be seized to satisfy the amount owed or why I should not be held as a civil prisoner if I fail to pay the amount owed. My lawyers have lodged an appeal at the Court of Appeal in Kenya but the appeal has yet to be heard. I am really scared and feel like running away. What do you advise me to do?

4th January 2010

We assume you want us to advise you on what to do in Court and not whether or not you should run away!

Your matter is not as complicated as it sounds. The Appeal in Kenya saves the day for you. That is good ground for you to pray in Court that the registration of the judgment be set aside pending the appeal. This derives from simple logic that the case is still pending in Kenya. We would be very surprised if your prayer is not granted.

Summons not received

A gentleman claiming to have come from the High Court Commercial Division came to my office six months ago. He had some papers from the Court which I told my secretary not to receive until I came back. On arriving, the officer had left my office. Is there something I should do? What would these papers be?

28th December 2009

It is very likely that the person was carrying a summons to appear. There is no law that disallows your secretary to receive Court summons. Six months is a long period and it is possible that the case is proceeding ex parte against you.

We suggest you immediately go to the High Court, Commercial Division and peruse the registry there to see if there is a case instituted against you, any members of your family or any company that you are directly or indirectly associated with.

Joined in a case

I am the second defendant in a case and have no clue why I have been joined. The plot of land which is the subject matter of the case does not belong to me and I am neither a neighbour nor a friend of anyone in the case. I do not know either party and am unsure what is going on. What should I do?

14th December 2009

We are unsure why you say you do not know the reason you have been sued. The plaint filed in Court will have all the details including why you have been sued. Unless there is something that you are concealing, it seems like you have been joined in the case by mistake.

This is a misjoinder i.e. where persons are wrongly joined as plaintiffs or defendants meaning that persons are made parties who ought not to be, which seems to be the case with you. You can make a formal application in Court to cease to be a party and the Court may, based on the reasons you adduce, make appropriate orders. This opinion will not hold if there are facts you have concealed.

Injunction ongoing, suit dismissed

I filed a case at the High Court Lands Division in Dar es Salaam, and got an injunction restraining the defendant from demolishing a building in which I am a tenant. The building is owned by the National Housing Corporation (NHC) who are the defendants in the case. NHC came up with a technical point and the case got dismissed on a pure technicality. Is that not unjust? My lawyer, however, assures me that the injunction we got is still valid as it has been typed and given to us prior? What should I do?

7th December 2009

An injunction is a judicial remedy whereby a person is directed to restrain from doing or to do a particular act or thing. It is very likely your injunction is temporary in nature. Usually no relief can be granted which goes beyond the main relief sought for in the main suit.

Whether it is just or unjust for your suit to be dismissed on technical grounds will depend on what those grounds are. Perhaps the plaint was faulty and incurable and hence the dismissal. Either way, your injunction is vacated and invalid as soon as your main suit is dismissed. Your lawyer is misleading you, in that your injunction still holds. It is immaterial if it is typed or not. In short, the dismissal of the suit paves way for the NHC to demolish your building if you do not reinstitute your suit and get the necessary injunction.

Powers of arrest when suspected of terrorism

Seven plain clothed police officers stormed into my shop to search my premises. They claimed that they suspected me of being involved in terrorism activities because I am in the hunting business. They did not find anything after a five hour search. What are my rights under the law? Should they have not come with a warrant to search or detain?

14th December 2009

The Prevention of Terrorism Act gives the police blanket powers to search and/or detain anyone or anything if they reasonably suspect that such a person or thing is going to be used in the commission in an act of terrorism. The Act allows the police officers, not below the rank of assistant superintendent, to conduct such a search in the interest of public security without a warrant. Hence in your case, the police officers had the right to conduct the search provided at least one of the police officers was not below the rank of assistant superintendent. You do not have to be in the hunting business for them to justify a search. It applies across the board to everyone in any industry.

Family problems as factor in sentencing

My son was convicted of stealing from his employer and sentenced to jail for a period of three years. I am a widow, my son is divorced and the whereabouts of his former wife are unknown. My son had custody of two children whom I have now started taking care of. All these were explained to the Magistrate yet he was given such an excessive sentence. Is there any way he can have his sentence reduced? Please assist.

21st December 2009

The three years sentence in your opinion is excessive. This is a subjective issue and perhaps the person from whom your son stole thinks he should have had a more severe sentence. All in all, we are unsure who your son stole from, but say it was a bank, then the Court in view of banks being there to serve the general public, will not reduce the sentence. We won't be surprised to see the High Court increasing the sentence from three years to five years, on appeal, and hence be very cautious on what grounds you raise in the appeal.

Answering your question, Court's will not generally mitigate a sentence on the ground that it is having an adverse effect on the offender's dependants. Every offender has a dependent, be it an ailing parent, a child or spouse – you must realise that the public needs protection and the Court's take the offence of stealing seriously. Offenders should think about the effects of their crimes on their own families and the people they steal from, before committing the offence. In any case, the family crises may be stated as one of the grounds of appeal to the High Court.

Terminated from employment and later charged on the same offence

My friend was employed as a storekeeper in a supermarket in Dar es Salaam. He was terminated from work on grounds of money theft. He informed me that there was a hear-

ing in which he admitted the charges. We are now astonished to see that the police arrested him a few weeks later on the same charges of theft. We secured his Court bail and he is now out. We heard that no one should be punished twice for the same offence. This is unfair to him, isn't it? Please assist.

28th December 2009

Although it is true that no one should be punished twice for the same offence, the facts of this case, as you have told us, are beyond the scope of this adage. Termination from employment after stealing does not make one immune to being charged in Court for stealing from an employer.

The former is an employer's disciplinary measure to protect his interest, while the latter is in the public interest to prevent crimes in society and ensure that no crime goes unpunished.

However, we feel compelled to comment that the regard for money is, fortunately or unfortunately, the one of the few universal characteristics in our civilisation, as is the belief that the love of unearned money is the root of all evil. The law is not prevented from taking one into the criminal justice system simply because of an employer's action of termination.

The best your friend can do is repent and pray for a lenient sentence from the Magistrate. If this is his first offence, he should mention it; it may help reduce the sentence.

Right of citizens to arrest

I am a farmer in Mikumu, Morogoro Region. Some six months back, just after midnight, we found a man jump our wall and run towards our chicken farm. Immediately upon being informed so, my sons and I went after him. We tied him up and took him to the police station, where he was detained. We have now received a summons to appear

in Court in which we are being sued for unlawful imprisonment. It shocks me how the cards have turned against us. The system in Tanzania is very unfair. Please advise me on what I should do?

30th November 2009

The facts you have given us, leave no doubt, that the circumstances in which the man was found, suggest that he had committed or was about to commit an offence. Our law, the Criminal Procedure Act empowers any person including private persons to arrest without warrant any person whom he finds lying or loitering in any garden or other place during the night and whom he suspects upon reasonable grounds of having committed or being about to commit an offence.

Although you are not a police officer, the law allows you to arrest a citizen whom you reasonably believe has committed an offence. We do not see anything wrong in the way you handled the situation, unless, of course, you used unreasonable force.

We do not wish to comment on the system in Tanzania being fair or un-fair. It is a very subjective question.

Appearance in Court

I witnessed the beating of a person in my home town in 2007. Shortly after the incident the police took my statement and I have been now served with a Court summons to appear and give evidence in the trial. Is there any way I can avoid going there? After all, the man was suspected of witchcraft.

23rd November 2009

First of all, you should understand that the summons of the Court to appear is a lawful order of the Court and any attempts to disobey it is punishable. Appearance in Court to give evidence cannot be avoided for it is the same evidence that you give that assists the Courts in administering justice. The obligation of a person to give his/her evidence is indispensable unless one is incompetent or a non-compellable witness, which the Court will decide on the day you appear.

In criminal matters, the Courts are empowered to commit to prison any person who appears in Court by virtue of being served a summons, or being present in Court and who being verbally required to give evidence, refuses to be sworn or affirmed, or to give answers to questions put to him or refuses to produce any document or anything which he is required to produce. In your case, we advise you to obey the summons of the Court and give evidence, unless you are exempted by the Court after appearing before it.

A man is innocent until proven guilty; the man, as you say, was suspected of practicing witchcraft. He has a constitutional right to defend himself in a Court with competent jurisdiction and the Court's will determine his innocence or guilt, not you.

Difference between conditions and warranties

I am signing a contract that has been drafted by the other party. After reading the contract, I have found some sections reading 'conditions' and other sections reading 'warranties'. What is the difference between the two? Are there any tricks I need to know before signing a contract?

23rd November 2009

We shall start with your 'trick' question. The 'trick' is not only to read the contract but also to understand it. If it is drafted in old medieval English, and you seem to understand the words but not the sentences, you better get help from a trained contract specialist. In short, make sure you understand the entire contract before signing.

The terms of a contract have been traditionally classified as either conditions or warranties. A condition is a basic term, non performance of which would render performance of the remaining terms something substantially different from what was originally intended. Consequently, the breach of such a term would entitle the party not in default to treat the contract as repudiated and itself as discharged from performance of all outstanding obligations under the contract. Conversely, a warranty is a minor term, a breach of which can be adequately compensated for by the award of damages. The breach of such a term will not therefore release the innocent party from performance of its contractual obligations. There are no tricks being played in dividing the terms as above. It is a standard drafting practice and it does make practical sense.

Hatred for the judge

Last month for the first time I went to Court in Mwanza and ended up hating the judge. He came in very late with no sign of apology. When I greeted him, he did not greet back and worst of all he postponed the hearing saying he had been summoned to Dar. What should I do?

30th November 2009

We are unsure what your question is. You seem to have a personality clash with the Judge, which is hard to cure. Just because the Judge did not greet you, this being your first time in Court, does not mean you start hating him. He will be indifferent and is not posted in that position to impress the people who appear before him.

A Judge dispenses justice. When you go to Court, it is for justice, not for social purposes. We are unsure where your hatred arises from. If there are other issues you have had with the Judge that have not been mentioned to us, you can raise an objection to this Judge presiding over your trial. There is no other magic formula.

Bail in anticipation

I am being investigated for a criminal offence and would like to know if I can apply for a bail before being taken to Court? In other jurisdictions, this is allowed so as not to cause inconvenience to the accused.

16th November 2009

What you are mentioning is anticipatory bail which is a direction to release a person on bail, issued even before the person is arrested. In jurisdictions like India, the law allows an accused to make such an application in Court. According to their laws, there are four conditions that are taken into account before the granting of such a bail. These are: the nature and gravity or seriousness of accusation as apprehended by the applicant; the antecedents of the applicant including the fact as to whether he has, on conviction by a Court, previously undergone imprisonment for a term in respect of any cognisable offence; the likely object of the accusation to humiliate or malign the reputation of the applicant by having him so arrested; and the possibility of the appellant, if granted anticipatory bail, fleeing from justice.

Unfortunately, in Tanzania, we do not have such a provision and hence you cannot apply for anticipatory bail.

Long contract, high lawyer fees

I engaged a lawyer to draft a sale agreement of machines for a company in neighbouring Rwanda. The sale was a simple one but the contract drafted was over fifty pages and contained irrelevant clauses towards the end. Is this a way lawyers charge for their services? Should I be signing such a contract?

2nd November 2009

It is very hard to answer you without reading the entire fifty page document. However, you must realise that a lawyer's job is to protect your interests and even if there is a slight possibility of anything happening that will affect you as a party to the contract, it is worth your lawyer mentioning it in the contract so that there is no ambiguity.

Many of the clauses you read, towards the end of the contract, are termed as 'boilerplate clauses' (standard clauses). For example; the likelihood of say snow falling in Mwanza is close to zero, but if such a possibility does exist, however slight, a good lawyer will cover it.

How lawyers charge can be very controversial. Many clients do not appreciate that a lawyer earns his or her living through time spent on a particular assignment. It is wise to agree with your lawyer on how you are going to be charged – hourly or a lump sum flat fee. If you are paying a flat fee, then your question becomes irrelevant as it will not affect the amount you pay whether you have a fifty page contract or a five page one. Lump sum billing is very common in Tanzania. In the event that you are paying hourly, and you think some of the clauses drafted were irrelevant and were inserted to increase the billable hours, you should have a dialogue with your lawyer. All in all, lawyers in Tanzania are much cheaper to work with than in many other neighbouring countries.

We wish not to comment on whether you should sign this contract or not.

Amendment of charge sheet

I am a convict writing from Ukonga prison. I was charged with the offence of assault against my neighbour with whom I have a dispute on plot boundaries. The Republic called five witnesses in total. To my surprise, after I had closed my defence case, the Magistrate entertained the prosecution prayer

to amend the charge sheet from offence of common assault to that of assault causing grievous bodily harm, of which I was finally convicted. Was the Magistrate proper in allowing the prosecution's prayer? I feel the Magistrate was biased against me. Are there any chances of success on appeal? Please advise me.

19th October 2009

From the given facts, it is difficult for us to decide whether or not the trial Magistrate was biased against you. However, our law, the Criminal Procedure Act, allows the Court at any stage of the trial, when it appears that the charge is defective in form or substance, to order amendment or alteration of the charge sheet. At any stage of the trial means stages from arraignment up to but excluding judgment, provided that when the Court decides to do so, it shall give the accused the right to the recalling of the prosecution witnesses, who have given evidence for further cross examination. This is mandatory and unless the procedure is adhered to, the whole proceedings become null and void. Unless you can establish that the above procedure was not followed, you cannot fault the decision of the trial Magistrate except on other substantive merits of the case, based on which you may appeal.

Out of Court in a criminal case

I own a business engaged in the exporting of logs. One of my servants stole money from my firm and was charged with 'stealing by servant'. When the charge was still pending in the Magistrate's Court, I wrote a letter to the Magistrate informing her of my wish not to proceed with the prosecution because I had been adequately compensated for the loss by the accused's father. The charges were thus removed. I have been informed, however, that the file has been called by the High Court. Is this correct? Why has the High Court called the file when I have decided not to proceed with the case since I am the complainant?

26th October 2009

This is the first time we are hearing of a Magistrate dismissing a criminal trial on grounds that it has been settled out of Court. 'Settled out of Court' is an expression foreign to criminal proceedings in Tanzania and elsewhere. Although you are the complainant, in criminal cases the parties to the case are the Republic and the accused and you would normally come in as a witness.

What has perhaps happened is that the Director of Public Prosecutions (DPP) has used his powers under section 91 of the Criminal Procedure Act to enter a *nolle prosequi* i.e. by stating in Court that the Republic does not intend to continue with the criminal proceedings.

Assuming the case has been dismissed, wrongly so, because of your letter to the Magistrate, the High Court has powers under section 372 of the Criminal Procedure Act to call for the file. This is basically for the purpose of satisfying itself as to the correctness, legality or propriety of any finding, sentence or order recorded or passed and as to the regularity of any proceedings of the Magistrate's Court.

In short, once you institute a complaint in a criminal matter, the prosecution of the accused is conducted by the public prosecutor and not by your team of lawyers. This would be different in a civil matter where your lawyer would take the lead role.

Defendant in suit dead

A few months ago I instituted a case against one of my business partners and the case is still going on at the High Court. I have just been informed that the partner against whom I have claimed (the defendant) died in a car accident. What is going to happen? How am I going to get my rights?

19ᵗʰ October 2009

It is an elementary law that the death of a plaintiff or defendant shall not cause a civil suit to abate if the right to sue survives. Under our law, when the sole defendant dies and the right to sue survives, the Court, on an application made in that respect, shall cause the legal representative of the deceased defendant to be made a party and shall proceed with the suit. The legal representative as defined under the Civil Procedure Code means a person who in law represents the estate of a deceased person and includes any person who intermeddles with the estate of the deceased and, where a party sue or is sued in a representative character, the person on whom the estate devolves on the death of the party so suing or sued.

In your situation and as per the facts you have provided, it is not known if the deceased defendant left a Will or not. In a situation where a person dies living a will appointing an executor, the person so appointed as executor represents the estate of the deceased testator as from the date of the death of the testator, unless the executor renounces the executorship. The executor therefore may be brought into the suit before the grant of probate and can carry on the proceedings without grant as far as possible until he has to prove his title, when of course he must establish the grant of probate, which is the proof or evidence of his title. To sum up, your rights in a civil case do not vanish when a party to the suit dies.

Brother misused my power of attorney

My brother and I bought a property together many years ago. Subsequently I had to travel overseas for a medical emergency whereby my condition did not allow me to come back to Tanzania for the past five years. Prior to departure I had given my brother a general power of attorney to act on my behalf should the need arise. I have just come back only to find that my brother has used the power of attorney and transferred my portion of the property into the name of his son. He tells me that the son will hold it in trust for me. All these years my brother has never cheated me – I have received my portion of the rental income on time and the correct amount. I continue to receive the rental income. Is there any cause for alarm?

26ᵗʰ October 2009

If you trusted your brother so much, you would not be writing this question to us. There is some element of mistrust that has arisen, which has brought some doubts in your mind and you are wondering 'why did my brother transfer the property using the power of attorney?' And that is precisely our concern.

A power of attorney in simple terms is power given to one person by another to act for that person. A transfer of title by the donee of power of attorney done without knowledge or consent of the donor is invalid. There are many similar cases where the Courts have ruled on this. Additionally, if the consideration for the transfer was love and affection, such consideration cannot be attributed to the donor of the power of attorney without his knowledge and consent.

Answering your question – is there a cause for alarm. Our answer is yes. However, try and sort this out amicably. If that fails, you have a good case and should pursue your rights. A word of caution – this property as we speak does not belong to you. If you die, it will become a bigger issue when the beneficiaries fight over it. There seems more to this than meets the eye.

Commercial Court too fast

I filed a case against a leading multination-

FB

l company at the High Court, Commercial Division in Dar es Salaam. The suit was filed in July 2009 after which I travelled to Europe for eight weeks. When I came back, I was shocked to see that the suit was disposed of and that not only had I lost the case, but also had to pay costs to the other side. My lawyer tells me that we did not even go into the merits of the case, because the other side raised an objection. How can the other side raise an objection that puts the matter to rest so fast?

12th October 2009

Most people complain that our Courts are slow in hearing and disposing of cases! This is the first time we are hearing a complaint that a case has moved too fast.

The Commercial Court is one of the fastest Courts in which to appear. It is efficient; it understands commercial issues very well and is perhaps one of the best Commercial Courts in the region. One of the draw backs of going to the Commercial Court is that it is expensive.

It seems like the defence side have successfully pleaded a preliminary objection that disposed of the case without having to go to the main suit. You still have a remedy to file an appeal to the Court of Appeal. One of the grounds of appeal that you may not use, that you may be thinking of using (from the tone in your question), is that the Court moved too fast! We suggest you contact your attorney and look at the chances of success on appeal before filing one.

Dual citizenship in Tanzania

I am Chinese by birth, currently residing and doing business in Dar. Having been here for over six years, I am now conversant with Kiswahili language and am married to a Tanzanian woman. I wish to apply for Tanzanian citizenship but wish to hold onto my Chinese passport. Can I not have both citizenships?

How do I apply?

5th October 2009

Many other countries including the US and other European countries allow dual citizenship – Tanzania does not allow this.

If you want to apply for citizenship, you will have to renounce your Chinese citizenship in case you are successful.

To apply for citizenship, the law provides that an application must be directed to the Minister concerned and the decision of the Minister is not subject to appeal or review in any Court, and hence final and conclusive.

Search by the police

I am a Congolese businesswoman residing in Dar es Salaam. On suspicion of being in possession of a stolen mobile phone amongst other items, policemen searched me. I was then taken to a police station where I was held for over twelve hours. I was not given any water and was also denied access to my medication for diabetes. Is this kind of behaviour allowed in Tanzania?

28th September 2009

The act of searching an individual is regulated by the law. Police officers have power to enter into a vessel, dwelling house, boat, aircraft etc. to conduct a search when there is a reasonable cause to suspect that there are any stolen goods, anything used or intended to be used in the commission of an offence or any offensive weapons, an article of disguise or any article prohibited under the law.

Subject to certain rules, the police are also allowed to search an individual. However, the law requires that whenever it is necessary to cause a woman to be searched, the search shall be made by another woman with strict regard to decency. In your case, this was not followed and hence the search on you was illegal.

As for the denial to access water and your medication, section 55 of the Criminal Procedure Act says that a person shall, while under restraint, be treated with humanity and with respect for human dignity. The section also further states that if the person under restraint makes a request to be provided with medical treatment, the police officer shall forthwith take such reasonable action as is necessary to ensure that the person is provided with medical treatment or assistance. Hence, denying you access to your diabetes medication was also illegal.

Limitations under power of attorney

In 2007, I bought an unsurveyed piece of land in Dar es Salaam. A few months later, I travelled to Malaysia for my post graduate studies. Before I left the country, I appointed a friend of mine under specific power of attorney to process the survey and finalise the registration of the property in my name, which he did. In 2008, my friend purportedly acting under the said power of attorney, mortgaged my property to secure a loan from a bank. My friend has defaulted the bank loan and now the bank is in the process to forfeit my property. Do I have any recourse against my friend? What about the bank? I now see this as an opportunity to make more money.

14th September 2009

If everything you are telling us is true, it is likely that the bank's move to forfeit your property will not succeed. Something of great importance is whether the authority you gave your friend under the power of attorney to process the survey and finally register the property allowed him to mortgage the property the way he did. Your attorneys will need to read the power of attorney carefully and study the wording, as surely a banker would not lend on a specific power of attorney the way you mentioned it in the question. There could be something you might be missing, though banks are known to make very silly mistakes.

Assuming the power of attorney is specific as you claim, your friend's act of mortgaging your property without your knowledge and/or consent is void and illegal, and therefore the mortgage is ineffective. The bank cannot enforce it. You can sue the bank and your friend and will need to get injunctive relief from the Court before the bank and/or its agents make any further move.

We are unsure how you see this as an opportunity to make more money. You can claim for various types of damages but be assured that the bank will also put up a long fight in Court. Banks are in the business of lending on securities and a default on a loan does not reflect too well on a bank's books. Be prepared for litigation that may take considerable time before the matter is finally disposed off.

Sued when I should be suing

I have been taken to Court by an agent at a time when I should be demanding money from him. How can the Court accept such cases? I have been living in Australia for years and have never seen anything like that. How can I be sued when I am the one supposed to collect the money? What should I do?

21st September 2009

Your agent is probably trying to diverge your energy from your collection spree to his suit. He surely has come up with a cause of action and sued you accordingly. He cannot have sued you to recover your money. You have not mentioned why he has sued you, but it is likely, based on a breach of contract.

Just because the case has been admitted in Court, does not mean that it has been

FB

decided. It is the Court's duty to look at both sides and decide. In this case, he is the plaintiff and you are the defendant. Court's are guided by principles and you have a chance to put a counterclaim in your defence.

A counterclaim is a cross claim brought by a defendant in civil proceedings that asserts an independent cause of action but is not a defence to the claim made in the action by the plaintiff. You can bring up your claim in the same suit but must also respond to the claims he is making against you. Just because you think that his claims are frivolous, does not mean that the Court thinks the same way. You need to convince the Court that no claim exists against you. This is standard legal procedure all over the world, including Australia.

Forceful HIV test

I am a 29-year-old male living in Lindi. I am being forced to take a HIV test which I am reluctant to take because of my religious beliefs. Unlike many other people who are scared of taking the test, I have no fear as I know the results will be negative. What are my rights?

24th August 2009

One has to respect your belief but it is normally advised that to undergo an HIV/AIDS test has more advantages than disadvantages.

Your question is whether you can be forced to undergo a test or not. The law comes to your protection – the HIV and AIDS (Prevention and Control) Act has clearly stated that one cannot be forced to undergo a HIV test unless the person voluntarily agrees to do such a test or there is a Court order compelling the person to be tested. The law also states that no consent shall be required from a person who is donating any organ or tissues or to a sexual offender. The Act further recommends that personal in the medical fraternity and expectant mothers should take the tests but

it is not compulsory.

From the facts you have given, none of the above are applicable to you and hence you cannot be forced to take the test. The eligibility to take a test does not matter on how old you are, where you are from or what religion you follow. It is an offence for anyone to forcefully ask you to take the test.

Survival of suits after death

My father died last year in a car accident. During his life time he had sued a newspaper for defamation. Can we, as his children continue with the law suit? We have reached a very good stage in the case and are being assured of 100% victory.

17th August 2009

It is quite interesting to note that someone has assured you of victory. We are unsure who that someone is and if it is your advocate who is assuring you of victory to that degree, you are being taken for a ride. We know that this is not the answer you are looking for.

The question invites us to explain in brief the effect of death on causes of action in different suits. Unlike in Criminal Law, where the liability of the accused person ceases with his death, the case is different in civil suits. Under Civil Law, there are some causes of action which survive the death of a person suing or being sued and some which do not. Under the Law Reform (Fatal Accident and Miscellaneous Provisions) Act, on death of a person all causes of action subsisting against or vested in that person shall survive against or for the benefit of the person's estate except for defamation, seduction, damages arising from adultery and inducing one's spouse to leave or remain apart from the other and all personal injuries not causing the death of the party.

The cause of action does not survive in respect of the defamation case because the injuries a person suffers in defamatory remarks do not necessarily cause damage to the estate of the person wronged.

Hence, in your case, the right of your father to sue the newspaper for compensation of defamation was his personal right and it died with your father. Therefore, the suit filed by your father abated on his death and you as a legal representative of your deceased father's estate cannot continue with the case (*actiopersonalismoritur cum persona* – a personal right of action dies with a person).

Ship on Tanzanian waters

I was passing about two nautical miles off the coast of Tanzania in my personal ship heading towards Durban when your coast guard stopped me and arrested my ship and refused us to exit. What does the law say about passing through Tanzanian waters?

17th August 2009

The band of sea between the limit of internal waters of a state and the high seas are the territorial waters of a country of which the country exercises sovereignty which includes an exclusive right to fish and exploit seabed and subsoil of the seabed and exclusive usage of airspace above the territorial waters. The law allows all foreign ships right of innocent passage through Tanzanian territorial waters i.e. the right to pass through, provided the ship does not prejudice the peace, security or good order of the country.

You claim to have been two nautical miles off the coast and hence on Tanzanian territorial waters. You have not mentioned why your ship was arrested but if you were just passing and posing no threat to security and that you had accordingly informed the Tanzanian coast guard, there should be no reason for arrest.

My lawyer confusing me

I have recently engaged a lawyer to chal- **lenge a contract that I have entered into. The words he uses are confusing me – sometimes I am told my contract is void, sometimes he says it is voidable. Initially I thought the two meant the same, only to realise they did not. What is the difference between a void and voidable contract?**

24th August 2009

We do not blame you – the words void and voidable sound quite similar but are different. A voidable contract is a contract, though valid when made, is liable to be subsequently set aside because of misrepresentation, some instances of mistake, non disclosure and/or undue influence.

On the other hand, a void contract is one that has no legal force from the moment of its making. Void contracts occur when there is a lack of capacity to a contract and sometimes by the operation of mistake. An illegal contract is void but not all void contracts are necessarily illegal.

Trial of drug dealer in the US

A Tanzanian who in the 1980s was suspected of having been involved in murder in Dar es Salaam, has apparently been nabbed in the US for dealing and distributing drugs. Can he stand trial here so that he can be convicted and get the death penalty?

3rd August 2009

From what we can make of your question, you want the suspect to be tried in Tanzania, be charged with murder and get the death penalty as opposed to being charged for a drugs related offence in the US which is bailable and only attracts a prison sentence.

What you effectively want is the extradition of the suspect to Tanzania. Extradition is the surrender of one state to another of a person accused of committing an offence in the latter. Unfortunately, Tanzania does not have an extradition treaty with the US and hence there is no automatic possibility of the trial in the US being moved to Tanzania. Just for your reference, some of the countries that Tanzania has extradition treaties with include Zambia, Kenya, Uganda, Australia, Mauritius, Malta and Singapore.

Bag taken by mistake

Last week I was on a bus from Mwanza to Dar. When I arrived in Dar, I mistakenly took someone's bag. I could not identify the owner of the bag. Later on two people came up to me and claimed a right over the bag. I have not handed over the bag to either one. The bag has some valuable contents – what should I do?

27th July 2009

You have a very interesting question. The Civil Procedure Code accommodates such scenarios by way of you filing an interpleader suit. Interpleader suits are suits instituted by a person who claims no interest over a certain property but to which two or more other persons have a claim. It is unfortunate that you have to file a suit but in the circumstances it seems to be the best thing to do. You should present to the Court a plaint and also state that you have no interest in the subject matter in dispute other than charges or costs incurred in storing the bag and instituting the suit. These charges are normally recoverable at the end of the suit.

We must point out that you should not be tempted to start using or disposing of the contents of the bag as you could be held liable for stealing.

Mentally challenged on the streets

I have just come back from the US to see so many mentally challenged people on the streets. Some of these people can be very dangerous. Isn't there anything that can be done?

20th July 2009

In protecting and monitoring the rights of persons with mental disorder, our law requires mentally disordered persons to be taken to mental health care facilities or reported to social welfare authorities. It is the duty of a police in charge of a station, justice of peace, social welfare officer, a religious leader, ward executive officer or village executive officer who has reason to believe that any person within the area under their jurisdiction is mentally disordered and is not under proper care or control, to immediately cause that person to be brought to a mental health care facility. We advise you to contact one of the above.

Mercy killing of sick patient

My father is seriously sick and doctors have given up hope on him. He has been in a coma for the past six months and one of our aunts who is a nurse has suggested we assist him die by injecting him with poison and reduce his suffering. Is this legal?

20th July 2009

There is an old adage that you cannot take what you have not given. Mercy killing or euthanasia is an act that ends a life in a painless manner, performed by someone other than the patient. This may include withholding common treatments resulting in death, removal of the patient from life support, or the use of lethal substances or forces to end the life of a patient, as your aunt is proposing.

Taking one's life intentionally is not excused under our law. If you assist your father die, you will be committing murder even though you aim at relieving him from his pain. Murder is a crime of unlawful homicide with malice aforethought and can lead to the death penalty.

There are, however, a few countries in the

world where euthanasia is legal. These include the state of Oregon in the US, Switzerland, Belgium and the Netherlands. Most of the laws in these countries require a physician assisted suicide, which should involve the fastest and least painful way of allowing the person to die. Whilst you can time how long it takes to die, it is very difficult to judge which is the most pain free way to die and this has also led to a lot of controversy.

The subject becomes even more controversial on who should decide whether the patient should die especially when the patient is in a coma. We do sympathise with you but wish to reiterate that the act of assisting or expediting your father's death is illegal.

Walking in public place with a pistol

I was stopped one evening by the police who found me with my pistol. I am a lawful and licensed owner of the said pistol. However, I have been charged with the offence of going out with an offensive weapon in a public place. What should I do?

6th July 2009

Provided you are a lawful and licensed owner of the pistol, going out with a gun in a public place is not an offence under our laws. Public places also mean public houses such as cinema halls and malls. Walking with a pistol only becomes an offence for instance, an owner of a gun starts, without any justification, to cause threat to those around him or to misuse the weapon. When this happens, then the possession of a gun/pistol becomes unlawful and the possessor is in possession of an offensive weapon in a public place. This is not the case here unless you have forgotten to renew your gun licence (please check). Unless there are facts that you are hiding, the charge you are facing is illegal and improper. You should seek legal advice.

Driving whilst disqualified

I am a mechanic undergoing practical training at a garage. I do not possess a driving licence and was caught by the traffic police for driving a client's vehicle which I was helping to tow. I was actually in the car that was being towed, only holding to the steering wheel since the engine was not running. I am being charged with the offence of driving a vehicle without a licence. It was only for a short distance and on a back street. Did I need to have a licence?

13th July 2009

The answer to your question is in the affirmative. Under the law, the Road Traffic Act (Cap 168 R.E. 2002) driving without a valid driving licence or a valid learner drivers' licence, is illegal. The definition of 'driver' is wide enough to cover steering a vehicle which is towed or pushed. Of importance is who is in control of the movement of the vehicle. You were controlling the vehicle by operating the brakes and steering-wheel and made the vehicle move. It is immaterial whether or not the drive is for a short distance or on a back street. You needed to have a licence and have been rightly charged.

Criteria for police bail

I was arrested by the police for a simple offence and was really harassed when it came to the issue of bail. What criteria do the police use to grant bail?

20th July 2009

Bail is the release by the police or Court of a person held in legal custody while awaiting trial. The police normally require sureties (guarantors) to undertake to produce the accused when required to do so. It is the contract by the surety and the Court or police that the accused will be made available when needed.

Bail is everyone's right. However, a police officer in charge of a police station or Magistrate has discretion to grant or refuse bail to an accused depending on several factors. These include the background of the accused, employment and family situation of the accused including his/her past record, the circumstances in which the offence was committed, the nature and seriousness of the offence and the likelihood of the accused absconding.

We are unsure as to what you mean by a simple offence. In any case, you are entitled to bail unless you were charged with murder, treason or armed robbery for which granting of bail has been expressly ruled out.

Temporary injunction refused

In a case, I had filed for a temporary injunction and the Court refused to grant it. The reason given by the Court was that I had delayed in filing for the injunction. Is such a refusal not illegal?
22nd June 2009

An injunction is a judicial remedy whereby a person is directed to restrain from doing or to do a particular act or thing. The former type of injunction is known as a restrictive injunction or prohibitory injunction, the latter is called a mandatory injunction. A temporary injunction is normally provisional in nature and is a preventative relief to preserve the status quo in respect of the subject matter of the suit. A temporary injunction maybe granted immediately, till the disposal of the application for temporary injunction. It is likely that you had applied for a restrictive injunction.

Amongst other factors, the Courts looks at the time at which you have filed for such orders. If a significant amount of time has elapsed from the time the cause of action arose to the time you filed for such orders, the

Court may refuse to grant you a temporary injunction and there is nothing illegal about this.

Right to call witnesses

I am a convict serving a thirty year sentence at the Ukonga prison. I was charged with armed robbery and was in remand from the date I was first arraigned in Court until the end of my trial. When the time to defend myself arrived, the trial magistrate refused to issue summons to call my witnesses. Can I appeal against the conviction?
8th June 2009

The accused's right to call his or her witnesses is statutory. The law governing the criminal proceedings in our legal system are the Criminal Procedure Act and the 3rd schedule to the Magistrate's Court Act.

For example, the Criminal Procedure Act, imposes mandatory obligation on the Magistrates to explain to the accused his rights to call witnesses in his defence.

It is trite law that once the accused has indicated his intention to call witnesses, the Court is duty bound to make sure those witnesses are available to testify at the right time by issuing Court summons, especially where the accused is not represented.

However, the Magistrate has discretion to refuse the accused the right to call witnesses and of course by giving reasons for such refusal, for example where such witnesses' evidence has no bearing upon the case or where the accused states that he has witnesses to call but his witnesses are not present in Court due to fault or neglect of the accused person. Whatever the reason, the same must be put on the Court record.

In your case, you have not told us the circumstances that led the trial Magistrate to deny you the right to call your witnesses nor the relevance of the evidence of your intended witnesses. However, if you think the evidence of your intended witnesses was material to your case and that the absence of your witnesses in Court was not to your fault or neglect such that the Magistrate ought to have adjourned the case, then you stand good grounds of appeal. The chances of your appeal to succeed also depend on the records of the Court.

Admitted murder still death sentence

My friend was involved in a robbery where the person who was being robbed got killed. My friend pleaded guilty to the charge of murder and has been sentenced to death. How soon will he be hanged? I thought that since he was honest in telling the truth, he would be given a prison sentence. Can the President reduce the sentence of death?

25th May 2009

Your 'honest' friend has assisted to save the Court's time and resources by telling the truth. In criminal offences, the admission of a certain offence, amongst other factors, may reduce the severity of the sentence.

Unfortunately, for your friend, the offence of murder under the Penal Code, attracts only one punishment – that of death by hanging. There is no mitigation of a sentence for a person charged with murder. The fact that your friend was honest does not change the fact that he murdered someone. Murder is a very serious offence and our law looks at it strictly.

Your friend will now be on death row waiting for the President's signature on the death warrant. Such a warrant will specify where the hanging should take place including the place of burial. However, the President is empowered to commute the sentence of death for any other punishment or even pardon the convict completely or with conditions.

Commercial Court fees high

Why must I file a large value business dispute at the Commercial Court? Is my lawyer trying to charge me more?

18th May 2009

You are unnecessarily suspicious of your lawyer. The Commercial Court has been set up to expedite and more efficiently handle commercial disputes. Such commercial disputes have been defined under our law and other Courts, such as the High Court, are not excluded from entertaining such disputes. Based on your lawyer's analysis of the case, it seems like the dispute will be better handled at the Commercial Court.

Because of its special set up, filing a case at the Commercial Court is normally more expensive. The Court fee is normally 3% of the amount you file for. This is a Court fee and not an amount made up by your lawyer. If you find the cost of filing a case at the Commercial Court expensive, you may file your case at the High Court. There is no mandatory requirement for you to file at the Commercial Court.

Suit time barred

I filed a case for breach of contract and the defendant raised an objection that the suit was time barred. The Judge surprisingly agreed with the application. Can I appeal?

11th May 2009

Different issues have different time limitations in which to file a suit. In the case of a contractual dispute, according to the Law of Limitation Act, the suit must be filed within six years of the alleged breach and hence any suit filed outside the time prescribed is not within the jurisdiction of the Courts. From the facts above, it seems that your suit was not filed within the six years and hence the defence lawyers have successfully raised a preliminary objection that has disposed of your suit. If you have good grounds on why you delayed to file the suit, you may apply to the Minister for Justice and Constitutional Affairs for extension of time to file such a suit. If the Minister is convinced of the reasons presented to him or her, then the Minister may grant an additional time in which to file your suit. Such additional time is half of the time that the law required you to file your suit in. In your case, the Minister may grant you a further three years and if the alleged breach was committed within the additional time, your suit will not be time barred.

In the alternate, if you think the trial Court has erred in computing time, you can appeal to the Court of Appeal. You will need to give a notice of appeal and apply for Court's proceedings, the ruling and dismissal order to be able to file your appeal.

Murder accused set free

I read in the papers that a few of the accused in a murder case were set free in between the murder trial, whilst others are still fighting it out in Court. How can the Court allow some to be set free in between a trial? I can smell something fishy.

18th May 2009

Once a person is charged with a criminal offence, it is the duty of the prosecution to lead evidence constituting the offence with which the person is charged. It is a legal burden upon the prosecution side, through testimonies of witnesses and other evidence, to prove beyond a reasonable doubt that the accused is guilty. If at the close of evidence in support of the charge, it appears to the Court that on the face of it, the case is not sufficiently made against the accused to require him to make a defence, the Court will dismiss the charge and acquit him.

The duty to adduce evidence sufficient to convict an accused person before the accused is required to defend himself is in legal terms known as establishment of a prima facie case. Therefore, in criminal proceedings the Court can acquit in between the trial if the evidence brought by the prosecution side is not strong enough to require any of the accused to make his/her defence. It is a law of procedure for the Court to examine and evaluate evidence brought by the prosecution side and rule whether or not the accused person has a case to answer. In answering your question, the accused that were set free in between the trial were those that the Court did feel to have had a case to answer. The others had a case to answer and the defence will then open/continue its case. There is nothing fishy about the procedure.

Long contracts, more money for lawyers

I have just entered into a contract with a foreign company and was surprised to sign a contract that was the size of a book. The details were simple but they had all sort of clauses in there. Why should I be signing such a long contract? The lawyers probably draft long contracts to charge more fees.

4th May 2009

You should have asked yourself this question before you signed the contract and not after. We have noted that many companies blindly sign documents only to start complaining later – your case seems no different. The length of a contract does not mean anything. You could have a contract the size of a book which is faulty and have a contract which is a few pages which is relevant and watertight.

The main objective of a written contract is to record what the parties have agreed to, to avoid any ambiguities and conflicts in the future. A long contract does not necessarily mean that it is faulty – it might be that the party drafting the contract has included what we call 'boilerplate clauses' to ensure that everything is covered, even the most remote possibilities.

It is very difficult for us to comment on the lawyers' intentions of drafting longer contracts to charge more fees. Whilst a lot of these boilerplate clauses are standard 'copy paste' clauses, sometimes drafting a shorter watertight contract takes longer and costs the clients more than a longer contract with standard clauses.

Motor vehicle as police exhibit

The police have confiscated my car and are not returning it to me. They claim that the car will be used as an exhibit in Court. Please advise.

13th April 2009

Under our law, the police are allowed to detain any property seized during the investigation of a criminal case until the last verdict in the case, provided that reasonable care is taken for preservation of such property. The reasons for such detention vary depending on the facts of each particular case. For example, there cannot be any justification for police detaining one's car involved in a road traffic offence, especially after preliminary investigations are complete. There are, however, situations where exercise of powers to seize and detain are necessary and justifiable such as when there are reasonable grounds to believe that the car in question was used in the commission of the offence and if tendered in Court, will afford evidence as to the commission of the offence in question. One of these situations is where it is alleged that the car in question was used in the commission of the offence in issue.

If your car has been confiscated because it was involved in the commission of an offence, the police can detain your car. You have

not mentioned the offence in question and hence we cannot give you a specific answer. Remember that for fair and just administration of justice, the police are justified to detain any property including motor vehicles, to be tendered as evidence.

Claim raised on a claim

I have filed a case in Court for an amount over TZS 150M for breach. I am shocked to hear from my lawyer that the defendant, in the same case, is now claiming TZS 1B from me. I cannot understand how this arose and am in a state of shock. How can the Court allow such demands that are only being made after I have taken the matter to Court? Please advise.

20th April 2009

The defendant's claim against you, in the suit that you have instituted, is called a counter claim. A counter claim is a cross claim brought by a defendant in civil proceedings that asserts an independent cause of action. Normally it is not a defence to the claim that you have made.

The law does allow the defendant to raise any counter claims. It is for your lawyers to make sure that they give the case a proper direction if the claim is fictitious and is intended to delay the trial. Counter claims can also be brought by the defendant towards any other person who might not even be a party to the suit and such claims need not necessarily arise from the same transaction. It is trite law that the Court must hear both parties to a case and hence you cannot stop the Court from listening to the counterclaim raised.

Father held for son's offence

While in a bar, my 21-year-old son and his friend fought over a woman. Using a beer bottle my son hit his friend on the head and caused him to suffer severe head inju-

ries. My son is now at large. Efforts by the police to arrest him have failed. The police have instead arrested my husband and they say they will not release him until my son is found. Is this just?

27th April 2009

The police cannot arrest your husband unless the arresting police officers have evidence to establish that your husband was involved in any way with the incident or is hiding your son i.e. obstructing them from discharging their duties. The act of arresting your husband violates his constitutional rights as to freedom of movement. Your son is a grown up person and therefore responsible for his own acts. It is trite law that a parent cannot be responsible for wrongs of his son or daughter. We advise you to consult a human rights group or engage an advocate for assistance.

Drunk driver in car

A few weeks back, my friends and I went to the national stadium to watch a match. After the match, my friend who was driving the car consumed a lot of alcohol and we got into an accident. I got seriously injured in the accident. Can I sue my friend?

27th April 2009

Yes, you can sue. However, you have not mentioned if all of you were drunk or if it was only your friend. It is likely that you were all drinking but even if you were not, the fact that you boarded the vehicle knowing that your friend was drunk, will reduce the amount you can claim.

Although your friend was negligent to drive under the influence of alcohol, there is no doubt that by agreeing to be driven by the drunk driver you also contributed to your injury. You could have avoided that by not boarding the car. Therefore, although you

have a maintainable cause of action against your friend for his negligent driving, he is likely to come up with a defence of contributory negligence. Hence if your suit is successful, the damages recoverable are to be reduced to such an extent as the Court thinks just and equitable, with regard to your contribution to the damages you suffered.

Am I compelled to testify?

My husband is a suspected offender. During the search of our house he was found with two packets of bhang. I have now received a Court summons requiring me to appear in Court and testify against my husband. I do not feel like going to Court. What should I do?

20th April 2009

Like in civil proceedings, every person in criminal proceedings is a competent witness, if he/she is of sufficient understanding to give evidence and to appreciate the nature and obligation of oath or affirmation. A competent witness is usually compellable to give evidence. Parties to cases usually determine their cases and submit to Court witnesses' for purposes of Court summons. Once a summons is issued, the concerned are compelled to attend. Apparently your name was presented in Court by the prosecution side because it thinks you are helpful to build up its case. However, being a wife of the accused you have a choice whether to give or not to give evidence against your husband. You will, however, have to attend Court as a summons has already been issued and explain to the Court your position.

Unhappy with Magistrate's Court

I have a claim against a party for USD 50,000 and have taken them to Court. I am not happy with the way the case is going. I can see that the magistrate is biased. I have been advised that I take the file to the High Court. Please advise me.

13th April 2009

A Judge or Magistrate is under duty not to adjudicate on cases in which he/she has either an interest whether personal, financial or due to race, sex and/or political background differences. To do otherwise amounts to adjudicating on his/her own case, which is contrary to a fundamental doctrine of natural justice i.e. no man should be a judge in his own case, in *latinnemoiudex in suacausa.*

If what you are saying is true, the trial Magistrate must certainly disqualify himself or herself from sitting on your case. The procedure is for you to raise your concerns to the Magistrate and in the event you manage to substantiate your allegations, the Magistrate will withdraw from conducting your case. You are therefore advised to make a formal application by way of chamber summons supported by an affidavit in which you will state your grievances against the trial Magistrate. It is important that justice should not only be done but it must manifestly be seen to be done. Please note that you cannot just 'take' the file to the High Court. You must follow the above procedure.

Moving with ID

What does the law say about moving with an ID card? Is it compulsory? A few months back, near Las Vegas Casino, I was stopped by police at night and harassed because I was not carrying an ID card. Please advise.

23th March 2009

In Tanzania, at least so far, there is no law governing the identity cards (IDs). In 1986, there was an enactment by the parliament to this effect but until now the law has not come into operation. There is no clear established national identity cards system issuing IDs in Tanzania. This does not mean that people do not have ID cards. Many Tanzanians carry their work IDs or even voting cards.

Strictly speaking, it is not compulsory for Tanzanians to move with their ID cards. However, it is advisable to carry a form of identification as we have seen people without IDs being denied bail and being refused release of their parcels from the post.

In neighbouring countries like South Africa or Kenya, where they have an established national identity cards system, moving with ID cards is compulsory. There, the police can stop any person, at any time and require them to produce their ID card. These are countries with national ID cards. The government also uses such cards to identify taxpayers and such people can access public health services and other social services by producing their IDs.

Summons to appear as a witness

A person brought me a paper from the Kisutu Resident Court asking me to appear before a magistrate as a witness for a case. I do not want to go. What should I do?

30th March 2009

Witnesses are vital in the administration of justice by the Courts. In any judicial system, cases are decided based on the facts of each particular case. However, Courts do not know facts of the cases they decide upon, except through witnesses. In practice witnesses attend to Courts through a summons. A summons of the Court requiring a person to attend and testify is a lawful order of that particular Court which is enforceable in case of non compliance.

It is a criminal offence punishable with imprisonment, for one to disobey the summons of the Court, unless there are any good excuses. In your case we do not see any.

Be informed that for the purposes of administering justice, the Courts of law have been empowered to even compel any person competent as a witness to appear before them and testify.

You must also note that when a witness is in Court and he or she refuses to swear or affirm or to answer any question, that person can be sent to prison for a period of eight days. This is in accordance with the Criminal Procedure Act.

In your case, we advise you to comply with the Court summons. There is no leeway. It is a lawful order of the Court. You have to testify for the administration of justice.

Arrested for not giving name

I was stopped by a policeman who asked me for my name and address. I refused to give him my details as I did not know what he wanted them for. I was then arrested and taken to the police station. Is this lawful?

23rd March 2009

Our law says that if a police officer suspects that a citizen has committed or is about to commit an offence, and the person suspected of the above refuses on the demand of the police officer to give his or her name and address, or if he or she gives a name and address that the police officer believes is false, such a person may be arrested by such officer in order that his name or residence may be ascertained and for preliminary inquiries.

In your case, if in the opinion of the police officer you had committed an offence, then he had the right to stop you and ask you for your name and address. From the facts you have given, it is likely that the arrest was legal.

You may also wish to note that you have the right to ask any police officer who stops you, his name, rank and place of duty. Further, be informed that it is an imprisonable offence for the police officer to refuse to give you his particulars or to lie about his particulars.

Permit refused to Tanzania

I am Sudanese and had applied for a resi-

dent permit in Tanzania. The Immigration department has refused to grant it. What should I do?

30th March 2009

Under our law, the power to issue any residence permit is vested with the director of Immigration services. Under the Immigration Act, every person is entitled, upon application and meeting certain conditions, to a residence permit unless he/she is a 'prohibited immigrant'. A prohibited immigrant includes a destitute person, a person dealing in dangerous drugs, a person against whom there is a force of deportation order or expulsion from Tanzania. In Tanzania we have three classes of residence permits. These are class A, B and C.

Class A permits are for persons who intend to enter or remain in Tanzania and engage in any trade and business. Class B permits are issued to persons who are offered specific employment in Tanzania in view of their qualifications and skills that are not available locally or are in short supply. Class C permits are offered to persons who are not granted a class A or class B permit. The director of Immigration Services shall specify such conditions upon which he shall grant a class C permit.

In your question, you have not told us under which class you are seeking for a residence permit nor reasons for refusal of your application by the director of Immigration Services. However, the decision of the director of Immigration Services not to grant your application for a residence permit is not final. You can appeal to the Minister responsible for matters relating to immigration for further consideration of your application.

Illegal arrest by the police

I was at home one evening with my family when two men claiming to be police

officers came and asked me to go to the Police Station. I refused. They subsequently forced me to go to the police station. Is that legal?

9th March 2009

Generally any police officer is empowered under the law to arrest any person for whom he has reasonable cause to believe that that person has committed a breach of peace in his presence or a warrant of arrest has been issued against such person. In your case we are not informed whether those police officers who came to arrest you carried with them any warrant of arrest or any such order mandating your arrest. We assume that they did not have either of these.

However, it is the law that unless the alleged offence for which the arrest is made is a serious one to enable the arresting police officer to arrest without warrant and with excessive force, the arresting police officer must inform the person to be arrested the cause for which the arrest is to be made. In your case, facts of the case speaks for themselves, that what the police officers did was illegal.

Fourteen days in police custody

My son has been in custody at the police station for fourteen days now. Police officers do not allow him to communicate with his relatives or allow me access to him. What should I do?

2nd March 2009

In Criminal Law, a suspect is deemed innocent unless the contrary is proved. This is true regardless of the nature of the offence the person is charged with. Although keeping a person in custody is in some circumstances necessary for smooth investigations by the police, the law allows every person under restraint to have access to reasonable facilities. These include right to communicate with

his/her lawyer, a relative or a friend of his or her choice and the right to police bail, if the offence is bailable.

The law commands that no person shall remain under police custody for more than forty eight hours before he/she is taken to Court. In this case, your son has been in police custody for fourteen days and that is unlawful. He should have appeared in Court or have been released by now. Not being allowed to communicate or having access to your son is also unlawful.

We advise you to engage a lawyer or contact a civil organisation for legal aid and assistance.

Two years, still no judgment

We have been waiting two years for judgment to be delivered in a civil case at the High Court. Our advocate refuses to follow up the matter claiming that it shall anger the judge. Please advise what recourse we have?

9th March 2009

It is the right of the parties to resort to Court whenever a dispute arises and they fail to resolve it amicably. The Court is the last resort for a person who feels that his/her rights have been infringed. The Court is also the custodian and determinant of the peoples' rights. It is also a policy of the law that cases should come to an end as early as possible. When the case comes to an end, it is the duty of the Judge to deliver the judgment within a reasonable time. Failure to deliver the judgment by the Judge within a reasonable time is unjust.

Your advocate is incorrect when he says that the Judge shall get angry. The Judge is dispensing justice, therefore no anger can be created by the act of you or your advocate following up for a judgment nor can a judgment be pronounced against you because of following up your rights.

This is your case and you also can follow up

at the High Court registry. Justice delayed is justice denied and the act of the High Court delaying the judgment for more than two years is denying your rights. However, such a delay is unusual and there is a huge possibility that there is something in the file that you are not aware of.

We suggest that you engage another lawyer or write a letter to the registrar of the High Court to inquire the status of the judgment.

Case dismissed by Magistrate

Is it right for a Magistrate to dismiss a case, in the presence of complainant, on a day of hearing after he/she was absent on a previous hearing date?

12th January 2009

For proper administration of justice, when the case is set for hearing, parties i.e. complainant and the accused must make sure the case continues on the date fixed for hearing. In this context complainant includes a prosecutor. Under the law, the Criminal Procedure Act, (Cap. 20 R.E. 2002) the Magistrate is empowered to dismiss the case and acquit the accused if the prosecution does not enter a proper appearance on the date of the hearing of the case. In your case, it seems that the complainant/prosecutor did not appear on the previous hearing of the case and the case was dismissed in the next hearing, in his presence.

If on the day, the prosecutor was not ready to call witnesses and came unprepared to Court to substantiate allegations against the accused, the case can be dismissed. It is not enough to just appear in Court.

Generally speaking, the Magistrate has discretion to dismiss the case if the complainant does not enter proper appearance especially when circumstances so warrant, for example if the conduct of the case by the prosecution has been pathetic or of gross inefficiency and negligence.

Civil case appeal

I had a civil case at the District Court of Ilala and judgment has been entered against me. I am not satisfied with the decision. What do you advise me to do?

19th January 2009

First of all, you should immediately make an application to the Court which passed the judgment for certified copies of judgment and decree. After you are served with the said copies you should file a Memorandum of Appeal to the High Court accompanied with a copy of the decree. The appeal should be lodged in Court within thirty days from the date of judgment.

The importance of the application letter to the Court asking for the certified copies of the judgment and decree is useful for computation of the thirty days within which you are supposed to file your appeal, meaning that the days in which you are waiting for the copies of the judgment and decree to be made available, are not taken into account in the computation of the thirty days.

Right to bail

Who has a right to Court bail? Why do some people get bail while others do not?

19th January 2009

Court Bail is the release by the Court, with or without conditions, of a person held in legal custody while awaiting trial. It is effectively a contract between the Court and the accused that the accused shall appear before the Court, when so required. The right to bail is automatic unless the offence is non bailable. Non Bailable offences include murder, treason, armed robbery, defilement and illicit trafficking in drugs. Even in offences that are bailable, the Court has a discretion whether to grant or refuse bail to the accused based on several factors, including when it appears that the accused person has previously been granted bail by the Court and failed to comply with the conditions of the Court, or absconded and if the Court thinks it is necessary that the accused be kept in custody for his own protection and safety.

You must note that for offences which are bailable, the Court issues certain conditions, upon fulfilment of which the accused is released on bail. Examples of some of the conditions that the Court may impose are two sureties to sign a bond, deposit of certificate of title or cash deposit and surrender of passport. If these conditions are not met, even if an offence is bailable, the accused will not be released from custody. Sureties to sign a bond, deposit of certificate of title or cash deposit and surrender of passport. If these conditions are not met, even if an offence is bailable, the accused will not be released from custody.

Appeal for imprisonment

My young brother was sentenced to three years imprisonment by the Kibaha District Court. He is not satisfied with the decision. What can he do?

12th January 2009

A person who is aggrieved with a judgment has a right to appeal. Your young brother should give a notice of intention to appeal within ten days from the date of judgment. He can then appeal to the High Court within forty five days from the date of judgment. This is as per section 361 (1)(a) and (b) of the Criminal Procedures Act (Cap 20 R.E 2002).

Also note that you will have to get a copy of the judgment which should be accompanied with the petition of appeal. It is advisable that he be represented by an Advocate in Court.

Defendant never in Court (civil)

I have filed a civil case against somebody in the Kisutu Resident Magistrate's Court. The defendant does not appear in Court as he has not been served with the summons. I have been appearing in Court alone, and the case always comes up for mention. I have been denied justice. Please advise.

19th January 2009

It is likely that your case is not moving forward because the other party has not been served with a summons. The law is very clear under Order V rule 20 and 21 of the Civil Procedure Code (Cap 33 R.E. 2002) that if you file a case against a person who cannot be easily traced for the purpose of serving him or her with the summons, you may make an application in Court to serve the summons by substituted service. This means that the summons shall be affixed to the place of his or her residence or place of business or sent by courier if the defendant is outside the country. The summons shall then be considered to have been duly served. The Courts have also accepted substituted service of summons by way of publication in a well circulated newspaper. If he or she does not appear after the substituted service, the Court shall proceed to hear the case ex-parte i.e. in the absence of the other party and you can prove your case and the Court shall enter a judgment accordingly.

Suing a tabloid

I am a working professional and had attended a party at one of the hotels in Dar. Whilst on the dance floor, I danced with my wife's friend, in the presence of my wife only to read in one of the Kiswahili tabloids that I was having an affair with this woman. My wife was equally shocked and luckily did not believe what she read. The newspaper also printed photographs of the two of us

dancing with a very nasty caption. What can I do?

5ᵗʰ January 2009

You can sue the magazine for defamation. Defamation is the publication of a statement about a person that tends to lower his reputation in the opinion of right thinking members of the community. Defamation is usually in words but pictures, gestures and other acts can be defamatory as well. To succeed in an action for defamation, the first test is whether it tends to lower you in the estimation of the right thinking members of society. From what you have mentioned, it is likely that that is the case. Second test is whether it referred to you. That is straight forward as the newspaper has also printed a photograph and it is likely that it has mentioned your name somewhere. Lastly, you will have to prove that this was published to a third party. Again this is straight forward since a newspaper is distributed across the country. You have a good case against the newspaper. Whilst we talk about defamation, some of the defences that may be available to the newspaper include justification (the truth) and fair comment – that the statement is a fair comment based on the true facts made in good faith on a matter of public interest. From what we can make out from the facts, you have a good case.

Crime

The next wave of big crime is electronic and cybercrime. It takes you unaware, causes permanent damage and difficult for law enforcement to catch up with. This is the new unseen crime era.

A fundamental principle of Criminal Law is that a crime consists of both a mental and a physical element. A person's awareness of the fact that his or her conduct is criminal is the mental element, and the act itself, is the physical element. Today most crimes, including common-law crimes, are defined by statutes that usually contain a word or phrase indicating the requirement of both the mental and physical element. Are criminal acts obvious to all? What is considered a crime? If you insult your employee is that a crime? Or If you lightly slap someone? This chapter will clarify what actions are considered criminal in the eyes of the law. Stealing, whether it be a big or small item, whether it be from your husband or wife, whether your intention is to give it back is still stealing and punishable by law. A person who commits a crime may be guilty even though he or she had no knowledge that his or her act was criminal and had no thought of committing a crime. If lack of common knowledge on what is right and wrong, what is a crime and what isn't, is your excuse, then the law will not take your side. It's quite simple, if you commit a criminal offence then you will face charges-which could be anything from paying a fine to imprisonment. And yes, even both a fine and imprisonment.

Admissibility of judgment in criminal trial

In early 2009, my car was severely damaged in a road accident. The driver of the vehicle which caused the accident was tried at Kinondoni District Court. At the beginning of trial, the driver denied the charges against him. After witnesses testified, the driver changed his plea to that of guilty. Following his change of plea he was convicted and sentenced to pay a fine. Thereafter, I instituted a civil case at Kisutu Court against the driver for compensation for my damaged motor vehicle. Unfortunately, my two witnesses are indisposed – one died last year and the other has disappeared and all efforts to find him have failed. I have requested the Court to consider their testimony made in the traffic case but the trial magistrate has denied my request. What should I do? Please assist, as I have suffered a very big loss.

18th April 2011

The Magistrate's refusal of your request is justifiable. A final judgment in criminal proceedings is merely relevant in that it declares any person to be guilty of the offence he was charged with at the time. The evidence submitted during criminal proceedings is not and cannot be used as evidence in a civil suit. All questions in a civil suit, even if the cause of action therein is connected with the criminal proceedings, must be determined independently. As far as your situation is concerned, the Magistrate in the civil suit is only called upon to determine claims for damages. He knows nothing of the evidence that was presented before the Criminal Court, because issues in criminal proceedings are different from claims for damages in the civil suit. As such, statements of evidence in criminal proceedings cannot be admissible in the civil suit. This is the law of the country as it stands today. The facts you have given do not tell us what evidence your two witnesses presented. You should continue with your case, because proving a case does not depend on the number of witnesses, rather on the weight of evidence provided. You should contact your lawyer for further advice.

Fighting in public on the streets

A police officer found a large crowd watching my son fighting in a street with another boy. My son also produced a razor blade that the other boy had attacked him with. Both boys have been charged by the police. My son claims that he was attacked first and was defending himself. Please advise.

11th April 2011

The act done by your son and his fellow is a criminal offence known as affray i.e. unlawful fighting in a public place. Under our Penal Code, the offence is punishable with imprisonment of six months or a fine not exceeding TZS 500.

In law, self defence has always been a good defence to justify infliction of bodily harm or even death provided no more force is used than necessary. To succeed in the defence to affray, one must be able to show that he was not fighting but defending himself for a man defending himself does not want to fight and he defends solely to avoid fighting. Considering the facts you have given us, your son will have to lead evidence to show that he was really attacked and defending himself and that there was no fight and consequently no affray. If he cannot prove this, the situation is inescapable.

Murder of Jessica Lal

I am a second year law student at a university in Dar es Salaam. I watched a movie and have read about the case of Jessica Lal, an Indian hostess who was killed by a politician's son in a night club in India. I learned with interest how the High Court called for the records of the trial Court and retried the murder case. Can the High Court in Tanzania do the same?

11th April 2011

The case you have referred to is a landmark Indian murder case where the son of a well-known politician shot to death a bar tender, Jessica Lal, in 1999, at a party where there was dim lighting and loud music. The accused was set free by the trial Court because, among other reasons, the prosecution did not prove beyond a reasonable doubt that the accused was present at the scene of the crime.

After the acquittal, the case was picked up by a well-known media outlet which started to investigate the murder. The investigation revealed a clear miscarriage of justice and raised a public outcry across India which resulted in the High Court, on its own accord (sua moto), calling for the records of the trial Court.

The High Court reversed the acquittal by the trial Court and sentenced the accused to life imprisonment. The accused then appealed to the Supreme Court of India, which is the equivalent to the Court of Appeal in Tanzania. The Supreme Court upheld both the conviction and sentence of life imprisonment awarded to the son of the politician, stating that the prosecution had proved beyond reasonable doubt the presence of the accused at the site of the offence. The Supreme Court added that the presence of the accused was proved by ocular evidence of the prosecution witnesses. The Supreme Court also pointed out that the conduct of the accused after the crime proved his guilt and sentenced some of the accuser's friends to prison after finding them guilty of destruction of evidence and obstruction of justice.

While the Court criticised the media for its reporting, it held that this did not cause any prejudice to the accused.

Returning to your question, according to the Criminal Procedure Act of Tanzania, the High Court of Tanzania has similar powers as those of the High Court in India. The High Court need not be necessarily moved by someone – it can move itself and address issues.

The Jessica Lal case is a matter which proves the important role the media can play in the administration of justice and reminds everyone that no one is above the law. It must be pointed out that there is no time limit when it comes to criminal law matters and an acquittal in one Court does not mean that a case cannot be reopened in another or tried again, of course depending on the new facts.

Mistreatment of animals

I own several dogs and keep them in small wood huts. As part of my business, I artificially induce them to mate and reproduce. Then, I sell them to people or hire some kids to sell them on the street. I am not very well-to-do and sometimes lack the funds to feed them. One day the kids that sell the dogs for me brought visitors to the house who wanted to see how I raise my dogs. I allowed them to do so, only later to be told that I was in breach of the basic standards of keeping and selling animals. I was subsequently arrested and am now facing criminal charges. I have never heard of such a thing – these are dogs and not humans. The prosecutors should be prosecuting the hard core criminals out there and not breeders of dogs. Don't they have better things to do? Is there no law that instructs such prosecutors to prioritise who they take to Court? What should I do?

14th February 2011

There is a law called the Animal Welfare Act of 2008. This law establishes an organisation responsible for the control and prevention of mistreatment or abuse of animals. An officer of this organisation, upon proof that a person is abusing animals or keeping them in conditions below the minimum standards established by the minister responsible for welfare of animals, can investigate the said person. If the officer finds that animals are being abused or forced to live in abusive conditions, he can then report the person to the director of Public Prosecution, who will prosecute. Furthermore, the law is clear that no cat or dog should be sold in a public place, except in appointed pet shops or approved areas. Also, note that if you are breeding the animals for commercial purposes, you are required to get a permit for such trading. Your letter makes no mention of you having such license. Not feeding the dogs regularly is considered to be mistreatment and we do not see why you should not be prosecuted. Though, we must mention that this is the first time we are hearing of such kind of prosecution. Lastly, there is no law that instructs prosecutors to prioritise who they take to Court.

Refused to go to police station

I was walking down a street and bumped into an elderly man. He was holding a bag and because of the collision his bag was apparently stolen. Within a minute of the incident I was surrounded by two policemen in uniform and two in plain clothes. They all started questioning me and asked me to go to the police station with them. I refused, and was slapped by one of them. What are my rights in such a situation? What should I have done? Was it necessary for me to go to the police station?

10th January 2011

It is quite surprising that four policemen appeared within such a short period of time. Citizens across the country usually complain that the police are late in arriving at the scene of any crime. In answering this question, we are going to assume that the four were indeed policemen and not some con artists, who are not in short supply in town.

To begin with, you cannot be slapped or hit by any police officer unless you have tried to escape or attack them, which does not seem to be the case here. Even if that were the case the police are not allowed to use more force than is reasonable. If you are a woman you can only be searched by a lady police officer. When under arrest you have the right to remain silent, you have the right to an attorney, and the right to inform a friend or a family member that you have been arrested, unless the officer finds it necessary to stop you from informing them on grounds that it will hinder the investigation process. You have right to ask why you are being arrested, including the right to know the name of the arresting officer, their badge number and what police station they are coming from.

What you cannot do is refuse to go to the police station, unless of course they are not real policemen. It is always advisable to inform at least two people of your arrest and to which police station they are taking you. It is quite interesting to note that you have not told us what happened in the end.

Identification of thieves

Late at night we were attacked by a group of four people, who stormed into our house armed with guns. We were ordered to lie down whilst they searched the house for money and a substantial amount was stolen. I reported this to the police officer who was at first reluctant to register the incident saying he was disappointed that we had kept such a large amount of money at home. After some hours of discussion at the police station, the incident was recorded. Four days later one of the culprits was caught and I identified him at the police station. The matter went to Court and he was surprisingly acquitted on grounds that the identification parade was improperly conducted and that there were chances that he might not be the one. This truly shocked us. Why would someone be acquitted after being identified?

6th December 2010

In Criminal Law, the Courts are faced with deciding the fate of an accused person that will ultimately lead to a custodial sentence. Hence, the Courts must be extra careful that the person it convicts is the actual offender. It is a known principle of law that evidence of facial identification must be carefully evaluated before it can be used to convict, unless corroborated by some independent evidence, which does not seem to be the case here.

Additionally, there are certain rules and procedures that must be followed for identification to be properly carried out; failing to do so means that the identification will fail in evidence. Some of the key points to note are that the accused person has a right, and should be made aware of his right, to have a friend, family member or lawyer present and that the officer in charge of the investigations does not carry out the identification. Additionally, witnesses should not see the accused before the identification, the accused should be placed with at least eight other persons of the same height, age and general appearance, and that the accused may take any position he chooses and may change his position after each witness has come for the identification. Care must also be exercised that the witnesses are not allowed to communicate with each other after they have been through the identification process, and the witness must touch the person who he or she identifies (merely pointing at him is not enough). At all times, the person conducting the identification parade must act with scrupulous fairness, otherwise the value of the identification as evidence depreciates considerably.

In this instance, there seems to be serious failure on the part of the police to ensure that a fair identification was conducted, which led to the case collapsing, and the accused being acquitted. The matter is also further weakened because you indicated in your question that you were asked to lie down during the attack. Generally, during an attack it is very hard to remember faces of people, one is fighting to get out of the situation alive rather than identify who is committing the crime.

As for the police officer querying why you are storing funds at home, we are unaware of any law that disallows a citizen to keep cash in their homes. It is advisable to avoid keeping large sums, but it is not illegal. We are truly surprised at the behaviour of the police. This matter should be reported to his seniors for appropriate action.

Arrested in bar after midnight

Just after midnight in September last year, my two co-tenants and I were arrested at a bar located along a street in Mkuranga District. The police alleged that it was an offence to be found in a bar at that particular time. They did not release us until the following day when we were bailed out by our relatives. Nevertheless, police have proceeded to charge us with the offence in the Primary Court. One police officer, a relative of the co-accused, has been urging us to plead guilty, alleging that the offence is punishable by only a minimal fine. However, I disagree with the police officer's advice, I feel we should plead not guilty, for we were arrested at a place around our home where we were drinking peacefully. Is this officer not misleading us? For years, I have been drinking at such a time without any problem? Please advise us.

11th October 2010

The Intoxicating Liquors Act prohibits any person, be it the owner of the bar, barmaid or any person to remain in the bar to consume beer after 11pm from Mondays to Fridays, or after midnight on Saturdays, Sundays and public holidays.

The facts of your case constitute all necessary ingredients of the offence under the Act and the fact that you have been drinking beyond such time for years without any problem is not an absolute defence. As you may have noticed, people do still consume or sell alcohol beyond the stipulated times – this is illegal under the law. People should not try to take cover of under our authorities' failure to discharge their duties as an excuse to break the law. Much as we would like to side with you, we subscribe to the advice of the police officer.

Charged with assault

I have been charged with assault after I punched one of my friends in the wee hours at a bar during Easter weekend last year. My case has not started, but I have been very unfairly treated as on the material day, another friend of mine mixed my Red Bull with some alcohol that resulted in this behaviour. It is well known amongst all my friends that I never drink alcohol. What should I do?

13th September 2010

We hope you are not trying to mislead us: on the one hand you do not drink, on the other hand you were in a bar till late at night. While we do know of few people who do not drink and go to bars, we know of fewer people who do not drink and are in bars till very late at night! In any case, we answer your question assuming that you really do not consume alcohol.

Our law is very clear in that intoxication shall not constitute a defence to any criminal charge. However, the law states that intoxication shall be a defence to any criminal charge if the person charged complained that or did not know what he was doing at the time of the act or omission, and the state of intoxication was caused without his consent by the malicious or negligent act of another person, and the person charged was by reason of intoxication insane, temporarily or otherwise, at the time of such act or omission.

In this case, you have a solid defence in that the criminal action was a result of lacing of your drink. There are many cases that have dealt with such defences and we do not see why you should not be able to defend yourself successfully. You will need to start working on witnesses who will testify for you.

Reconciliation in criminal matters

My son is charged with raping my neighbour's daughter. During the pendency of the trial at the District Court, family members met, discussed the matter, and concluded that the matter would be better resolved out of Court in order to promote harmony and good neighbourliness. The neighbour is someone I have grown up with and a close friend of mine. The elders managed to convince him to instruct the girl to withdraw the charges. Shockingly, the trial magistrate has refused to accept our request without assigning any reasons. Is this not illegal? Why should my son be prosecuted when two parties have agreed to forgive each other?

6th September 2010

Criminal Law seeks to maintain peace and harmony in society and the authorities responsible for criminal administration of justice are therefore encouraged to settle issues amicably and expeditiously. However, this reconciliation of offences does not apply to all offences. It only applies to minor offences such as common assault, or offences of personal or private nature. Our

Criminal Procedure Act empowers Courts to stay proceedings in a fit case depending the outcome of the settlement out of Court.

The nature of the offence your son is being charged with is not a fit case capable of reconciliation under the law. Rape is not an offence of personal or private nature; it is a serious offence in which the Court cannot promote reconciliation. The fact that you are neighbours and have known each other from childhood is irrelevant. That does not give your son the right to rape your friend's daughter. Put yourself in the shoes of the neighbour and look at it from his perspective – would you, as a father, forgive your neighbour's son for raping your daughter? Your 'neighbour's argument' is dangerous, unintelligible, absurd, and has no basis.

We are glad to hear that the Magistrate did not act with emotion and allow this kind of 'off Court' settlement in a serious offence like rape. Nowhere in the question have you denied what your son has done, and it might be prudent to counsel him.

Forfeiture of surety's bond

I stood as surety to secure my brother's release for bail in a criminal case he is facing in the District Court. While on bail, the accused failed to appear in Court. I showed up to inform the Court that he could not attend because of illness. The trial magistrate did not accept my explanation and instead ordered me to forfeit the TZS 500,000 that I had executed on the bond. Was this proper and fair? Is there anything I can do to get back my money?

6th September 2010

We are not sure if you have told us the entire story. Though in answering this question, we assume that you have disclosed all material information.

In our opinion, the trial Magistrate overreacted and acted in a biased manner against you. Generally, Courts have powers to take sureties to task when the accused they stand for defaults on bail conditions, as is the case here. If there is nothing to forfeit, the Court may also send the person who stood as surety to jail. However, before invoking these powers, which are normally discretionary, Courts are required first to ascertain whether or not the reasons given for the accused's default of appearance are genuine. In circumstances like yours, the Court ought to have adjourned the proceedings and required the accused to provide evidence that he was sick. The order was hence prematurely issued.

These orders are appealable, and if you present your facts properly, your appeal should be successful and you can get your money back.

Powers of Criminal Courts to order compensation

In January 2009, my uncle was charged and convicted of stealing a cow. The evidence upon which his conviction was based was that he was found in possession of skin which the complainant stated was of his cow. Upon his conviction, he was also ordered to compensate TZS 700,000 to the complainant, this being the value of the stolen cow and costs incurred by the complainant. Was this evidence sufficient to warrant conviction? Was it correct and fair for the trial Court to order for compensation against my uncle? Please advise us on the chances of success should my uncle appeal the conviction.

6th September 2010

We cannot give you an exact answer to the question without perusing through the Court records and understanding the way the case preceded. For example, we do not know what evidence was given by the complainant in identifying the skin of his cow, or whether the evidence given implicated your uncle as the actual thief, or merely the receiver of the alleged stolen cow and/or skin. It is also quite surprising to note how the complainant could identify the skin – we wonder what was so unique about this skin?

As to the order for compensation, be informed that our Criminal Courts have powers to order compensation depending on the nature of the offence the accused is charged with and circumstances of the case concerned. However, in your particular case the Court went beyond its jurisdiction in ordering compensation. In this instance, the jurisdiction of the Criminal Court was limited to determining the criminality of the accused persons before it. Issues such as the value of the stolen cow and/or costs incurred by the complainant in tracing his cow are matters which need to be proved in a civil case. To this extent, we are at least sure that your uncle's appeal will be successful, though he should have appealed within thirty days of the date of judgment. In case he has not appealed, he will have to make an application to seek leave to appeal out of time and cite reasons for the delay. The Court may or may not accept such reasons.

Criminal action on pending land case

I own a plot of land in Mwanza. Recently, my neighbour, who has always had an eye on a portion of my plot, started building on my area. I ended up filing a case against him at the High Court in Mwanza. While the suit was still pending in the High Court, he complained to the Police that I had trespassed on his plot. I was arrested and now there is a criminal case pending at the District Court against me. I am worried that I might get convicted and whether such a conviction would work against me in the High Court? Please advise.

16th August 2010

There are a number of High Court judgments which have held that 'no one can be convicted of an offence of trespass if there is a pending suit in any Court to determine as to who is the true owner of that particular plot'. In your case, there is a strong chance that the criminal case against you will not proceed, pending determination of the suit filed at the High Court.

Picked for murder

A friend of mine and I were enjoying drinks in a bar when I teased him about something he did not like. He punched me in the face and in self defence I knocked him out. He ended up unconscious, and we rushed him to hospital where he died the next day. I was picked up by the police and have been in remand for the past fifteen months. A number of my friends who have visited me in remand prison advise me that I have been wrongly imprisoned, and that I should be charged with manslaughter, not murder. What should I do? I expect to be taken to the High Court in Dar as Salaam, as the Kisutu Court cannot entertain this matter. Please advise.

16th August 2010

The Kisutu Court cannot entertain such matters, and neither can it give bail. Only the High Court has jurisdiction to try this case. The information (charge sheet) is prepared by the Director of Public Prosecutions (DPP), and will be read out to you at the High Court.

You must understand that you have not yet been charged, as the Kisutu Court only deals with preliminaries that will ultimately lead to trial at the High Court, if the DPP decides so. Also note that it is for the DPP to decide whether you should be charged with murder or manslaughter.

From the facts, assuming you are not hiding anything from us, we agree with your friends that you should be charged with manslaughter and not murder. And unless you are charged with manslaughter, you will not be entitled to bail.

Selling of pangas, knives on streets

I have on many occasions seen people in possession of, and sometimes selling, spears, bows, arrows, knives and pangas along the streets of Dar es Salaam. These sellers even approach you in your car with these items and offer to sell them. Are these activities legal?

9th August 2010

Roads and streets within a city are public places. We wish to inform you that the sale and possession on the roads of the items you have mentioned is both unlawful and illegal. This is not only because the sellers do not have valid licenses to sell the items, but also because the items are dangerous weapons. Under the Local Government (Urban Authorities) Act, selling of the said items is classified as dangerous or offensive trade. It is also an offence to be in possession of any of these items in a public place, unless the items are required for lawful purposes.

Right to appeal in criminal cases

After I reported a theft in my house, a criminal case was instituted against the son of my neighbour, and the case was called at the District Court where the Public Prosecutor prosecuted the case. Unfortunately, judgment was passed in favour of the accused (the neighbour). I want to appeal to the High Court, but I have been informed that because it is a criminal case, I cannot appeal. It is only the District Court Prosecutor who can lodge the appeal. I have hence followed up with the District Court Prosecutor's office, only to be informed that he has no intention of appealing the case. Is it true that I cannot appeal to the High Court in such a matter?

12th July 2010

There are two types of cases in law, criminal and civil. In criminal cases like yours, the Prosecutor of the District Court represents your interests in Court, and you are merely a complainant. In cases where judgment is passed against the Prosecution, the Prosecutor is the only one who has the mandate to decide whether to appeal or not, depending on the strength of the case at hand. In your case, it seems that there may not be enough evidence to convict the said accused person, and the Prosecutor has decided not to appeal.

On death row for fourteen years

After spending seven years in remand, my brother was convicted of murder and has been on death row for the past fourteen years. Who decides when his execution shall take place? Where is the execution carried out? Can he get his death sentence converted to life imprisonment?

16th August 2010

Death row sheets are forwarded to the President for authorisation to be carried out. We are informed that in the last ten years, no President has signed any death row sheet, and hence no execution has taken place.

The execution is carried out at the prisons by hanging to death, in the presence of a judicial officer and doctor. The doctor certifies that death has occurred before burial. As for the conversion of the sentence, only the President has such power.

Defence of alibi in murder

I was visiting a friend of mine in neighbouring Mwanza and in the guest house that I was staying, there was someone who was strangled to death. My room was two doors away from where this happened. I have been picked up by the police for murder although I was away on the day of the murder. However, the police claim there are witnesses who

have mentioned me. What do I do?

22nd February 2010

Alibi is a defence to a criminal charge alleging that one was not at the place at which the crime was committed and so could not have been responsible for it. The burden of proving an alibi does not rest on you – it is the prosecution who has to disprove your alibi. A conviction cannot be entered, if the evidence adduced in support of an alibi raises reasonable doubt as to the guilt of an accused person. In other words, if there is even the slightest doubt that it might not have been you, you shall be acquitted.

In your case, if your alibi is strong enough, it is a solid defence. The biggest challenge you face at this juncture is time in remand prison as when you are charged with murder, you cannot get bail. Murder in Tanzania, as in many other countries in Africa and beyond, attracts the death penalty. You must make sure you prepare a solid defence

Possession of illegal firearm

Ten years ago, to curb the increase in armed robberies, the Kilimanjaro Regional Police Commander announced publicly that all those in possession of illegal firearms should surrender them to the police and no questions or criminal proceedings would be instituted against such persons. Contrary to his promise, on surrendering my weapon, the Regional Police Commander ordered for my arrest. I was accordingly charged, convicted and sentenced. During the trial I defended myself on grounds that my possession of the firearm was lawful because I had surrendered the weapon after the announcement. The trial Court did not listen to my defence and proceeded to convict me. Was this legal?

15th February 2010

It is undisputed that your possession

of the firearm before, during and after the announcement remained to be illegal. That the Government (through the police) invited you to surrender, for whatever consideration, does not alter the law or provide lawful excuse for your possession.

To take you further, not every act of compliance with a Government direction would supply a lawful excuse. The direction itself might be unlawful. You will not like this but in short what the Court did was appropriate in the circumstances.

Husband stealing from wife

I have been married for three years and blessed with a child. I take care of the child and ensure that the house is in order. My wife is better off than I am with an excellent job at one of the leading banks in Tanzania. Recently, I was in need of funds and took money from my wife's purse without informing her. She was initially under the impression that the maid had taken it and reported the matter to the police. The maid was interrogated and made a remark that she suspected I had taken the money. I was arrested and have been charged with theft. My wife was not amused and told the police to do their job. Although I gave the police my marriage certificate, they have strangely refused to let me go. What should I do?

18th January 2010

According to our Penal Code, a husband and wife are two separate persons. A husband can steal from his wife and vice versa. Since you took money from your wife without her prior consent then you have committed a criminal offence and you will be charged with theft and if there is enough evidence to convict you, you will be imprisoned.

Under the Law of Marriage Act, a husband and wife are also treated as two different persons and each can own their own property. Unfortunately for you, even if your wife is better off than you, or if you take care of the kids whilst she earns, that does not mean her belongings are yours. That is the law.

Intentional spread of AIDS

I am a 32-year-old male and have been dating a widow for the past few years. Before we became intimate, I insisted that we go for a HIV/AIDS test. Since we were working in different parts of the city, we went for the test separately. Both results came out negative. Recently, I went for another HIV/AIDS test because I wanted to propose to her. My results are shockingly positive although I have been very faithful. One further revelation is that her husband actually died of HIV and not a cardiac arrest as she had claimed. She knew the cause of death as over the period that her husband was ill, she had taken care of him. After getting all this information, I confronted my partner who admitted that she had forged her HIV results. We have since separated but I now hear that she is dating another man. It seems like she is intentionally spreading the disease. Is this legal? What can I do?

14th December 2009

According to our Penal Code, it is a criminal offence for a person to knowingly or negligently spread any disease which is contagious and is a threat to another human life. The HIV and AIDS (prevention and control) Act also states that it is an offence for any person to wilfully and intentionally transmit HIV/AIDS to other persons and any person who commits such an offence is liable to imprisonment for not less than five years and not exceeding ten years. This issue can be reported to the police for their necessary action.

Hunting in Tanzania

I have been hunting in Tanzania for the past seven years. Out of the seven times I have visited, I have spotted officers of the military hunting with semi-automatic weapons. They literally spray bullets on the animals and at times do not even have enough space in their vehicle to take all of them leaving behind the dead. These soldiers also hunt at night with very high intensive lights. Do the hunting laws of the land allow such behaviour? Does it exempt members of the army who always overpower the rangers? Does the law have any protection for pregnant animals to protect them from being hunted?

21st December 2009

Hunting activities are governed by the Wildlife Act of 2008 which is very clear in all of the above.

The Act specifically disallows hunting using any automatic or semi-automatic firearms capable of firing more than one cartridge as a result of one pressure of the trigger or of reloading itself more than once without further action by the operator.

The Act says that anyone who contravenes this commits an offence and shall be liable on conviction to a fine of an amount not less than TZS 1M but not exceeding TZS 2M or to imprisonment for a term not less than one year but not exceeding three years, or to both. The same applies to hunting at night which is strictly prohibited and an offence under the Act.

The law does not exempt anyone including members of the armed forces from the provisions of the Act.

As for pregnant animals, the Act is very specific and states that any person who holds a licence, permit, or written authority to hunt an animal of any species, hunts the young of that species or the female of that species which is apparently pregnant or is accompanied by its young, unless the hunting of such young or such female is expressly authorised by the licence, permit or written authority, commits an offence and shall be liable on conviction to a fine of not less than twice the value of such animal or to imprisonment for a term of not less than three years or to both.

The law does protect the pregnant in the interest of maintaining enough animal stock. The word 'apparently' appearing before the word pregnant is important to note and has a subjective interpretation.

Stealing from a thief

Twelve months ago, I was caught stealing cattle from a herdsman in Northern Tanzania. I have since been charged in Court and am depending on the defence that the person I was stealing from is a big thief. What are my chances of success?

2nd November 2009

Your story sounds like the story of Robin Hood – the English hero and outlaw who was stealing from the rich and giving to the poor. There are also many proverbs that will support your claim. One famous proverb reads (and we quote) 'It is no crime to steal from a thief.' Unfortunately the law does not support Robin Hood, the proverb or your defence.

Theft is the dishonest appropriation of property belonging to someone else with the intention of keeping it permanently. Appropriation is the assumption of the rights of the owner of the property and includes any act showing that one is treating the property as one's own.

A crime consists of two elements: *actusreus* accompanied by a specific *mens rea*. The *actusreus* is normally the act of doing something wrong. The *mens rea* is the state of mind. These two must exist for you to be found guilty.

In your case, you are admitting that you did steal and knew what you were doing, hence both the *actusreus* and *mens rea* exist.

And since your 'robin hood' type defence is not going to be accepted, you will very likely be convicted. The offence of theft attracts a custodial sentence and there are high chances that you will be sentenced to imprisonment.

Husband violence kills wife

My brother is charged with murder for causing the death of his wife. Admittedly he used to mistreat his wife with considerable violence. One eventful date, the deceased locked the husband out of the matrimonial home on the second floor of an apartment building. My brother threatened to kill her and started banging on a glass window which ultimately broke. Upon hearing the breaking of the glass, the deceased panicked and jumped out of a window and broke her backbone. She was paralysed for two years and recently died because of the injury. My brother is now charged with murder and is not getting bail. Can my brother be charged with murder? Isn't the deceased to blame for her death?

5th October 2009

In principle if one creates in another's mind an immediate sense of danger which causes such a person to try to escape, and in doing so that person injures oneself, the person who creates such state of mind will be responsible for the injuries. The same principle will apply in this case.

Under our Penal Code a person is deemed to have caused the death of another person although their act is not the mediate or sole cause of death, if by actual or threatened violence he causes that other person to perform an act which causes the death of that person.

We are not told if your brother was armed with any weapon and how close the window was that your brother was trying to break in from where the deceased was.

Both these would enable us determine whether or not in the circumstances, these caused an immediate apprehension of violence in the mind of the deceased. It is likely that it did.

The fact that she died two years later is very critical to the charge of murder since under our law a person is not deemed to have killed another if the death of that person does not take place within one year and a day. That alone exonerates your brother from the offence of murder.

Answering your questions, in view of the time that elapsed between the fall and the death, your brother cannot be charged with murder. However, based on his previous behaviour, he may be charged with manslaughter. Your second question should be answered by yourself – be reasonable when you think about it and forget that the accused is your brother. Don't you think that the death was caused by the threat of violence that the deceased anticipated? Our opinion is that any reasonable person will answer this in the affirmative. You may also want to consider medical treatment for your brother to control his violent behaviour.

Female Genital Mutilation (FGM)

My aunt who comes from a traditional background forcefully had my sister undergo FGM without any medication or anaesthesia. My sister has suffered depression ever since. My aunt has been taking care of us as both of our parents died some years ago of HIV/ AIDS. What do you suggest I do?

7th September 2009

It does not matter whether your aunt comes from a traditional background or she takes care of both of you or not. She has broken the law. Under the Sexual Offences Special Provisions Act, any person who, having the custody, charge or care of any person under 18 years of age, ill treats, neglects or abandons that person or causes female genital mutilation or procures that person to be assaulted, ill treated, neglected or abandoned in a manner likely to cause suffering or injury to health, including injury to, or loss of sight or hearing, or limb or organ of the body or any mental derangement, commits the offence of cruelty to children. And any person who commits the offence of cruelty to children is liable on conviction to imprisonment for a term of not less than five years and not exceeding fifteen years.

You should report the incident to the police and any women support organisation in your area. We do understand that your aunt may be the only person who is raising the two of you and reporting her is difficult but the law is on your side.

Charged with murder twice

A Judge recently acquitted all the accused persons in Zombe's case and ordered the police to look for the responsible person(s) for the killings. If the wanted persons are apprehended and charged, can the acquitted persons be re-charged together with them on the same charge of murder?

31st August 2009

Essentially, there is no controversy under our laws over the question you have asked. The acquitted persons were tried by adducing evidence and they were finally acquitted, meaning that the case was decided on its merits. They cannot be charged again with the same offence. Our legal system protects a person from being charged twice over the same offence. The law also goes as far as protecting persons from being convicted twice on the same offence.

Our Criminal Procedure Act makes it an absolute defence, legally termed as *Autrefois Acquit*, which bars any criminal prosecution for the same offence, against any person who has already been tried and acquitted by a Court of competent jurisdiction.

Things would have been different, if the accused had been discharged. In such a situation, there is no bar for subsequent prosecution on the same offence but this is not the case in Zombe's case. In this case the only available remedy for the Republic is to appeal to the Court of Appeal of Tanzania. Short of that, the matter as far as the acquitted accused are concerned, has been put to rest.

Arrested equipped for stealing

My son was seen acting suspiciously in a residential area. He had a torch, gloves and two screwdrivers, which he threw away when he saw a police officer. He was subsequently arrested and charged with the offence of attempting to commit burglary. What should I do?

17th August 2009

Whether or not there are chances of success will depend on the evidence that the prosecution will present to prove the charge against your son. The torch, gloves and screwdrivers are not articles which were made or adapted for use in committing theft or burglary but Courts are entitled to draw inferences from their nature and the circumstances in which the suspect was in possession of them in order to determine intent.

The facts of the case are leading to implicating your son – you will need to seek legal assistance immediately. This is a criminal charge which can lead to a custodial sentence for your son.

Threatening sms to kill

Someone I do not know sent me an anonymous message on my mobile phone that they would kill me if I do not pay up a sum of money. What can I do?

13th July 2009

The offence of demanding by threats is sometimes known as demanding money with menaces. In other jurisdictions it means blackmail. It can be a threat to injure a person or to gain a property. It can be a threat to cause injury to the third person intended to be injured or to induce the person to whom the menaces are addressed to part with money or valuable properties. A conduct could amount to menaces if it is of such a nature and extent that the mind of an ordinary person of normal stability and courage might be influenced or made apprehensive so as to accede unwillingly to the demand. What is a menace will differ from circumstances of each case, meaning that what would be a menace to an ordinary person could not be a menace to the person to whom it was addressed or vice versa.

Before the Court could rule a conduct to be a menace, it has to consider all the circumstances including the accused's knowledge of the victims' state of mind to find whether or not the victim was menaced by the accused when the unwarranted demand was made. Demanding money with view to gain includes demanding money lawfully owing to the person making the demand.

Demanding money or any other property by threats is an offence punishable with imprisonment of up to fourteen years. In your case, you do not seem to know who has sent you the threatening message. We advise you to immediately report this incident to the nearest police station. Bear in mind that in the absence of a mobile phones register, it may be very difficult for the police to find out the culprit. It is not normal for someone to 'just' receive a message like this. There might be more information that you have not told us, that you can tell the police, to enable them to conduct a thorough investigation.

Tendency to steal

My sister has a tendency to pick things in supermarket and put them in her pocket. She just cannot stop doing that. We have tried to stop her but to no avail. How can we protect her?

6th July 2009

Picking things like that amounts to stealing. However, it is very likely that you sister is kleptomaniac, a condition recognised in law. This is a mental disorder leading to the irresistible impulse to steal. Irresistible impulse is an uncontrollable urge to do something and is usually not a defence in law unless it arises out of a disease of the mind. We suggest that your sister see a medical practitioner and get checked for this abnormal condition.

Indecent assault on a woman

My brother was walking down a narrow road and saw a very attractive woman walking ahead of him. He followed her and held her lightly on her waist and her thighs, and made a comment. The lady turned out to be the daughter of a minister. My brother is charged with indecent assault. What do you advise us?

29th June 2009

This is a high street drama case. Let us start with some irrelevant things you have mentioned. It does not matter whether a woman is attractive or not. It also does not matter whether she was the daughter of a minister or not. The law looks at her as a resident or citizen of Tanzania and protects her accordingly.

Indecent assault is the crime of making an assault or an actual physical contact with a person involving an element of sexual affront or harm, without that other's consent and against the other's will. Under the Penal Code (Cap.16 R.E 2002), as amended by the Sexual Offences Act No. 4 of 1998, the offence of indecent assault is punishable with imprisonment for a term not exceeding five years or to a fine not exceeding TZS 300,000 or to both the fine and imprisonment. The law prohibits both men and women to commit acts of indecent assault, such as uttering words or sounds or making gestures with intent to cause sexual annoyance to another person. The words, sounds or gestures become offensive in law, if the maker thereof intends them to be heard or seen by the other person. An assault becomes indecent if it is accompanied by circumstances of indecency towards the person assaulted and it is not a defence that there was no indecent motive in the mind of the maker (the accused).

In the case of your brother, unless the lady consented or knew him in a close manner, neither of which seems to be the case, touching her the way you have described, even 'lightly' (whatever that means) amounts to an indecent assault. Our opinion is that your brother has a high chance of being convicted. You should, however, seek further legal advice.

Disposal of exhibits

I am a businessman trading in transportation. My truck was impounded on allegations of carrying suspected stolen goods and later tendered in Court as an exhibit. Criminal proceedings were conducted and culprits convicted but the police have refused to release my truck. What should I do?

22nd June 2009

An exhibit is a document or thing produced for the inspection by the Court, or shown to a witness when giving evidence or referred to in a deposition. Whether to produce exhibits in Court will depend on the facts of each particular case. Unless you have concealed some facts from us, our opinion is that there was no need to impound your truck. The major issue before the Court was that of the goods allegedly stolen.

All in all be as it may, after Court proceedings you were entitled to your truck unless there was an order of the Court as to forfeiture or claim of a title by any person over the truck. Under the Criminal Procedure Act Cap 20 (R.E. 2002.), the Court at any stage of the proceedings, is empowered to order the return of an exhibit, if it is satisfied that it would be just and equitable to do so.

In your case, in the absence of any forfeiture orders by the Court, continuing to hold your truck is unlawful and actionable for compensation. You can apply to the Court for an order to release your truck.

Nasty text messages

I am a business woman, now residing in Shinyanga. Before I lived in Dar es Salaam and happened to share a boyfriend with a certain woman also living in Dar. I have now been receiving abusive text messages from her and have reported the matter to the police, but no action has been taken by them. What should I do?

1st June 2009

It is very interesting to note that you 'share' a boyfriend with another lady. However, your question is on the abusive text messages that you have been receiving, possibly from a jealous woman and hence we shall not comment on the 'sharing'.

Using abusive language against another is a criminal offence against public tranquillity. Under the Penal Code, such an offence is punishable with imprisonment for a term of six months. The law looks at such abusive language in view of the breach of peace that it may cause. If such abusive language will or is likely to cause a breach of peace, for example by two parties or other third parties engaging into a fight, it becomes a criminal offence. The intention of the law is at all times to maintain peace and calm amongst the public.

In your case, unfortunately you are in Shinyanga and it is very unlikely that because of the distance, there could be any breach of peace. It seems to us that this is the way the police are looking at it. This is a very general way of looking at the question though. For further guidance, we suggest you meet your attorney in Shinyanga.

Cruelty to animals

I own a guard dog for security, since we live in a farm area and have recently moved to Tanzania from overseas. The dog is always in our compound. Nonetheless my neighbour has a dislike for our dog. A few months ago, the neighbour jumped over the fence and hit my dog, likely with a large stick and the dog can hardly walk now. What should I do?

18th May 2009

From the facts, it seems your neighbour has hatred towards your dog and perhaps even you. As far as the law is concerned, your neighbour's act of beating and injuring your dog is unacceptable. Under the Animals (Protection) Act, the act of your neighbour is a criminal offence punishable with a fine not exceeding TZS 500,000 or imprisonment for a term not exceeding six months or both fine and imprisonment. We advise you to report the matter to the nearest police station for the necessary action. The law in Tanzania, as in other countries, does provide protection to animals against cruelty. Your neighbour is also liable in tort. The dog is a property. By beating your dog, your neighbour has committed the wrong of trespassing into your property. You can also sue him for both special and general damages.

Shots fired, neighbour killed

A few months back our house was robbed by armed gangsters. In the course of pursuing the robbers, my father fired and a neighbour, who was coming to assist us, was killed. My father is charged unfairly with murder. Please advise me.

11th May 2009

We sympathise with you and your father – from the facts, your father did not intend to kill your neighbour. It was an accident. In Criminal Law, the state of mind (*mens rea*) of the suspect is of paramount importance to determine guilt. As far as murder is concerned, this state of mind is known as malice aforethought i.e. an intention to kill a person.

There are three types of malice: particular, general and transferred. In particular malice, the particular victim aimed at is affected. In general malice (sometimes called universal malice), no particular victim is targeted. And when one intends to kill Y and instead kills X, is what we call transferred malice. The fact that your father killed his neighbour instead of the robbers, does not make any difference. In law, he killed.

Your father can use the defence of protecting property. He must, however, establish that the act of firing, had he even killed the robbers, was reasonable. This being the case, he can get away with a lesser offence of manslaughter. The punishment for manslaughter is imprisonment for life or less, and sometimes even a conditional discharge sentence, depending on the circumstances under which the offence in question was committed. One fact, however, remains – that there was someone killed and the law is very strict about this. Your father will also not get bail in the offence of murder and it is for you to make sure that the investigation and trial is expedited.

Obligations of a surety

My cousin was arrested for a criminal offence and taken to Court. I was a surety for him for bail and have been attending the trial since. I am not happy with his behaviour in and out of Court. What should I do?

4th May 2009

A surety is a person who binds himself to satisfy the obligation of another. As far as criminal proceedings are concerned, before the Court can grant bail to the accused, it requires a surety to commit on the appearance of the accused person on certain days and time. The surety hence commits himself for the appearance of the accused person. The Court must be satisfied that the surety is reliable and of good character. There is no statutory provision that strictly specifies the criteria which are to be applied in assessing the suitability of a surety. Factors that are commonly taken into consideration also include the surety's financial standing, history and sometimes even the relationship of the accused to the surety.

You must note that if the accused does not appear before the Court on a given date and time, the Court may arrest you as guarantor. You have mentioned in your question that you are not happy with the behaviour of the accused. We are not sure what you dislike but whatever that it is, if that dislike is due to a suspicion that the accused may flee or involve himself in anything criminal again, we advise you to go to Court and request to be discharged from the obligation of being a surety. That is the safest option you have. If the circumstances permit, you may also want to inform the accused of your intentions so that he can organise any alternative surety otherwise he will be rearrested.

Abortion to go to school

My daughter successfully completed standard seven and was selected to join secondary school in Dar es Salaam. However, before joining the school I discovered she was pregnant. She underwent an abortion in order to continue with her studies. My daughter and I are now charged with the offence. What are the available defences to us?

27th April 2009

Under our law, the Penal Code, abortion is an offence punishable with imprisonment for a term up to fourteen years. The fact that your daughter and you knew that she was pregnant and performed an abortion is illegal. If the prosecution manages to establish this case against you, both of you may be convicted and imprisoned.

From the facts above, the defence that might work for you is that of necessity. Necessity is the pressure of circumstances compelling one to commit an illegal act. In your case, you may try and convince the Court that you aborted in order for your daughter to be able to continue with her studies. Backed by the position of the law today, it is very unlikely that you will succeed as yours was a personal necessity, which in law cannot be justification for a crime. Other defences for example of not knowing that one was pregnant and abortion on medical grounds are not available to you. There could be other facts that might be important in the case that you may have not informed us about. We suggest you get yourself an attorney and disclose all material facts.

Lawyers prosecuting in criminal trials

A few months back, I was robbed and the robber was brought to Court. I have been following the Court proceedings and can see that the public prosecutor is not aggressively pushing the case. It really hurts me to see how this case is being handled. It is very unlikely that the hard core robber will ever go to jail. Why don't private lawyers prosecute such people? Can I appoint a lawyer to fight this case for me?

6th April 2009

You have not told us how long the case has been in Court and the stage it has reached, to enable us assess whether or not the public prosecutor is contributing to the dragging of the case. However, there are several factors that make cases take long before they are finalised. These include adjournments due to incompleteness of investigation, failure of witnesses to come to Court when summoned to testify and other reasons beyond the public prosecutor's control such as the Magistrate' indisposition.

If you think that the delay of the case is due to the prosecutor's inactiveness, we advise you to complain to the offices of the Director of Public Prosecutions (DPP) for his action. Under the law, i.e. both the Criminal Procedure Act and the National Prosecutions Act, the DPP has control over prosecutions of all criminal cases in the country. He can at any time and stage intervene or take over the conduct of any criminal proceedings and/or appoint special prosecutor (state attorney) to conduct the prosecution of a case, in the public interest.

If you fail to get a proper response from the DPP's office, you can look into initiating a private prosecution. The Criminal Procedure Act allows private persons, upon seeking and obtaining leave of the Court, to initiate or institute private prosecutions against any person who commits a criminal offence punishable under our law. Robbery is an offence punishable under the law.

The procedure to initiate private prosecution is to file an application in Court, by way of a chamber summons supported by an affidavit, in which you will state among others that you have moved the prosecution authority to prosecute the suspect for the riminal offence committed but in vain.

It might be wise to engage a private lawyer to explain to you what the current stage of the case is, before you start making any applications in Court.

n remand for four years

My brother has been charged with murder and has been in remand for the past four years. Every time the case comes before the Resident Magistrates Court, the prosecutor says that the investigation has not been completed. My brother did not commit murder. What should I do to expedite the investigation?

30th March 2009

Murder is a serious offence attracting only one sentence, death, in the case of conviction. It involves, as far as the deceased is concerned, loss of life of an innocent person. In all fairness and justice for both the accused and the deceased, a thorough investigation is required. However, under normal circumstances four years is, without any doubt, a very long period to complete investigations for a murder case.

You may also wish to note that the Resident Magistrate's Court has no jurisdiction to conduct murder trials. The offence of murder is only triable by the High Court. Therefore the trial of your brother has yet to even begin.

The only person to intercede the delay of investigation of your brother's case is the Director of Public Prosecutions (DPP). Under the Criminal Procedure Act, it is only the DPP who has the power to intervene. He has the power to speed up the process or call for examination of the criminal investigation files by the police and if in his opinion the available evidence on file is insufficient to stand the charge of murder, he can order for the discontinuation of the investigation and discharge your brother. If in the opinion of the DPP, the file has enough evidence to prosecute, the DPP can expedite the trial date.

We therefore advise you to lodge a complaint to the DPP's offices, at Mwanza zonal offices or at the headquarters in Dar es Salaam and explain the delay.

Slapping on the face

I am a very short tempered individual and have recently slapped quite a number of people in my office after they irritated me. I did apologise to them. However, recently I slapped one of the employees again, who now wants to report me. When I slapped him, I honestly could not control myself. If I am taken to task, do I have a defence? Please advise.

23rd February 2009

Slapping someone is an offence and called common assault under our laws. It is punishable by imprisonment.

In Criminal Law, most offences have defences depending on the circumstances in which the alleged offence was committed.

In your case, you have not mentioned what specific circumstances led you to slap the employees. Irritation alone is not a defence. Defences that would be available to you would include provocation and maybe self defence. These defences will depend on what actions were taken by the employee against you that resulted in the slapping.

Provocation is conduct or words causing someone to lose his or her self control. Generally, provocation is not a recognised defence in Criminal Law but reduces the severity of the offence for example murder to manslaughter.

From the facts you have given us, it seems like you have an irresistible impulse to slap people. Irresistible impulse is an uncontrollable urge to do something. It is not usually a defence in law and will not afford a defence of insanity unless it arises out of a disease of the mind. We advise that you also seek medical attention and stop slapping people.

Murder and death penalty

Do we still have the death penalty in our laws? Is it appealable? Is the penalty fair?

9th February 2009

Yes, it is true that we still have the sentence of death under our Penal Laws. Under the Penal Code, (Cap.16 R.E. 2002), once it is established that a person has caused death of another, the only available punishment is sentence of death by hanging. Causing death has, in law, legal meaning for one can cause death through dangerous driving or in due course of executing a lawful order. This is not causation of death in this context.

Under the penal Code in order for one to establish the offence of killing (murder), one has to prove beyond a reasonable doubt that the person said to be killed died an unnatural death, that the death was due to an unlawful act and due to ill intent (legally termed as malice aforethought). Offence of murder is only triable by the High Court or by a subordinate Court with extended jurisdiction.

The sentence of death is indeed appealable. A person convicted and sentenced to death can appeal to the Court of Appeal of Tanzania within sixty days from the date of judgment. The procedure for appeal is preceded by the notice of appeal, which has to be filed within fourteen days from the date of judgment. In case of a delay to lodge notice of appeal or the appeal, the Court can allow extension of time to do so. However, no application of extension of time to file notice of appeal or appeal can be allowed after the President has signed for execution of the sentence. You must take note that after the High Court passes a death sentence, the execution can only take place after the President signs off. There are many convicts presently in prison who are on death row as the President has not signed for the execution to take place. However, there are situations where despite being found guilty of murder, the Court does not impose the sentence of death by hanging. These situations include, where the convict was at the time of the commission of the offence below 18 years of age or where the convict is a woman who at the time of her conviction is found to be pregnant. In these situations, the Court has normally imposed the sentence of imprisonment for life.

Your question of whether the death penalty is fair or not is subjective. Many of the family members of the person murdered normally say it is fair – the notion of an eye for an eye. Amnesty International thinks the death penalty is the ultimate, irreversible denial of human rights and is working towards the abolition of the death penalty worldwide. From Amnesty International reports, we are informed that around 137 countries have abolished the death penalty. Countries like China, USA and Tanzania have not done so.